The North End
Italian
COOKBOOK

"Not your ordinary pasta compilation . . . [this] cookbook provides a gastronomic gold mine of over 150 original family recipes. . . . She brings the tastes of the Old World to the New, never losing her family's Northern Italian heritage."

> —*Boston Woman*

"I found it near impossible to read Buonopane's recipes without getting hungry. . . . No Italian kitchen, or any kitchen, should be allowed to continue pretending to be purveyors of delectable meals without the presence of Buonopane's cookbook, at least kitchens where cooks intend to be successful."

> —Claude Marsilia, *Post-Gazette*, Boston

"Do yourselves and your family a great favor and get this cookbook!"

> —*The News,* Southbridge, Massachusetts

"Buonopane has won a culinary reputation that has grown beyond her Italian-American neighborhood. . . . [She] has concentrated on her favorite dishes plus selections from family and friends. One thing hasn't changed. The book remains Italian-American to the core."

> —Copley News Syndicate

The North End *Italian* COOKBOOK

Fourth Edition

Marguerite DiMino Buonopane

The Globe Pequot Press

Guilford, Connecticut

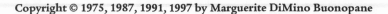

Cover design by Saralyn D'Amato-Twomey

Cover photo by Janet Knott; cover inset photo by Shaffer/Smith Photography

Text design by MaryAnn Dube

Photos on pages vi, 231, 251, and 291 by Janet Knott. Photo on page 227 courtesy of Boston Convention and Visitors Bureau. All others by Ben Lipson.

Fresh Mushroom Soffritto recipe on page 24 reprinted with permission from the *Post-Gazette*, Boston, Massachusetts, May 7, 1993 issue.

Library of Congress Cataloging-in-Publication Data
Buonopane, Marguerite DiMino.
        North End Italian cookbook / Marguerite DiMino Buonopane. -- 4th ed.
            p.   cm.
        Includes index.
        ISBN 1-56440-990-2
        1. Cookery, Italian.   I. Title.
    TX723.B785 1997
        641.5945--dc20
        DNLM/DLC
                                                                96-27596
                                                                CIP

Manufactured in the United States of America
Fourth Edition/Thirteenth Printing

 # Contents

Mama

 # Acknowledgments

For this fourth edition of the *North End Italian Cookbook,* I again want to acknowledge my beautiful mother. In my life I never remembered her ever saying no. Never did she complain about cooking, babysitting, shopping for us, or just being around to comfort us when we were ill.

Thank you to my daughter, Lisa Mediano. Your bright knowledge and keen mind helped me through some befuddling moments. And many thanks to you for our beautiful twins, Tessa and Savannah. Thank you Barney Waxman, my computer glitch fix-it man. You were never too busy to help. Thank you Laura Strom for being my mentor. So warm and soft and understanding. You were my guiding light.

As they say at the academy awards, the list goes on and on. So . . . thank you Angelo, my husband, for your inspiration. Love you Sal and Dina, David, Michael, Stephen and Gina, Cesarae, little Steve, and baby Michael. Also, thank you to my school chums Barbara, Claire, Joanie, Margaret, Marie, Patty and Patty, and dear Tillie. We spent much time reminiscing about all the good food we ate in our younger years and talking about the importance of keeping our family traditions alive.

Thank you, Charles Everitt, for your time and patience as you carefully guided me through the many befuddling moments that faced this novice writer. Thanks also to my brother, Dom Capossela, and Toni Lee for all the wonderful recipes you shared with me from your famous restaurant. To Pamela, editor of the *Post Gazette,* and Frances, this foodie is glad to be a part of a most cooperative staff.

I appreciate each and every one of you.

Papa

 # Introduction

Why another *North End Italian Cookbook?* Well, why not? Can anyone ever get enough of the delicious repetitions of Italian cuisine—the pastas, the tomatoes, the cheeses, the herbs, and the olive oil? Judging from the requests, suggestions, and prodding of friends, readers, and neighborhood people, I have concluded the answer is no. So, in this edition I have renewed every treasured recipe from my earlier cookbooks, plus I've added seventy-five more tried-and-true favorites. Many are family recipes, cooked in the way I remember my mother and grandparents used to cook. I call it peasant style, as our family recipes are from the Roman region of Italy, where these were the foods of the common people. But many were created right here in Boston's North End. All in all, I have both recaptured days gone by and preserved the present-day traditions of North End Italian cooking.

To some people food means something to eat, nothing more. To cooks in my neighborhood, food is a poem, an adventure. It means eye-appealing colors, nose-tingling aromas, mouth-watering tastes—ideas that stir the imagination. Cooking can become truly exciting if you follow my Old World–style recipes. As my guide, I chose two New World–style principles. Each dish must appeal to the average family, and the ingredients must be commonly available. Collected over many years, the recipes come from my family, my friends, myself, and, of course, from my mother and grandmother. Using these recipes as guides, you can incorporate over time a style of your own, one that suits your family's tastes. And with this book you will be guided every step of the way in the art of cooking Italian. It's as if you were taking a cooking class in which you are the only student.

When you blend the golds of Italy—olive oil, garlic, and Italian herbs and spices—you create a fragrance fit for the gods as well as the hungry mortals who will come begging for a sample. If you use these recipes, you will satisfy that hunger and create or rekindle your own history of Italian favorites.

Don't get discouraged by the lengthier recipes. Do you think your grandmother had it easy? When you enjoyed her wonderful pastries and pastas, you shared the fruits of her efforts. Now you can create them, too. Allow yourself the joy she felt as you prepare these dishes. Allow yourself also to improvise as she did. Add or substitute a little more or a little bit less of this or that ingredient. Experiment. Make cooking a piece of personal artwork. Through improvisation, many cooks have become great. With this cookbook, you too can become a great cook, pleasing your friends and family with the wonderful aromas and delicious tastes of Italian cooking.

Antipasto, Salads, and Appetizers

 Antipasto Salad Platter

I serve antipasto as a way of keeping my guests happily eating while I'm in the kitchen putting the finishing touches on the other courses. The salad dressing is also good on any garden salad, and it will keep indefinitely in the refrigerator.

> **1 head romaine or iceberg lettuce, washed and drained**
> **1 red bell pepper, thinly sliced**
> **1 green bell pepper, thinly sliced**
> **4 large mushrooms, wiped clean and sliced**
> **¼ pound Provolone cheese, thinly sliced**
> **1 8-ounce can chickpeas, drained**
> **¼ pound Genoa salami, thinly sliced**
> **½ cup small black pitted olives**
> **1 large tomato, cut in wedges**
> **1 medium onion, thinly sliced**

1. Trim the lettuce and tear the leaves into bite-size pieces. Arrange the leaves on a large serving platter.

2. Add the remaining ingredients, spreading them evenly over the lettuce.

Salad Dressing

> **½ cup olive or vegetable oil**
> **¼ cup lemon juice**
> **1 teaspoon salt**
> **½ teaspoon freshly ground black pepper**
> **⅛ teaspoon dried crushed red pepper flakes**
> **1 garlic clove, crushed**
> **1 tablespoon snipped fresh basil leaves, or 1 teaspoon dried basil**

1. Combine the ingredients in a jar with a tightly fitting lid. Shake until well blended.

2. Pour the dressing onto the antipasto ingredients and toss gently, using two large spoons. Serve.

Serves 8

 # Cold Stuffed Eggplant

This makes a wonderful appetizer, lunch, or light dinner, served with a salad and garlic bread. It is a very unusual and hard-to-come-by dish. I once made this on television, and the cast devoured it in no time. Serve warm or cold.

> **3 medium-size, firm eggplants**
> **olive oil**
> **1 cup onions, chopped**
> **2 garlic cloves, mashed**
> **3 ounces canned tomato paste (or slightly more)**
> **¼ cup chopped fresh parsley**
> **3 anchovy fillets, chopped**
> **1½ tablespoons dried oregano**
> **pinch of dried red pepper flakes**
> **salt and pepper to taste**
> **drop of Tabasco (optional)**
> **1 pound ground beef**
> **¾ cup freshly grated Romano or Pecorino cheese**
> **1 cup or more fresh bread crumbs**

1. Wipe eggplants with a paper towel and cut in half, lengthwise. Scoop out the pulp, leaving a ½-inch shell. Chop the pulp into small cubes. Turn the pulp onto paper towels and drain for a half hour.

2. Heat ¼ inch of olive oil in a large skillet. Saute the chopped onions and mashed garlic until soft.

3. Add the chopped eggplant pulp and cook for a few minutes.

4. Put the mixture in a large bowl. Add the tomato paste (you may need more to achieve a rich color), parsley, anchovies, oregano, red pepper flakes, salt, pepper, and Tabasco. Toss the mixture until well blended.

5. Brown the meat in any remaining juices in the skillet. Drain and discard all fat. Season the meat with salt and pepper.

6. Combine the meat with the eggplant mixture, grated cheese, and just enough bread crumbs to hold the mixture together (about 1 cup). Put the filling into the eggplant shells.

7. Place the filled shells in a baking pan and pour in water or stock to slightly cover the bottom of the pan. Cover the pan tightly with aluminum foil.

8. Set the pan on the middle rack of a preheated 375-degree oven. Bake for 1 hour. Then remove the foil and bake 10 more minutes on the top rack.

9. Serve at room temperature or refrigerate for a couple of days. Cut into thick slices just prior to eating.

Serves 6

 Warm Green Beans and  Potatoes Insalata

When fresh beans are available, my guests always enjoy this simple peasant salad, which is delicious warm or cold. Serve it for lunch with leftovers or as a side dish at dinner.

> *1 pound fresh green beans, tips removed, and snapped in half*
> *½ pound small potatoes, unpeeled*
> *⅓ cup olive oil*
> *3 tablespoons wine vinegar*
> *2–3 garlic cloves, chopped*
> *1 tablespoon (or more) dried oregano*
> *1 tablespoon chopped fresh parsley*
> *pinch dried red pepper flakes (optional)*
> *salt and freshly ground black pepper to taste*

1. Steam the beans for 8 to 10 minutes, until tender. Drain and place on a serving platter.

2. Boil the potatoes until tender. Drain (do not rinse), let cool, and then cube, leaving the skin on. Add to the green beans.

3. Using a large spoon, gently toss the beans and potatoes with the remaining ingredients.

4. Serve the salad at room temperature or refrigerate for a marinated flavor.

Serves 4–6

 Arugula and Radicchio
Salad

Arugula has to be my favorite of all lettuce. Add other vegetables, if desired, or just serve with this delicious dressing. The dressing is on the rich side, so use only as much as needed and reserve the rest for another day.

Salad

> **2 bunches arugula**
> **2 small heads radicchio**

1. Rinse and trim the arugula.

2. Cut the cores from the radicchio, rinse, and tear the leaves into bite-size pieces.

3. Dry arugula and radicchio. Wrap in paper towels, place in a plastic bag, and refrigerate until cold, about 30 minutes.

Creamy Garlic Dressing

> **½ large egg yolk**
> **juice of ½ lemon**
> **1 tablespoon red-wine vinegar, plus additional to taste**
> **1½ teaspoons mustard (Dijon), plus additional to taste**
> **1 clove garlic, minced**
> **salt and freshly ground pepper to taste**
> **¼ cup olive oil**
> **2 tablespoons vegetable oil**
> **2 tablespoons chopped fresh parsley**

1. Whisk the egg yolk, lemon juice, vinegar, mustard, garlic, salt, and pepper.

2. Gently mix in the oils until the mixture forms a creamy consistency.

3. Just before serving, place the greens in one or two large salad bowls. Divide the dressing evenly between the bowls. Toss well to combine. Garnish with parsley.

Serves 6

Tomatoes with Fresh Basil and Olive Oil

Simple and delicious —use only fresh ripe tomatoes for this recipe.

1 pound yellow, orange, or red plum tomatoes
   OR cherry tomatoes (whatever is in season or readily available)
¼ cup fruity olive oil
10–15 fresh basil leaves
salt and freshly ground pepper to taste
8 ounces buffalo mozzarella, cut in chunks (optional)

1. Place the tomatoes in a colander; rinse well under cold running water. Drain and pat thoroughly dry with paper toweling.
2. Toss the tomatoes with the olive oil, basil leaves, and salt and pepper to taste in a medium bowl. If using, add the mozzarella and toss again.
3. Let stand at room temperature until serving time, tossing occasionally. This makes a nice appetizer or side dish.

Serves 3–4

This recipe can also be prepared with regular-size fresh ripe tomatoes, sliced. Simply brush the slices with a little olive oil and sprinkle with salt, pepper, and the basil leaves. Add some pitted, dry-cured black olives for garnish.

◆◆◆ Fennel and Tomato Salad ◆◆◆

Hopefully you have access to some fresh, ripe tomatoes from your garden or your neighbor's. The anise bite of fennel and the zest of orange give this tomato salad a continental flavor.

1 bunch red leaf lettuce
6 medium tomatoes, quartered
1 bunch fennel, thinly sliced
½ cup arugula, cut into small strips
1 dozen Sicilian dry-cured olives, pitted (or use canned)
6 tablespoons olive oil
2 tablespoons lemon juice
2 garlic cloves, finely chopped
1 teaspoon grated orange peel
¼ teaspoon salt
freshly ground pepper to taste

1. Arrange lettuce leaves on a decorative platter. Reserve.

2. In a medium-size bowl, add quartered tomatoes, fennel, arugula, and olives.

3. In a screw-top jar, mix the oil, lemon juice, garlic, orange peel, salt, and pepper together.

4. Pour dressing over the salad and toss lightly.

5. Place tomato mixture over lettuce on platter.

6. Serve at room temperature or refrigerate, covered with plastic wrap, for no more than 2 days.

Serves 8–10

Cannelini Beans Insalata

I love this salad so much that I always keep some on hand for unexpected guests. It makes a wonderfully healthy lunch or an excellent appetizer. Beans were always so plentiful as I was growing up that my mother created plenty of different ways to use them. In the ingredients list, I have given you several options for enhancing the recipe. What I like to do is toss in anything appropriate that I find in my refrigerator.

2 cups cannellini beans, or any beans, fresh or canned
2 tablespoons lemon juice, freshly squeezed
¼ cup olive oil
salt and freshly grated pepper, to taste
¼ cup fresh parsley, chopped
2 garlic cloves, chopped
½ cup Sicilian dry-cured olives, pitted and halved (optional)
¼ cup goat cheese, crumbled (optional)
¼ cup sun-dried tomatoes, chopped (optional)
¼ cup red pepper, cut in strips (optional)
Red onion slices (for garnish)

1. Place drained beans on a decorative platter; sprinkle with lemon juice, olive oil, salt and fresh pepper to taste, parsley, chopped garlic, and remaining ingredients, if using.

2. Garnish with onion slices.

3. Serve warm or refrigerate at least 1 hour to allow flavors to blend.

VARIATION: For a wonderful quick pasta e fagiole, add a ladle or two of the bean mixture to the reserved broth. Add fresh chopped tomatoes or tomato sauce to give the broth a rosy color, adjust seasonings, and add some cooked pasta. Don't forget the grated cheese.

Serves 6–8

If you are using fresh beans for this salad, it is not necessary to soak the beans overnight. Just rinse them thoroughly, remove any stones or foreign objects, and boil in enough water to cover. Don't add any salt to the water, for the salt will hinder the cooking process. When the water comes to a boil, simmer beans for 15 minutes. Then add a drizzle of olive oil, one crushed garlic clove, and pinch of chicken bouillon powder. Simmer for 1 to 1½ hours, or until tender. Remove beans from broth (reserve broth), add beans to a serving platter, and continue with above recipe.

 Lentil Salad

3 cups lentils, picked over, washed, and drained
⅓ cup red-wine vinegar
½ cup olive oil
¼ cup red onion, finely chopped
½ cup scallions (white part only), finely chopped
2 tablespoons fresh mint, chopped
2 tablespoons fresh parsley, chopped
salt and freshly ground black pepper to taste

1. Bring a large saucepan of water to boil. Drop in the lentils and return the water to a boil, stirring often. Lower the heat and let the lentils simmer steadily for 20 to 25 minutes or until they are tender.

2. Drain them into a colander, shake to remove excess moisture, and pile into a bowl.

3. While still hot, add the vinegar and oil and stir gently but thoroughly. Let them sit until they cool completely.

4. Add the onion, scallions, mint, parsley, salt, and pepper; stir again.

5. Cover with plastic wrap and leave at room temperature for 1 hour for the flavors to mellow, stirring occasionally.

6. Taste for seasoning and serve at room temperature.

Serves 6

 Insalata di Fagioli

BEAN SALAD, ITALIAN STYLE

A short version of my bean salad, this appetizer will introduce you to the combined flavors of fresh cheese, peppers, and olives.

> **1 20-ounce can red kidney beans or black beans, rinsed and drained well**
> **2 tablespoons lemon juice**
> **olive oil**
> **salt and freshly ground pepper to taste**
> **¼ cup fresh parsley, chopped**
> **2 cloves garlic, chopped**
> **black dry-cured olives (optional)**
> **1 red bell pepper, chopped into bits (optional)**
> **½ cup goat cheese (optional)**

1. Place the beans in a serving dish large enough to accommodate the beans neatly.
2. Toss them gently with fresh lemon juice, olive oil, salt and pepper, fresh parsley, and chopped garlic.
3. Garnish with black olives, which have been pitted and cut in half, and red pepper for crunch and color. Serve at room temperature.
4. Sprinkle goat cheese over mixture and serve at room temperature.

Serves 2

If you have any leftover bean salad, just throw it in a blender and grind away. Add a drop or two more of olive oil, and you will have the best bean dip ever. Serve with crackers or crusty bread.

 Gnocchi Insalata

Gnocchi doesn't have to be eaten warm to be enjoyed! This chilled version is a nice change from the ordinary. It makes a wonderful lunch or does well as an appetizer or as part of an antipasto plate.

1 pound gnocchi, cooked and chilled
1 cup green peas, fresh or frozen
½ cup Sicilian dry-cured olives, pitted and halved
1 green bell pepper, seeded and chopped in bits
½ cup red onion, finely chopped
½ cup fresh basil leaves, chopped
pinch of dry mint or fresh mint, chopped

1. Place the chilled gnocchi in a decorative serving platter.

2. Drop the peas into salted boiling water and cook until tender, about 3–5 minutes.

3. Remove peas and allow to chill.

4. Combine the gnocchi, peas, black olives, green pepper, onion, basil, and mint; stir gently until well blended.

5. Toss with dressing (recipe below).

Dressing

3 tablespoons olive oil
2 tablespoons red-wine vinegar
2 tablespoons tomato paste
salt and ground pepper to taste

1. Place all ingredients in a glass jar and shake until well blended.

2. Pour over gnocchi salad and refrigerate.

3. Serve cold.

Serves 6–8

Eggplant Frittelles

Try this easy recipe if you need to add another quick, delicious appetizer or side vegetable dish to your meal. Don't expect these to taste like eggplant. Excellent either plain or topped with marinara sauce; they are very similar in texture to meatballs and a great meat substitute for vegetarians. I get nothing but raves over this recipe.

> **1 pound eggplant**
> **1 cup fresh bread crumbs, grated**
> **¾ cup Parmesan cheese, grated**
> **2 fresh garlic cloves, chopped**
> **¼ cup fresh parsley, chopped**
> **2 eggs**
> **salt and pepper to taste**
> **flour for dredging**
> **olive oil**
> **marinara sauce for dipping (optional)**

1. Peel the eggplants and halve them lengthwise.

2. In a large pot of water, simmer eggplant halves for 40 minutes or until they are tender.

3. Drain eggplant well, and puree in a food mill or processor until texture is smooth.

4. Transfer eggplant to a medium-size bowl and add bread crumbs, grated cheese, garlic, parsley, eggs, and salt and pepper to taste; mix well using a wooden spoon.

5. Flour your hands and shape eggplant mixture into little balls.

6. Roll the balls in flour and set aside.

7. Heat olive oil in a small saucepan (about 2 inches of oil). When oil is very hot, deep-fry the eggplant balls, two or three at a time, until crisp and golden.

8. Drain on paper towels and remove to a warm platter. Serve immediately if possible.

Serves 4

 Roasted Peppers Salad

This tried-and-true recipe is one of my old-time favorites, handed down from three generations. It's sure to be a big hit at family reunions, get-togethers, or parties. I like a combination of red and yellow peppers, but one or the other alone will do fine. A good brand of canned peppers will suffice if you are unable to obtain fresh ones. Anchovies are salty, so use them with discretion.

4 whole red bell peppers (or 2 yellow, 2 red)
½ cup pure olive oil
½ cup fresh parsley, chopped
4 garlic cloves, chopped
1 can flat anchovy fillets, chopped
½ teaspoon red pepper flakes
black Sicilian dry-cured olives, pitted and halved
salt and pepper to taste

1. Heat broiler, then place whole peppers on lowest rack from heat, turning often until the skin is charred and blistered, about 10–15 minutes. (Use tongs to turn, so peppers won't bruise.)
2. Remove peppers and place in heavy paper bag, closing tightly so steam won't escape. Place bag in a bowl, and let cool.
3. Scrape cooled peppers, using your fingertips, and peel away the charred skin.
4. Carefully tear the peppers in long strips, place them on a decorative platter, and cover them with olive oil.
5. Scatter the remaining ingredients evenly over the peppers, cover with plastic wrap, and refrigerate at least 1 hour to blend flavors.

Serves 4

Pepper salad will keep in the refrigerator for at least 3 days.

 Fried Mozzarella Sticks

1 pound mozzarella cheese
all-purpose flour, for dredging
3 eggs, beaten
salt to taste
4 ounces bread crumbs, finely grated
1 cup olive oil

1. Cut mozzarella in 3-inch square chunks.

2. Put flour in a shallow dish, the eggs in a small bowl, and the bread crumbs on wax paper.

3. Roll cheese in flour, then dip into eggs, and roll in bread crumbs.

4. Once again, dip into eggs and bread crumbs. Reserve.

5. Using a heavy skillet, heat 1 cup olive oil, on medium-high heat.

6. Fry cheese bits until golden brown.

7. Drain on paper towels and serve immediately.

Serves 6

 Spinach and Mushroom  Salad

Salads can be very boring, so I thought I would share this favorite of mine. Very tasty and low in calories, it makes a wonderful lunch. For best results, use fresh, coarsely grated Parmesan cheese.

1 package spinach, washed and cleaned
1 pound mushrooms, thinly sliced
2 stalks celery, very thinly sliced (optional)
3 garlic cloves, chopped
⅓ cup olive oil
3 tablespoons lemon juice, freshly squeezed
salt and freshly ground black pepper to taste
¼ pound whole piece Parmesan

1. Tear spinach into bite-size pieces and put in large salad bowl.

2. Add sliced mushrooms, sliced celery, and chopped garlic.

3. Sprinkle olive oil and lemon juice over salad; toss lightly.

4. Add salt and pepper and toss well.

5. Generously grate fresh Parmesan over vegetables.

6. Serve at room temperature.

Serves 4–6

 # Stuffed Eggplant Rolls

This recipe is a wonderful variation for eggplant. You need not remove the skin; it will help keep the slices from tearing. You will need my recipe for marinara sauce. The Sicilians are noted for using hard-boiled eggs in their cooking, and we are doing the same here.

> **2 large eggplants, thinly sliced**
> **olive oil**
> **1 onion, thinly sliced**
> **1 cup soft bread crumbs, freshly grated**
> **½ cup Parmesan cheese**
> **2 cups shredded mozzarella**
> **2 hard-boiled eggs, chopped**
> **1 tablespoon fresh parsley, chopped**
> **salt and pepper to taste**
> **marinara sauce**

1. Heat ¼ cup olive oil in a heavy skillet, using high heat.
2. Saute slices of eggplant in hot oil until they are golden brown on both sides.
3. Drain on paper towels and reserve.
4. Using same skillet, heat 2 tablespoons of olive oil over medium heat and saute the sliced onion until golden brown.
5. Lower heat and add the soft bread crumbs.
6. Quickly stir mixture until bread is golden in color.
7. Turn off the heat and, to the same skillet, add the Parmesan cheese, shredded mozzarella, chopped eggs, fresh parsley, and salt and pepper to taste. Toss well.
8. Preheat oven to 350 degrees.
9. Spread each eggplant slice with 1 teaspoon of the bread crumb stuffing mixture and 1 teaspoon of marinara sauce.
10. Roll up slices and secure with toothpicks.
11. Place rolls, seam side down, in an oiled baking dish.

12. Spread remaining bread crumbs over eggplant and drizzle each roll with olive oil.

13. Cover with remaining Parmesan cheese and 1 tablespoon chopped parsley.

14. Bake in hot oven for 15 minutes, or until bread mixture is crusty and browned.

15. You may top cooked eggplant rolls with extra marinara sauce and cheese if desired.

16. Serve as an appetizer or side dish with pasta or meat.

Serves 4

 # Panzanella

STALE BREAD AND TOMATO SALAD

For this salad you may add any leftovers from your refrigerator. Be sure to adjust the vinegar, oil, and seasonings to taste.

> 8 slices crusty italian or french bread, 3 days old
> ½ bunch fresh basil, stems removed
> 1 pound soft, ripe tomatoes, chopped
> 1 ripe cucumber, peeled and thinly sliced
> salt and pepper to taste
> ¼ cup olive oil
> 3 tablespoons red-wine vinegar
> ½ red onion, thinly sliced
> ½ cup fresh parsley, chopped

1. Cut bread into bite-sized pieces and put in a large bowl. Sprinkle bread with a little cold water to slightly dampen.

2. Pick over, wash, and dry the basil leaves; cut them into thin strips.

3. Add tomatoes and their juice, sliced cucumber, and basil to bread in bowl and toss well. Add salt and fresh ground pepper to taste.

4. Drizzle olive oil evenly over salad until glistening but not soaked; add vinegar and toss well. Adjust seasonings.

5. Decorate with sliced onion and chopped parsley. Allow salad to develop its flavors for at least 1 hour before serving it. For a more dramatic effect, bread salad may be put on a bed of lettuce leaves on a platter.

Serves 4

 Melanzana con Olio  e Aceto

PICKLED EGGPLANT

salt
1½ pounds eggplant, sliced very thin
3 cloves garlic, cut into large pieces
2 basil leaves, chopped fine OR ½ teaspoon dried basil
½ teaspoon oregano
1–2 hot green peppers (optional)
1½ cups wine vinegar
oil

1. Sprinkle salt very lightly on the sliced eggplant. Let stand about 30 minutes.

2. Put the slices into a pile and press until most of the liquid drains out. Squeeze well and wipe dry.

3. Arrange the slices in a 1-quart screw-cap jar that has been sterilized.

4. Add the garlic, basil, oregano, peppers, and vinegar to every other layer until all ingredients are used. Press down firmly and pour enough olive oil to cover the eggplant mixture.

5. Store in refrigerator at least 48 hours. Serve as an appetizer with crackers or toasted French bread.

Yield: 1 quart

 Mom's Potato and  Egg Frittata

A frittata is an Italian peasant version of the French omelette. It was used to turn eggs into a full meal. Use this recipe for a quick lunch or serve in crusty rolls as sandwiches. We can't get enough of this, especially when sprinkled with extra cheese and black pepper or even a shot or two of Tabasco.

> **8 large eggs**
> **3 tablespoons milk**
> **¼ cup freshly grated Parmesan cheese**
> **2 tablespoons fresh parsley, chopped**
> **salt and pepper to taste**
> **¼ cup plus 1 tablespoon olive oil**
> **2 medium potatoes, peeled and thinly sliced**
> **1 medium onion, thinly sliced**

1. In a large mixing bowl, beat the eggs with a whisk or fork until foamy. Add the milk, grated cheese, parsley, salt, and pepper.

2. Heat ¼ cup of oil in a heavy skillet over high heat. Sprinkle a dash of salt on the bottom of the pan and add the sliced potatoes (the salt will prevent potatoes from sticking). Fry about 5 minutes or until crisp.

3. Add the sliced onions and cook until tender, tossing gently with a spatula.

4. Put the potato and onion mixture in the bowl of beaten eggs. Stir gently.

5. Return the skillet to the heat. Drizzle in the tablespoon of olive oil to coat the pan sides, using a rotating motion. Pour the egg mixture into the pan, reduce the heat to medium-low, and stir briskly with a fork, pulling the cooked egg from the sides to the center of the pan. Continue stirring until the mixture starts to set. Cook slowly until the edges start to brown.

6. Remove the frittata from the heat, cover, and let rest for 5 minutes. Cut into wedges and serve.

7. If you prefer to brown both sides of the frittata, place a large plate on top of the skillet and slide the frittata out. Then, flip it upside down back into the skillet so that the uncooked side is down. Cook for 5 minutes more. Remove from the heat and let rest 5 minutes.

Serves 6

Frittata Arrabiata

HOT AND SPICY OMELETTE

This recipe is a fancy version of a plain omelette. Serve it to friends or just when you feel like going all out. Enjoy!

6 eggs
2 tablespoons warm water
¼ cup freshly grated Parmesan cheese
2 tablespoons fresh parsley, chopped
salt and pepper to taste
⅓ cup olive oil
1 medium onion, thinly sliced
¼ pound mushrooms, sliced
3 large hot vinegar peppers, sliced
2 tablespoons grated mozzarella cheese
6 pitted black olives, halved
2 ounces canned roasted peppers, cut in pieces
pinch of fresh basil or mint

1. In a large mixing bowl, whisk the eggs until foamy. Add the water, grated cheese, parsley, salt, and pepper.

2. Heat the oil in a large skillet over medium heat. Add the onions, mushrooms, vinegar peppers, and a shake of salt and pepper. Saute.

3. When the vegetables are tender, raise the heat to high. Slowly drizzle the egg mixture over the vegetables in the pan, gently pushing the edges of the batter to the middle of the pan where it is the hottest. This will enable the omelette to set properly.

4. When the omelette is three-fourths firm, sprinkle with the mozzarella cheese, olives, roasted peppers, and pinch of basil or mint. Cook a few more minutes.

5. Turn off the heat, cover the pan and let the omelette set for 5 to 7 minutes, or until it is moist and firm. Cut into wedges and serve immediately.

Serves 4

Prosciutto and Melon

This recipe makes an excellent, light, and tasty appetizer. If you like a decorative look, serve it on a bed of lettuce with a few black olives on the side. The color combination is very attractive!

1 large cantaloupe or honeydew melon
8 ounces imported prosciutto, thinly sliced
1 lime, cut in 8 wedges

1. Cut the melon into 8 wedges. Remove the seeds from each wedge, but leave on the skin.

2. Make crosswise cuts ½ inch apart into each wedge, cutting down close to the skin. Lay the wedges on serving plates or a serving platter.

3. Drape a piece of prosciutto across the top of each wedge of melon. Top with a lime wedge.

4. To eat, squeeze the lime onto the prosciutto. Cut into the prosciutto where the melon has been cut, and then lift up a piece of melon and prosciutto on your fork.

Serves 8

Mozzarella en Carrozza

MOZZARELLA IN A "CARRIAGE"

This is an Italian version of a grilled cheese sandwich. For this recipe, you may use any favorite large loaf of Italian bread. But if you are lucky enough to have an Italian bakery nearby, specify a bastone. *This is a crusty bread shaped into a large loaf that is slit on top. It is ideal for this recipe.*

> **1 long loaf Italian bread**
> **¾ pound mozzarella or fontina cheese, sliced ¼ inch thick**
> **1 2-ounce can anchovy fillets, washed and drained**
> **2 medium eggs**
> **3 tablespoons milk**
> **½ cup olive oil**
> **lemon wedges for garnish**
> **fresh parsley sprigs for garnish**

1. Cut the bread into 14 half-inch slices. Make 7 sandwiches, by adding a slice of cheese and 1 anchovy fillet to each.

2. Whisk the eggs with the milk. Dip each sandwich in the mixture and set aside.

3. Heat the olive oil in a large heavy skillet over medium heat. Fry the sandwiches on both sides until golden brown. Drain on paper toweling, slice in half, and serve immediately.

4. Garnish with the lemon wedges and fresh parsley.

Serves 5–7

Fresh Mushroom Soffritto

This recipe is so good and easy! The tomato paste gives the mushrooms a sweet, pungent flavor, which gets tastier as it reaches room temperature. Try to use button mushrooms, especially if serving as an appetizer. If you choose large mushrooms, cut them in big chunks. These are great to take on a picnic or even as a side dish with your favorite roast. I love them for lunch with some Tuscan bread and an arugula salad.

> olive oil
> 2 pounds fresh mushrooms
> 5 garlic cloves, chopped
> 3–4 small red hot peppers, chopped (optional)
> salt and pepper to taste
> 2 large onions, thinly sliced
> 3 red bell peppers, thinly sliced
> 3 green bell peppers, thinly sliced
> 1 small can tomato paste
> 20 Sicilian dry-cured black olives (pitted)
> 2 tablespoons oregano

1. In large skillet, add enough olive oil to cover bottom of pan.

2. Using medium heat, saute mushrooms, garlic, and hot peppers (if using). You may substitute 1 teaspoon crushed red pepper flakes for the hot peppers if you wish. Salt and pepper to taste.

3. When mushrooms are lightly browned, reserve to a platter.

4. In same skillet, add more oil if needed and saute onions and peppers until tender.

5. When pepper and onion mixture is slightly limp, add the cooked reserved mushrooms. Saute a minute or so to blend all the flavors.

6. Add 1 can of tomato paste, and, using a wooden spoon, stir gently until the paste is dissolved and the vegetables are nicely coated with the sauce.

7. Add oregano, pitted olives, and additional salt and pepper if needed. Toss gently and simmer 1 minute.

8. Serve at room temperature.

Serves 4–6

Soups

Old-Fashioned Chicken Soup

My mother passed on this wonderful recipe to us, and I am sharing it with you.

1 3½-pound fowl, quartered
2 tablespoons salt
1 tablespoon black pepper
4 medium carrots, scraped and sliced
3 celery stalks with leaves, chopped
4 fresh parsley sprigs
4 small potatoes, peeled
3 fresh tomatoes, chopped, or 1 cup canned tomatoes
2 large onions, quartered
about 10 tablespoons freshly grated Parmesan or Romano cheese

This broth is a good do-ahead recipe, as it should be refrigerated for a day before using it to let the fat congeal so it can be discarded. This broth also freezes perfectly.

1. Wash the fowl thoroughly and remove and discard excess fat. Place the fowl in a large stockpot and add the vegetables and seasonings. Add cold water to 1 inch above the height of the ingredients.

2. Bring the pot to a gentle boil, then reduce to a simmer. Cook slowly, uncovered, for about 2 hours. (The fowl may be removed after 1½ hours if it is cooked through, but the stock should continue cooking for another half hour.) Reserve the fowl.

3. Cool the broth and then refrigerate. The next day, remove and discard the congealed fat from the top of the broth. Remove the vegetables. Process the vegetables and add back to soup for a thick texture. I like to keep them chopped and added to the soup bowls along with the shredded chicken.

4. Reheat the broth and serve with about a tablespoon of grated cheese on each serving.

VARIATION: Just before serving, add 2 cups of cooked rice to the strained broth and heat until the rice is hot. Or cook ½ pound tiny pasta such as *acini di pepe* in 2 quarts boiling water, drain, add to the strained broth, and serve immediately. Note: If pasta remains in the soup for a period of time, it will absorb much of the broth and thicken it. Only add pasta when the broth is ready to serve. The farina dumplings (page 27) are a good alternative to the rice or pasta.

Serves 10 (generously)

 Farina Dumplings

These dumplings are traditional additions to meatless soups, often used when the pasta and trimmings of a soup were eaten up after the first serving. You can save this recipe for day two of a big pot of soup, or make them right from the start for a hearty addition to a lighter soup.

Farina is a light flour that can be purchased at any market. This type of flour was a staple in the Italian homes in my neighborhood, and many a good recipe was created because of its availability. The dumplings in this recipe are boiled in water first, then added to the broth.

¼ pound butter
3 eggs
salt to taste
½ pound farina (about 1¼ cups)

1. Using a medium bowl, whip butter till light and fluffy.

2. Add eggs, salt to taste, and farina.

3. Stir slightly (batter should be lumpy). If batter seems too thin, add a little more flour. Let stand 15 minutes.

4. Drop small lumps of batter from a teaspoon into a medium-size pot of boiling water. Cover and simmer 10 minutes.

5. Remove from heat and let stand an additional 10 minutes.

6. Remove dumplings from water and drain in a colander.

7. Drop into hot soup and stir to coat with broth. Serve with soup in bowls.

Serves 6–8

Chicken Soup with Escarole and Polpettini

Once you accomplish making a homemade soup, it will become a simple and enjoyable task. The secret to this is the secret to all Italian cooking—having the basic ingredients on hand. That will always encourage you to plunge into almost any recipe without fear.

1 plump fowl, about 4–5 pounds
2 celery stalks with leaves, halved
2 fresh parsley sprigs
2 scraped carrots
1 large ripe tomato, chopped
salt and pepper to taste
1½ pounds escarole, well washed and cut crosswise into thin shreds
½ cup water
1 pound ground beef
2 tablespoons freshly grated Romano cheese
1 teaspoon fresh parsley, chopped
½ pound tiny pasta such as pastina, orzo, or acini di pepe

1. Clean and wash fowl well. Discard excess fat. Place fowl in a soup pot and add cold water to cover. Bring it slowly to a boil and skim the surface often.

2. When the water stays fairly clean, add the celery, parsley, carrots, tomato, salt, and pepper.

3. Cover the pot tightly and cook slowly over low heat until the fowl is tender, about 2½ hours. Strain the broth. (The chicken may be used for chicken salad sandwiches another day or the white meat may be boned and added to the broth.) Refrigerate the broth until the fat has congealed on top. Remove and discard the fat.

4. Reheat the broth over medium heat. Put the escarole in a large skillet with the ½ cup water.

Simmer for 3 minutes, strain, squeeze out excess water, and add to the broth.

5. Combine the ground beef, cheese, parsley, and salt and pepper to taste. Shape into balls no larger than a filbert (dip hands in water to keep the balls smooth and round), and drop into the hot, semi-boiling soup. These are the *polpettini* (tiny meatballs).

6. Cook the soup for ½ hour on low heat to combine the flavors thoroughly and to cook the meat.

7. Cook the pasta in 2 quarts of boiling salted water. Drain, do not rinse, and add to the soup just before serving.

Serves 10–15

This soup can be refrigerated for several days. It also freezes well.

 # Zuppa di Pesce with Brandy and Cream

When I make fish soup, I always buy the cheaper, but very fresh, fish from our local fish market. You should use a boneless chowder fish, such as cod, scrod, or flounder, for this recipe.

1½ pounds fish fillets, cut in bite-size pieces
3 tablespoons olive oil
2 medium onions, chopped
2 cloves garlic, crushed
½ teaspoon thyme
1 teaspoon turmeric (or saffron, if available)
salt and pepper to taste
1 teaspoon Tabasco sauce
¼ cup tomato paste
1 cup white wine
5 cups water
4 tablespoons brandy
2 cups cream

1. Rinse the fish in cold water and reserve.

2. Using a large, heavy skillet, saute the onions, garlic, thyme, and turmeric until transparent.

3. Add the fish, salt and pepper to taste, and Tabasco and cook for 5 minutes, tossing gently.

4. Stir in the tomato paste (use a wooden spoon), wine, and water. Bring to a soft boil, then reduce heat, and simmer for 5 more minutes.

5. Remove from heat and slowly add brandy and cream, stirring gently.

6. Return to heat and simmer for 5 more minutes.

7. Serve immediately in soup bowls with side dishes of salad and crusty bread.

Serves 6

 Stracciatella Soup

"LITTLE RAGS" SOUP

This is a quick soup that looks elegant on the table but takes very little work in the kitchen. It will keep in the refrigerator for at least 3 days, and it freezes well. Use your own homemade broth or canned broth.

> **2 eggs**
> **⅛ teaspoon salt**
> **freshly grated Parmesan cheese**
> **1 quart homemade chicken broth (see page 26), or canned**
> **¼ pound cooked acini di pepe or orzo pasta**
> **chopped fresh parsley for garnish**

1. Combine the eggs, salt, 2 tablespoons of cheese, and 3 tablespoons cool broth in a mixing bowl. Beat with a wire whisk for about 3 minutes.

2. Bring the remaining broth to the boiling point. Add the egg mixture slowly, stirring constantly with a fork. Let the soup simmer for at least 5 minutes.

3. Add cooked pasta to soup and simmer 5 minutes more.

4. Pour the soup into individual bowls and sprinkle with parsley and more grated cheese, if desired.

Serves 4

 # Nonna's Beef Soup

1 to 2 beef soup marrow bones, with marrow, cracked
1 pound beef chuck or eye of round
3 fresh tomatoes, chopped, or 1 8-ounce can tomatoes, squeezed to break into
    small pieces
2 carrots, scraped
1 large onion, quartered
1 potato, peeled
3 celery stalks with leaves, halved
3 parsley sprigs
salt and pepper to taste
½ pound pastina or acini di pepe, cooked and drained just before soup is ready to serve
freshly grated Parmesan cheese for garnish

1. Place the soup bones in cold water and boil for 3 minutes. Drain and rinse well. You may need to repeat process until water is clear of residue.

2. Place the washed bones, beef, vegetables, and seasonings in a large soup pot. Cover with cold water, two inches above the ingredients. Slowly bring to a gentle boil, removing any foam that may form on top.

3. Simmer, covered, for about 2½ to 3 hours, stirring from time to time. Remove bones, meat, and vegetables. Shred the beef and reserve. The vegetables may be served as a side dish to this soup.

4. Strain the broth into another large pot and return to the heat. Add the cooked pasta and shredded beef. Pour into individual soup bowls and sprinkle with grated Parmesan cheese.

Serves 6

This soup freezes well or can be refrigerated for at least 3 or 4 days.

 # Soup Meat Insalata

When my mother made beef soup, she always used lots of beef. After the soup was placed in our bowls, she would take the remaining beef and tear it into shreds, placing it on a decorative platter. Then she would tear vinegar peppers into strips over it so that the juices would cover the meat. This mixture of peppers and beef would be drizzled with pure olive oil and sprinkled with salt and pepper to taste. We would cut crusty Italian bread and devour this wonderful meat salad. This is one of the lost recipes that I would like to share with you.

1 pound cooked beef chuck or eye of round, taken from soup and shredded
4 large vinegar peppers*
olive oil
salt and pepper to taste

1. Place the warm, shredded beef on a serving platter.

2. Tear the vinegar peppers and their juices over the beef.

3. Drizzle enough olive oil to generously cover the meat and peppers.

4. Add salt and pepper to taste.

5. Toss well and serve warm.

Serves 4

*Vinegar peppers may be purchased from the supermarket in jars, or you can make your own using the recipe on page 219.

My Homemade Minestrone Soup

I concocted this recipe at a North End Union luncheon, using the leftovers of the previous day. You might find it a good way to use your leftovers. You may omit some ingredients or add others. Use only what you have on hand, just adjust the seasonings. Garlic bread makes an excellent accompaniment.

1 quart cold water
1 medium onion, chopped
1 8-ounce can whole green beans, undrained
1 8-ounce can chickpeas, undrained
1 8-ounce can red kidney beans, undrained
1 small zucchini, unpeeled and diced
1 celery stalk with leaves, chopped
2 carrots, peeled and thinly sliced
1 16-ounce can chicken broth or 2 cups homemade broth
1 medium cabbage, chopped (remove center core)
1 8-ounce can medium-size peas, undrained
Quick Pesto Sauce (optional; see recipe opposite)
1 8-ounce can tomato sauce or 1 cup Marinara Sauce (see page 46)
½ cup cooked pastina, tubetini, acini di pepe, or raw rice
salt and pepper to taste
freshly grated Parmesan or Romano cheese

1. Place the first 11 ingredients in a large pot and bring to a slow boil. Lower heat and simmer uncovered for 1½ or 2 hours, stirring often.

2. Add the pesto sauce and tomato sauce to the soup. Adjust seasonings.

3. Bring sauce to a soft boil and add cooked pasta of your choice.

4. Ladle the soup into bowls and sprinkle with grated cheese.

Serves 6–8

Quick Pesto Sauce

> ¼ *cup olive oil*
> 1 *garlic clove, chopped*
> 1 *tablespoon chopped fresh basil leaves*
> 1 *tablespoon chopped fresh parsley*
> ½ *cup freshly grated Parmesan or Romano cheese*

1. Blend the ingredients in a blender until smooth.

 # La Minestra Mom's Way

Straight from my grandmother, her mother, and her mother's mother, this recipe reflects a truly "old style." It takes a while to prepare but is very nourishing and flavorful. It should be started the day before you wish to serve it. See your butcher for a fresh prosciutto bone. Don't concern yourself with its size, but have the butcher cut it into small pieces.

> 1 *cup white navy or pea beans*
> 1 *fresh prosciutto bone with meat attached*
> ½ *pound pepperoni, cut in chunks, OR 2 pounds spareribs, boiled, drained,*
> *and rinsed well, OR 2 pigs' feet, boiled, drained, rinsed well*
> 7–8 *garlic cloves, crushed*
> 1 *large Savoy cabbage, outer leaves removed, quartered*
> ½ *cup olive oil*
> *salt and pepper to taste*
> *dried red pepper flakes for garnish*

1. Wash the beans well, removing any imperfect ones. Soak overnight.

2. Soak the prosciutto bone for 6 to 8 hours in a bowl of water in the refrigerator, changing the water often.

3. Boil 6 cups of water. Gradually add the beans to the boiling water. Simmer 2 minutes, and remove from heat. Set aside to soak for 1 hour. Then rinse beans and strain.

4. Boil the prosciutto bone and the meat of your choice for 20 minutes. Rinse and strain. This will remove any fat or residue.

5. Put the clean prosciutto bones, your chosen meat, and the prepared beans in a large heavy pot. Cover with cold water to an inch over the bone and beans. Add 3 cloves of garlic. When the water comes to a boil, lower the heat and simmer. When the prosciutto meat starts to pull away from the bone (about 30 minutes), shut off the heat. Separate the meat from the prosciutto bones and put the meat back in the pot.

6. In a separate large pot, cook the cabbage until tender. Do not overcook. Strain, reserving some of the liquid. Put the cabbage in the pot with the beans and prosciutto.

7. Fry 4 or 5 cloves of garlic in the ½ cup of olive oil until brown. Add to the cabbage and beans. If the sauce seems too thick for your taste, add some of the cabbage broth. Simmer the entire mixture for 5 minutes, stirring with a wooden spoon. Add salt and pepper to taste (be careful with the salt, as prosciutto and pepperoni are highly salted).

8. Remove the pan from the heat and let rest for at least 2 hours so that all the flavors will be well combined. Refrigerate until ready to serve.

9. When you are ready to serve, reheat *La Minestra* on a low burner, heating only as much soup as needed. Serve in large bowls, topped with red pepper flakes. It is excellent with crusty Italian round bread.

Serves 6–8

 # Pasta e Fagioli

PASTA AND BEANS

We ate this very popular and easy-to-prepare soup at least twice a week as a filler before the main course. It can be used as a lunch dish or as a first course at dinner.

To Prepare Beans

> *½ pound white navy or pea beans*
> *6 cups cold water (sometimes I use leftover or canned chicken broth*
> *for a richer flavor)*
> *¼ cup olive oil*
> *2 garlic cloves, crushed*
> *salt and pepper to taste*

1. Wash the beans thoroughly and discard any imperfect ones.

2. Put the cold water in a large pot. Add the beans, garlic, oil, salt, and pepper.

3. Simmer until the beans are tender, about 1½ hours.

Marinara Sauce

> *1 garlic clove, chopped*
> *pinch of dried red pepper flakes, basil, and mint*
> *3 tablespoons olive oil*
> *1 8-ounce can tomatoes*
> *salt and pepper to taste*

1. In a small heavy skillet, slowly saute the garlic and seasonings in the olive oil on low heat until golden brown.

2. Add the tomatoes and a pinch more of each of the seasonings. Add salt and pepper to taste.

3. Simmer, uncovered, for 10 minutes on low heat.

To Finish Soup

> *1 teaspoon salt*
> *2 quarts water*
> *½ pound ditali, small shells, or elbow macaroni*
> *freshly grated Parmesan cheese*

1. Put the salt in the water and heat to boiling in a large saucepan.

2. Gradually add the pasta. Boil rapidly, uncovered, about 12 minutes or until al dente. Reserving 1 cup of liquid, drain the pasta in a colander, rinsing under cold water to prevent sticking. Reserve.

3. When the beans are tender, add the drained pasta and the marinara sauce to the pot. If more broth is desired, add the 1 cup of liquid from the pasta. Simmer 10 to 15 minutes.

4. Ladle into large soup dishes and sprinkle with grated Parmesan cheese. Serve immediately or the pasta will swell and absorb all the soup.

Serves 4–6

 # Pasta e Piselli

PASTA AND PEAS

This soup was a familiar one while I was growing up. I didn't appreciate it then, but I love it now. It makes a tasty and nourishing lunch, especially with garlic bread.

¼ cup olive oil
1 small onion, chopped
1 large garlic clove, chopped
2 teaspoons tomato paste
1 14-ounce can peeled Italian plum tomatoes
pinch of dried basil, mint, and red pepper flakes
1 8-ounce can medium-size sweet peas
salt and freshly ground black pepper to taste
1 pound small shells, ditali, or elbow macaroni
freshly grated Parmesan or Romano cheese for garnish

1. Heat the olive oil in a heavy saucepan, and saute the onion and garlic. When transparent, add the tomato paste. Mix well.

2. Add the canned tomatoes and juices, squeezing the tomatoes to break them up. Saute for a minute or two, then add basil, mint, and red pepper flakes. Stir gently for about 3 minutes over medium-low heat. Add the undrained can of peas. Simmer the sauce while you cook the pasta, adding more seasonings if desired and salt and pepper to taste.

4. Meanwhile, bring 2 quarts of salted water to a boil. Add the pasta. Boil rapidly, uncovered, about 10 minutes or until tender. Drain in a colander, reserving 2 cups of the water. Do not rinse. Transfer the pasta back to the pot, and add the tomato sauce and peas mixture.

5. Stir gently and add the pasta water until the sauce produces a nice broth texture.

6. Serve immediately with plenty of grated cheese.

Serves 6–8

TO BLANCH FRESH RIPE TOMATOES

Cut a cross along the bottom of each tomato. Drop in boiling water and cook for 1 minute or until skin loosens or splits (touch with a knife to ensure splitting). Remove from water and dip in cold water; then peel off skin. Blanched tomatoes can be frozen for future use in soups or stews.

When marinating, use a non-aluminum container to prevent the acid from discoloring the pan.

Italian-Style Split Pea Soup

This is great for lunch or as a first course, especially with a ham dinner. It can be refrigerated for several days or frozen.

> **1½ cups green split peas, picked over, washed, and drained**
> **1 large onion, chopped**
> **2 celery stalks, chopped**
> **1 large leek, chopped**
> **1 large garlic clove, halved**
> **1 large ripe tomato, chopped**
> **1 large carrot, peeled and chopped**
> **3 quarts cold water**
> **¼ cup olive oil**
> **salt and pepper to taste**

1. Place the peas in a 4-quart stockpot with the vegetables and the cold water. Drizzle with the olive oil.

2. Let the stock come to a boil. Stir well and add salt and pepper. Simmer for about 1½ hours, or until the peas are cooked tender but not mushy.

3. Ladle into large soup bowls and serve with croutons or garlic bread.

Serves 6–8

A good way to begin preparing a recipe is to have the basic ingredients on hand. The basics for Italian cooking are usually tomatoes—canned and/or fresh—fresh garlic, fresh parsley, freshly grated Italian cheese (Romano or Parmesan), fresh bread crumbs, and good olive oil.

 Lentil Soup

Even if you do not like lentils, you will not be able to resist this soup. My daughter used to turn up her nose at lentil soup when she was young. Now, as a married woman, she keeps containers of it in the freezer to serve to her friends gathered around the fireplace on a cold winter night. And she doesn't hesitate to accept the rave reviews!

½ pound lentils, picked over, washed, and drained
1½ quarts cold water
2 or 3 celery stalks with leaves, finely chopped
2 small carrots, chopped
1 tablespoon chopped fresh parsley
1 onion, chopped
1 garlic clove, chopped
1 tablespoon olive oil
3 ripe tomatoes, peeled and chopped, or ½ cup canned tomatoes
salt and pepper to taste
½ pound ditali, small shells, or elbow macaroni
freshly grated Parmesan cheese

1. Place the lentils in a large pot with the cold water. When the water comes to a soft boil, add the remaining ingredients, except the pasta and grated cheese.

2. Simmer, covered, for ½ hour or more, until tender.

3. Meanwhile, cook the pasta in 2 quarts of salted water until al dente. Drain the pasta, reserving 1 cup of liquid. Add the pasta to the soup.

4. Taste for seasonings and simmer 5 minutes. if the soup seems too dry, add some or all of the reserved pasta water.

5. Ladle into large soup bowls, sprinkle with grated cheese, and serve immediately for lunch and dinner along with a garden salad or antipasto.

This soup freezes well or can be refrigerated for several days.

Serves 4–6

 # Mediterranean Three-Bean Soup

The use of string beans in this soup gives it a distinct taste. It is important that you use fresh beans to appreciate the combination of the different bean flavors.

⅓ **cup olive oil**
2 leeks, coarsely chopped
2 stalks celery, coarsely chopped
2 cloves garlic, minced
4 cups chicken broth, fresh or canned
1 teaspoon thyme
1 teaspoon marjoram
1 bay leaf
pepper to taste
1½ cups cooked kidney beans
1½ cups cooked garbanzo beans
1 pound string beans, cut into 1-inch pieces
grated cheese

1. Heat the oil over moderate heat in a large soup pot.

2. Add the leeks, celery, and garlic and saute 3 to 4 minutes. Add the remaining ingredients except for the string beans and grated cheese.

3. Bring the soup to a boil; then lower heat. Simmer for 20 minutes.

4. Add the string beans and simmer for 15 to 20 minutes more, until the string beans are cooked but still crunchy. Serve with grated cheese.

Serves 4

 # Zuppa di Ceci con Acciughe

CHICKPEA SOUP WITH ANCHOVIES

Beans, beans, beans! What would we ever do without them? They are such a great staple and so adaptable to any recipe. Whether you prepare them fresh or from cans (in which case the texture might be softer), their flavor never changes. Use any small pasta for this recipe, or just enjoy the soup and beans alone.

> **olive oil**
> **pinch of dry basil**
> **1 garlic clove, finely chopped**
> **red pepper flakes**
> **1 ounce anchovy fillets, chopped**
> **2 tablespoons tomato paste**
> **½ cup water**
> **2 (16-ounce) cans chickpeas**
> **1 pint water**
> **salt and pepper to taste**
> **½ pound small shells or elbow pasta, cooked**
> **grated Parmesan cheese**

1. Using a medium stock pot, heat olive oil and saute basil, garlic, red pepper flakes, and anchovies on low heat until dissolved.

2. Dilute tomato paste in ½ cup water.

3. Add tomato paste solution to anchovy mixture; mix well, using a wooden spoon, and simmer for 10 minutes.

4. Add chickpeas (with canning liquid) and 1 pint water.

5. Bring to a boiling point and add salt and pepper to taste and a pinch of red pepper flakes.

6. Simmer about 10 minutes, then add cooked pasta.

7. Stir well and serve immediately in bowls; sprinkle well with grated Parmesan cheese.

Serves 6

Veal Soup

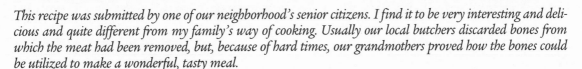

This recipe was submitted by one of our neighborhood's senior citizens. I find it to be very interesting and delicious and quite different from my family's way of cooking. Usually our local butchers discarded bones from which the meat had been removed, but, because of hard times, our grandmothers proved how the bones could be utilized to make a wonderful, tasty meal.

> **2½ pounds veal, with bone**
> **enough water to parboil the veal**
> **1 pound beef chuck**
> **6 quarts cold water**
> **2 stalks celery, chopped**
> **1 onion, thickly sliced**
> **2 carrots, cleaned and chopped**
> **¼ bunch parsley sprigs**
> **3 ripe tomatoes, chopped**
> **salt and pepper to taste**
> **1 cup tubettini pasta, cooked**
> **2 eggs, slightly beaten**
> **grated Romano cheese**

1. Bring a large pot of water to boil, add veal, and cook for 5 minutes.

2. Remove the veal from pan and drain, rinsing meat a few times until the rinse water is clean.

3. Refill the large soup pot with 6 quarts of fresh, cold water; add veal and bring to a soft boil.

4. Add beef, all vegetables, and salt and pepper to taste.

5. Simmer for 1½ hours, or until both meats are well cooked, skimming any residue from top of pan.

6. Remove meats, and when cool, tear into small pieces; reserve.

7. Strain the broth into another large soup pot, return to heat, and add the shredded meats.

8. Heat broth with meats and add cooked tubettini pasta.

9. Using a small bowl, beat eggs with grated cheese.

10. Slowly stir eggs into soup, turning with a large fork to keep eggs somewhat shredded.

11. Adjust seasonings.

12. Stir broth well and serve immediately with additional grated cheese.

Serves 8

 # Marinara Sauce

The difference between plain meatless tomato sauce and marinara is texture and color. Tomato sauce is prepared with tomato paste, giving it a darker, richer body and flavor. Marinara sauce is light, almost pinkish, and can be cooked in 10 or 20 minutes for a delicate effect. It also can be frozen. Use it over cooked thin spaghetti or linguine.

> **½ cup olive oil**
> **2 garlic cloves, chopped**
> **1 teaspoon dried red pepper flakes**
> **1 teaspoon dried basil**
> **1 teaspoon dried mint**
> **1 28-ounce can crushed or whole plum tomatoes, with juice, or 12 peeled fresh**
>   **tomatoes**
> **salt and pepper to taste, plus pinch more of above seasonings**
> **1 tablespoon fresh parsley, chopped**

1. In a large heavy skillet, on low heat, very slowly heat the oil, garlic, and the red pepper flakes, basil, and mint. Let cook for about 5 minutes or until the garlic is golden brown.

2. Raise the heat to medium-high. When the oil is really hot, add the tomatoes. (If you are using the plum or fresh tomatoes, crush them in your hands or put them in a blender for 1 second before adding them to the pan. This will speed up the cooking process and give a smoother consistency to the sauce.) Let the sauce come to a soft boil.

3. Add salt and pepper to taste, and a pinch more of red pepper, basil, and mint. Add the chopped parsley. Let the sauce simmer, uncovered, for about 15 minutes, stirring occasionally with a wooden spoon.

VARIATIONS: This is a wonderful sauce to use as the basis of other recipes. Add a can of clams, or sliced mushrooms, or sliced black olives. Be inventive! I gradually add the juices from the canned clams or mushrooms to the sauce as well, until I produce the texture my family enjoys. Other additions might include a can of crabmeat or a pound of cut-up baby squid or lobster meat.

Yield: 4 cups

 # Sunday Gravy

This tomato sauce with meat is called gravy because the meat drippings become the base for the sauce. It is meant to feed the whole family abundantly. You may cook up to 3 pounds of pasta and have enough sauce and meat to make everyone happy. It refrigerates and freezes well. You may use any or all of the meats listed.

1 pound sweet Italian sausages
2 pounds meatballs (page 129)
4–5 lean pork chops
1 pound lean spareribs
1 pound piece of beef or pork
½ cup olive oil
1 medium onion, chopped
1 garlic clove, chopped
pinch of dried basil, red pepper flakes, and mint
1 6-ounce can tomato paste
1 28-ounce can peeled and crushed tomatoes
1 28-ounce can water
salt and pepper to taste

Pork added to the gravy will make an oily—though delicious—gravy. When you are using a significant amount of pork, skim the excess oils off of the top of the sauce. Pork also tends to produce a thin sauce, so go easy when adding additional water, or add an extra can of paste at the beginning of the preparations. This will help maintain the body of the sauce.

1. Fry the meats of your choice in ¼ cup of the oil in a large heavy saucepan.

2. When they are browned, transfer them to a platter. Add the remaining ¼ cup of oil to the residual juices in the pan. When the oil is hot, saute the onion, garlic, and seasonings until transparent.

3. Stir in the tomato paste and blend well. Add the tomatoes and stir until blended with the tomato paste and oil. Stir in an extra pinch of the seasonings. Add water, using the 28-ounce can from the tomatoes. (Keep adding water until the sauce remains the thickness you desire. I use a full can.)

4. Let the sauce come to a full boil and add salt and pepper to taste and an additional pinch of herbs. Return the meat to the pan. Then simmer over medium heat, uncovered, for at least 1 hour or until all of the meat is fully cooked. Stir gently every 15 minutes or so, using a large wooden spoon.

5. Serve the sauce over pasta, reserving some additional sauce for individual servings at the table.

Serves 10–12 generously

 # Fresh Eggs in
Marinara Sauce

How lucky we were to taste the mint (fresh from my grandfather's farm) cooked in tomato sauce. My grandfather carefully added several dropped eggs to the sauce and cooked them until they were firmly set. The eggs are a wonderful substitute for meat, and they can be added to any leftover sauce to stretch it for another meal.

1 dozen fresh tomatoes, blanched and peeled
¼ cup olive oil
1 small onion, chopped
1 small carrot, chopped
1 stalk celery, chopped
red pepper flakes
salt and pepper to taste
1 tablespoon fresh mint, washed
2 garlic cloves, chopped
6 fresh eggs
¾ pound linguine or other thin pasta
enough water to boil linguine

1. Put whole tomatoes into boiling water until skins split.

2. Cool and, with your fingertips, remove the skins.

3. Put peeled tomatoes in a blender, process briefly just to coarsely mash them.

4. Using a large, deep skillet, saute in olive oil the chopped onion, carrot, and celery until translucent.

5. Add tomatoes, red pepper flakes, and salt and pepper to taste. Mix well and simmer for at least 5 minutes, stirring with a wooden spoon.

6. Chop mint and garlic together (cut the garlic into julienned strips); add to sauce and stir until well blended.

7. Adjust seasonings and simmer for at least 15 minutes, stirring well.

8. Raise heat to medium-high and bring sauce to a soft boil.

9. Crack eggs, one at a time, onto a small plate and slide each raw egg, uncrowded, into the tomato sauce; continue until all six eggs are used.

10. Lower heat, cover skillet and cook for 5 minutes.

11. Uncover and, with a wide wooden spoon, gently coax the eggs away from each other without breaking them.

12. Ladle sauce over the tops of the eggs to better cook them.

13. Cover and simmer for about 15 minutes or until the eggs are firm and set. At this point you should be able to move them around without breaking the yolks. Reserve.

14. Cook pasta separately in salted boiling water according to package directions.

15. Drain and put on a serving platter.

16. Add sauce to linguine or other pasta.

17. Place eggs on top of the pasta or serve on the side.

Serves 4

Tomato Gravy with Beef and Pork

This sauce uses tomato paste, which gives us a heavier texture than that of the Quick Meat Sauce recipe.

> ½ cup olive oil
> 1 medium onion, chopped
> 1 large garlic clove, chopped
> 1 pound lean ground beef (or ½ pound ground beef and ½ pound ground pork)
> 1 6-ounce can tomato paste
> salt and pepper to taste
> 1 28-ounce can peeled and crushed or Italian plum tomatoes
> 1 teaspoon dried basil
> 1 teaspoon dried mint
> 1 teaspoon chopped fresh parsley (optional)
> ¼ teaspoon dried red pepper flakes (I use a little more)
> 1 tomato-paste can water

1. Heat the olive oil in an enamel or stainless steel heavy saucepan. Add the onion, garlic, and the ground meat. Stir with a wooden spoon and work it over well to break up any possible chunks of meat.

2. When the meat is browned and sort of crusty, but not burned, add the tomato paste. Blend well and sprinkle in a little salt and pepper.

3. Add the tomatoes and blend well. (If you are using the plum tomatoes, put them through a sieve or in a blender to crush them.) Sprinkle in the seasonings and more salt and pepper. Stir well. Simmer, uncovered, for at least 20 minutes on low heat, stirring occasionally and gently with a wooden spoon. After 10 minutes of simmering, pour in the can of water until you reach the consistency you desire.

4. Serve the sauce over pasta, eggplant, lasagne, or manicotti.

Yield: approximately 6 cups

 # Quick Meat Sauce

The total cooking time for this sauce is approximately ½ hour; it can be cooked ahead and reserved. The sauce refrigerates well for several days and freezes excellently.

> ¼ cup olive oil
> 1 pound ground meat (½ pound beef, ½ pound pork)
> 1 small onion, chopped
> 1 garlic clove, chopped
> pinch of dried basil, red pepper flakes, and mint
> salt and pepper to taste
> 1 28-ounce can peeled and crushed tomatoes

1. Heat the oil in a large skillet. When it is rippling hot, add the ground meat and start to brown it, stirring with a wooden spoon. When partly browned, add the onion, garlic, and seasonings. Continue browning until the meat is a little crisp on the bottom of the pan.

2. Add the can of tomatoes and mix until the sauce starts bubbling. At this point lower the heat and add additional salt and pepper to taste, stirring well. If the mixture is too thick, add some warm water to smooth it a bit.

3. Sprinkle in an additional pinch of basil, red pepper flakes, and mint. Let the sauce simmer, uncovered, on low heat for about 20 minutes, and stir it often.

4. Serve over a pound of cooked pasta, or use as a topping for eggplant, lasagne, manicotti, ravioli, or stuffed peppers.

Yield: approximately 6 cups

TO FREEZE OR REFRIGERATE SAUCES AND SOUPS

Place meal-size portions of soups and sauces in freezer storage bags and secure tightly. The bags will take up less space than containers, and the sauce or soup can be reheated in the microwave right in the bag.

 Bolognese Sauce

There are many old versions of this authentic sauce. Although only fresh tomatoes were used at the time of its creation, in later years canned tomatoes made it easier for the working person to recreate this sauce. The ground tomatoes used here give the sauce good body and texture. This sauce is wonderful with homemade pastas.

**¼ cup olive oil
1 pound ground meat (preferably ½ pound each of beef and pork)
3 garlic cloves, chopped
1 small onion, chopped
1 tablespoon each of dried basil, mint, and red pepper flakes
1 small can tomato paste
1 cup dry white wine
1 28-ounce can kitchen-ready* tomatoes
salt and pepper to taste
½ cup heavy cream or half-and-half**

1. Heat olive oil in a large, heavy, stainless steel skillet.
2. Add ground meat and cook on high heat until partly browned but not burned, stirring often with a wooden spoon.
3. Add the chopped garlic, onion, and seasonings.
4. Brown the meat totally until the meat is a little crisp on the bottom.
5. Lower heat and add tomato paste, stirring constantly until paste is well blended.
6. Add wine, mix well, and cook on medium-high heat at least 2–3 minutes, stirring often.
7. Add can of tomatoes and keep stirring until sauce is bubbly.
8. Lower heat, adjust seasonings to taste, and simmer sauce for about 10–15 minutes, stirring often.
9. Add ½ cup cream or half-and-half; stir and simmer a few minutes or until sauce is creamy.
10. Serve over manicotti, lasagne, ravioli, or homemade fettuccine.

Serves 6–8

*Peeled and ground tomatoes—no puree added. Pastene is a good brand.

Cooked Fresh Tomato Sauce

The difference in this sauce is its sweet, fresh taste. The recipe makes enough sauce to coat at least 1 to 1½ pounds of any bought or homemade pasta. If you desire to add some fish or meat to the sauce, you may do so immediately after the sauce is prepared and just keep cooking until the fish or meat is cooked.

12 ripe tomatoes
½ cup olive or vegetable oil
1 carrot, scraped and chopped
1 small celery stalk with leaves, chopped
1 medium onion, chopped
1 garlic clove, chopped
pinch of dried basil, mint, and red pepper flakes
salt, freshly ground black pepper

1. To blanch the tomatoes, make an X-cut in the skin and put them into boiling water for a couple of minutes. After the skin begins to shrink from the fruit, remove them from the water and run under cold water to finish the process of peeling.

2. After the tomatoes are peeled, put them in a pot with no water. Let them boil until they are cooked, about 10 minutes. Then mash or blend them in a blender until they have the consistency of a cooked sauce. Now they are ready for use.

3. Heat the oil in a large heavy saucepan. Add the carrot, celery, onion, garlic, and a pinch of basil, mint, and red pepper flakes. Saute until the vegetables are tender, but not burned.

4. Pour in the tomatoes and mix well. Let the sauce come to a soft boil. At this point you can determine if you wish to add some water. You also can add salt and pepper and additional basil, red pepper, or mint.

5. Stir for a couple of minutes, lower the heat, and let simmer for ½ hour or more, stirring often, but gently, with a wooden spoon. I like the oils to accumulate on top of the sauce at this point because I feel they seal in all the flavors. So I stir very gently, trying to scrape the bottom of the pan without disturbing the accumulation of oils.

6. Add meatballs, ground meat, or fish, if you choose, and cook until they are cooked through. Serve over pasta.

Yield: approximately 6 cups

 Uncooked Fresh  Tomato Sauce

This is a different and exciting way to use your fresh garden tomatoes. Serve on linguine or thin spaghetti as a main dish with a barbecue of meat, fish, or chicken.

> **1 pound red ripe plum tomatoes**
> **1 garlic clove**
> **1 shallot clove**
> **4 fresh basil leaves**
> **salt and pepper to taste**
> **¼ teaspoon dried red pepper flakes**
> **½ cup olive oil**

1. Peel the tomatoes and remove the hard stem. Cut into small cubes and remove seeds (squeeze with hands). Place in a blender or a food processor with the garlic, shallot, basil, salt, black and red pepper, and olive oil. Blend at high speed for one or two seconds, or until the tomatoes are somewhat crushed and combined with the other ingredients. Do not overblend. Serve at room temperature.

2. This makes enough sauce for ½ pound pasta. Sliced black olives and chopped parsley make a nice garnish for the dish. The sauce is also good as a pizza sauce.

Yield: approximately 2 cups

 # Aglio e Olio

GARLIC AND OIL SAUCE

This is the original and widely used peasant sauce we enjoyed while growing up. This sauce is delicious on spaghetti (about ½ pound is the right amount). If you like garlic, you would also like this sauce with shrimp, as shrimp scampi, or as a sauce with clams.

> **1 cup olive oil**
> **5 garlic cloves, slivered**
> **salt and freshly ground black pepper**
> **¼ teaspoon dried red pepper flakes (optional)**
> **1 tablespoon fresh parsley, chopped**
> **1 teaspoon fresh basil, chopped (optional)**

1. Using a medium-sized heavy skillet, heat the oil until warm. Add the garlic and simmer slowly for about 5 minutes or until the garlic is golden. Do not burn. You may remove the garlic at this point or leave it in if you enjoy a strong garlic flavor.

2. Add the salt, black and red pepper, parsley, and basil. Let simmer about 5 minutes to blend flavors; use as desired. If using with pasta, add some of the hot pasta water to sauce in skillet and let slightly boil about 3 minutes, add to hot strained pasta and serve immediately with lots of fresh grated black pepper and grated cheese.

Yield: 1 cup

 # Vongole a
la Marguerita

RED CLAM SAUCE A LA MARGUERITE

This sauce is another favorite tried and true. A variation of linguine vongole, it is prepared with a marinara sauce. It is best served over pasta or even as a topping for pizza when cooked with whole clams, it translates into a wonderful broth.

10 littleneck clams, in shell
approximately 4 cups heated marinara sauce
   (see page 46 or use your favorite recipe)
2 tablespoons dry white wine
fresh parsley, chopped
salt and freshly ground black pepper to taste

1. Scrub the clams thoroughly with a clean brush. Rinse under cool running water.

2. Put the clams in a pot with the marinara sauce and wine. Cover. Let the clams steam for about 5 to 7 minutes, or until they open. Remove the clams as soon as they have opened, to prevent toughness.

3. Add parsley and salt and pepper to taste.

4. If you serve this sauce with pasta, toss the noodles with about 4 tablespoons of butter to keep them from absorbing too much of the sauce. Arrange the clams in their shells on the sides of the platter of pasta. Sprinkle the pasta with grated Parmesan or Romano cheese.

Yield: approximately 4 cups

 # Pesto Sauce

This excellent recipe for pesto came from Dom's Restaurant. This sauce is served uncooked, at room temperature, over cooked pasta. It makes an elegant dish when used with tortellini, fettuccine, and other favorites. It is also excellent when added to minestrone or pasta primavera. When all the ingredients are on hand, the sauce takes about 5 minutes to prepare. It also can be refrigerated or frozen indefinitely for future use; just warm it up at room temperature.

> **2 cups olive oil**
> **2 firmly packed cups whole fresh basil leaves**
> **2 cups fresh parsley leaves**
> **4 garlic cloves**
> **½ cup pignoli (pine nuts)**
> **1 tablespoon freshly ground black pepper**
> **1 teaspoon salt**
> **1 cup freshly grated Pecorino or Romano cheese**
> **½ cup lemon juice**

1. Put all the ingredients except the basil into a blender and grind thoroughly. Then add the basil and grind until a creamy texture is achieved. No cooking is needed.

2. This amount of sauce is enough for 1 pound of pasta of your choice.

Yield: 2 pints

 # Puttanesca Sauce

This is such a zesty and robust sauce that it was named after the gypsies. I have omitted the salt because of the anchovies, but you be the judge. If you're not the daring type, you can omit some of the seasonings also. The first six ingredients, however, are important to the flavor of the sauce and should not be left out.

> 2 tablespoons olive oil
> 1 large onion, halved and slivered
> 6 garlic cloves, coarsely chopped
> 2 28-ounce cans Italian plum tomatoes
> 1 heaping teaspoon tomato paste
> 2 cans (2 ounces each) anchovies in oil
> ¾ cup Sicilian dry-cured olives, pitted and coarsely chopped
> 4 tablespoons capers, drained
> 1 teaspoon each basil, oregano, and red pepper flakes
> black pepper to taste
> 6 quarts boiling water
> 1 pound pasta of your choice
> grated Parmesan (optional)

1. Heat 2 tablespoons of olive oil in a heavy saucepan.

2. Add onion and garlic and cook on low heat until transparent.

3. Add tomato paste and blend in well.

4. Crush tomatoes slightly and add to the pan along with their juices. Cook for 5 minutes on medium heat.

5. Coarsely chop the anchovies and add to the saucepan, along with their oil, stirring gently with a wooden spoon.

6. Stir in the olives, capers, basil, oregano, red pepper flakes, and black pepper to taste. Blend gently and simmer over medium heat for about 20 minutes, stirring occasionally.

7. While sauce simmers, bring a large pot of water to a boil.

8. Add pasta of your choice, such as fettuccine, rigatoni, or linguine. Cook until al dente, about 15 minutes.

9. Drain pasta and place on decorative platter. Top with the hot Puttanesca Sauce.

10. Pass the Parmesan and serve immediately.

Serves 6–8

 # My Angelo's Red Pepper Sauce

Because we had an abundance of peppers, thanks to a neighbor with a huge garden, my husband Angelo concocted this recipe to accompany our pescia fritta. We think it is so wonderful that it is now a must with our family's fried-fish dinners.

> **4 long finger peppers (hot or sweet)**
> **3 ounces raspberry vinegar**
> **½ cup milk**
> **2 tablespoons soy sauce**
> **4 tablespoons lemon juice**
> **1 teaspoon fresh parsley, chopped**
> **½ teaspoon garlic salt**
> **1 garlic clove**
> **¼ stick butter**
> **flour**

1. Cut stems off peppers, slice, and put in food processor.

2. Add all other ingredients except butter and flour.

3. Blend well until mixture forms a smooth texture.

4. Heat butter in a medium skillet and add pepper mixture; simmer uncovered for 2–3 minutes.

5. Stirring well, using a wooden spoon, add flour as needed until mixture has slightly thickened.

6. Serve immediately over any broiled or batter-fried fish.

**Yield: 12 ounces, enough for
at least 4 servings of fish**

Spinach Sauce

> ¼ cup butter or margarine
> 1 10-ounce package frozen chopped spinach
> 1 teaspoon salt
> 1 cup ricotta cheese
> ¼ cup grated Parmesan cheese
> ¼ cup milk
> ⅛ teaspoon ground nutmeg

1. In a 2-quart saucepan over medium heat, in hot butter, cook spinach and salt 10 minutes.

2. Reduce heat to low; add remaining ingredients. Mix sauce well and cook until just heated through (do not boil).

Yield: 2½ cups

Walnut Sauce

> ¼ cup butter or margarine
> 1 cup coarsely chopped walnuts
> ½ cup milk
> 2 tablespoons minced parsley
> 1 teaspoon salt

1. In a 9-inch skillet over medium heat, in hot butter, lightly brown walnuts (about 5 minutes), stirring occasionally.

2. Stir in remaining ingredients; heat.

Yield: 1⅓ cups

Creamy Broccoli Sauce

1 bunch of broccoli (about 1½ pounds)
¼ cup olive oil
4 garlic cloves, chopped
salt and pepper to taste
¼ teaspoon dried red pepper flakes
1 cup heavy cream
¾ cup grated Romano or Parmesan cheese

1. Cut broccoli into flowerets.

2. Cook in water uncovered until tender; drain well and set aside.

3. Heat oil in medium-size saucepan.

4. Add garlic, salt, pepper, and red pepper flakes.

5. Saute slowly on low heat until garlic is lightly browned, about 5–7 minutes, and remove garlic.

6. Add cream and cook 20 minutes to thicken.

7. Add cooked broccoli and cheese to sauce mixture; stir to blend.

8. Serve over cooked gnocchi, ravioli, or any homemade pasta.

Yield: 3½ to 4 cups, enough to cover 1 pound of pasta

Pasta

Some Tips for Cooking and Serving Pasta

Since all pasta is cooked the same way, it is not necessary to repeat the cooking directions for each dish. However, here are a few general pointers so that your pasta will not be cold and gummy before the sauce is done.

Store-bought pasta will take about 10 to 15 minutes to cook; homemade or fresh pasta from the delicacy shop only takes about 3 or 4 minutes. These cooking times are measured from the time the cooking water returns to a full boil after the pasta is added.

There should be plenty of water in the cooking pot to allow the pasta to float around easily and uncrowded. Always have the cooking water rapidly boiling when you first put the pasta into it, and softly boiling as the pasta is cooking. Don't start cooking the pasta until your sauce is ready, or the ingredients for the sauce are fully ready.

After the pasta has been cooked and sauced, it should be served immediately. Don't let it stand at room temperature; don't even try to keep it warm or hot in the oven while you eat your appetizer. The pasta should be served as soon as it is prepared. The only exception would be primavera, which keeps well and therefore can be made in advance.

A true Italian serves the pasta as the first or main course, with the meat and salad coming after it.

◆◆◆◆◆◆◆◆◆◆ Ravioli ◆◆◆◆◆◆◆◆◆◆

Because this recipe can be somewhat tedious, I suggest you invite a friend over to prepare it with you. That way you can share both the work and the rewards. If you make the ravioli one day and freeze them, and the sauce another day and freeze it, you'll be putting together your meal without a lot of last-minute fuss. To make the ravioli, you will need a lightly floured, flat, unpainted surface; I use my kitchen counter or an old table without any veneer. A heavy rolling pin on ball bearings will make the dough much easier to roll out. Don't get discouraged! It will take you a few times to get comfortable with making ravioli.

Basic Ravioli Dough

6 cups unsifted unbleached flour (King Arthur preferred)
3 eggs
1 teaspoon salt
boiling hot water (about ¾ cup)

1. Pour the flour on your preparation surface and form a well in the center. Add the salt to the well. Add the eggs to the well, breaking them gently with your fingers. Mix the flour and eggs together until they form a cornmeal texture.

2. Make another well and gradually add hot water, constantly shifting the flour on top of the water (so you won't burn your hands), until you are able to handle the mixture. The dough should be soft and pliable. If you find it too moist, add more flour to the working surface and knead the dough directly on top of it. If the dough is too dry, keep wetting your hands with warm water as you work the dough until it handles well.

3. The dough should be kneaded for about 8 minutes or until it becomes smooth enough to roll. A thorough kneading mixes the ingredients and develops elasticity in the dough. Knead dough by folding the opposite side toward you. Using the heel of your hand, gently push the dough down and away from you. With your fingertips, squeeze it and push it back to you. Fold the dough over envelope-style, and repeat the process over and over. When the dough has been kneaded enough, its surface will feel satiny and will look smooth. For a beginner, this might take 10 to 12 minutes, while an experienced person may need 5 or 8 minutes. Throughout this process, use as little additional flour as possible.

4. Place the kneaded dough in a bowl, pat it with some water, and cover with a clean cotton cloth or an inverted bowl to prevent drying. Let it rest for 30 minutes before

Many people feel that they should add at least a half dozen eggs to this recipe, because that's what Grandma used to do. That is fine, but it should be remembered that the resting period for a dough with this amount of eggs must be longer—at least an hour. Working people without much time should keep this in mind. A dough with many eggs that is not sufficiently rested will simply "bounce back" in the rolling process.

◆ 65 ◆

attempting to roll it out. Remember, the dough should be very smooth in order to work well. While the dough is resting, you can make the filling.

Ravioli Filling

> **2 pounds ricotta cheese**
> **3 medium eggs plus 2 additional egg yolks**
> **½ cup freshly grated Parmesan or Romano cheese**
> **1 garlic clove, pressed**
> **½ cup chopped fresh parsley**
> **salt and pepper to taste**

1. Mix the ingredients thoroughly in a large, wide bowl. Reserve.

To Finish Preparation

> **1 recipe Quick Meat Sauce (see page 51)**
> **1 pound, approximately, freshly grated Parmesan or Romano cheese**

1. Divide the dough in half, keeping the other half covered with an inverted bowl. Roll out the dough on a lightly floured surface until it is about ⅛ inch thick. Repeat with the second half.

2. Drop teaspoonfuls of filling about 2 inches apart on one sheet of dough until the filling is used. Cover with the other sheet.

3. With your fingertips, gently press around each mound of filling to form a little filled round. Cut apart into 2-inch squares with a pastry cutter or a special ravioli cutter (available at a specialty shop in all sizes and shapes). Make sure the edges are well sealed. Sprinkle the finished ravioli with a little flour and let rest until the water is boiling.

4. Meanwhile, bring approximately 8 quarts of salted water to a boil in a large pot.

5. Using a spatula, gently lift the ravioli into the rapidly boiling water. The ravioli will keep rising to the top of the water during cooking, crowding each other. Lower the heat to medium and gently press the ravioli back down into the water, using a large, flat, slotted soup skimmer. This step is important because it allows the ravioli to cook evenly. Continue for at least 10 minutes.

6. Taste to see if dough is tender enough to serve. (I always wait for the pasta to cool before sampling; somehow it changes its texture after it is out of the water.)

7. Strain gently and thoroughly, one third at a time, and place on a large serving platter. Form three layers of ravioli, gravy, and grated cheese. Continue until all the ravioli is on the platter, ending with gravy and grated cheese.

Yield: 5–6 dozen

Ravioli can be made earlier in the day it will be served; just sprinkle with flour and cover with a dry cloth. Ravioli can also be frozen in the following manner: Place a few pieces at a time in single layers on a cookie sheet and place in the freezer. When they are frozen, place them in a plastic freezer bag. Continue this process until all the ravioli are frozen. They will keep indefinitely in this way. When ready to use, gently drop into boiling water as you would any fresh product.

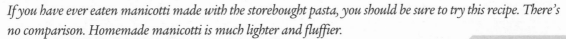

Manicotti

If you have ever eaten manicotti made with the storebought pasta, you should be sure to try this recipe. There's no comparison. Homemade manicotti is much lighter and fluffier.

Basic Ravioli Dough (page 65)
2 pounds ricotta cheese
2 pounds spinach, boiled, drained, squeezed dry, and chopped
4 large egg yolks
2½–3 cups freshly grated Parmesan cheese
1 cup shredded mozzarella cheese (optional)
1 large garlic clove, pressed
¼ cup chopped fresh parsley (reserve 2 tablespoons for topping)
salt and pepper to taste
½ recipe Quick Meat Sauce (page 51)

Manicotti may be prepared in advance and refrigerated uncooked. When ready, bake as usual. Stuffed peppers and a salad complement this elegant meal nicely.

1. Follow the ravioli dough recipe until the rolling-out stage. Then, divide the dough in half and roll it on a lightly floured surface until it is paper thin. Cut into 5- by 6-inch rectangles. Continue until all the dough is used up.

2. Cook the pasta rectangles in 8 quarts of boiling salted water in a large pot. Add a drizzle of oil to prevent the pasta from sticking together. Cook about 12 to 15 minutes or until tender, stirring often with a wooden spoon. Rinse well under cold water, but be careful or pasta will tear. Drain well and reserve while you make the filling. Run the noodles under cold water occasionally and loosen them with your hands. Pat dry on paper towels and reserve.

3. Mix together the ricotta, spinach, egg yolks, 1 cup of grated cheese, ½ cup shredded mozzarella (if using), garlic, parsley, salt, and pepper to taste.

4. Spread 2 tablespoons of the mixture on each piece of cut pasta. Roll envelope-style, carefully tucking all ends together halfway through the roll to prevent the filling from oozing out.

5. Place the filled manicotti side by side in a baking pan with the tucked ends on the bottom of the pan. Cover the manicotti with a layer of gravy and grated cheese and ½ cup shredded mozzarella (if using). Sprinkle with the 2 tablespoons of reserved parsley.

6. Bake in a preheated, 400-degree oven, covered with foil, on the middle rack, 15 to 20 minutes. Remove from oven and let rest 20 to 30 minutes; then serve with additional gravy.

Serves 8–10

 # Crepes for Manicotti

We usually make our manicotti like pie crust, rolling it out and using forms to cut out the dough. Then we wrap them around an aluminum tube and fry them. This recipe, however, is a batter dough, which you can use as a manicotti shell or a cannelloni, putting in any filling of your choice. This is a very popular style in many regions of Italy.

4 eggs, well beaten
1 cup all-purpose flour
pinch of salt
1 cup water
olive oil
tomato sauce
grated Parmesan cheese
basil (optional)

1. Place beaten eggs in a large mixing bowl.

2. Sift flour with pinch of salt.

3. Add flour to the eggs gradually, while beating with an electric mixer on slow speed, until mixture is smooth.

4. Add water and 2 tablespoons olive oil to bowl; mix on slow speed until mixture is lump-free. (If small lumps remain, stir with a wire whisk or put batter through a strainer.)

5. Cover bowl with a damp cloth and let rest 30 minutes.

6. Heat a 9-inch nonstick skillet over medium-high heat; brush pan lightly with olive oil.

7. Remove pan from heat, stir the batter in the bowl, and pour 2 tablespoons into a single spot at the edge of the skillet, tilting so batter just coats bottom.

8. Cook crepe until bottom is set, about 5 seconds, loosening the edges and underside with a spatula.

9. Turn the crepe over and cook until second side is set but not browned, about 5 seconds. (Lower heat as needed, to keep pan from burning crepes.)

10. Continue until all batter is used up, stirring batter occasionally.

Crepes can be prepared in advance by placing each crepe between 2 sheets of waxed paper and allowing to cool completely. Put in plastic bags and refrigerate for up to 3 days. You can also freeze these for at least 1 month. Bring to room temperature before using.

11. Remove finished crepes to a warm platter, stack, and cover with a clean towel until needed.

12. Fill crepes with 2 tablespoons of your favorite filling, such as ricotta, meat, or a combination of the two.

13. Roll each manicotti and place in an ovenproof dish, seam side down.

14. Pour 2 heaping spoonfuls of tomato sauce over manicotti and 1 tablespoon of grated Parmesan cheese.

15. Bake in a hot, 400-degree oven for 20 minutes.

16. Serve at room temperature with more hot sauce to cover, garnish with basil.

Serves 6–8

 # Lasagne Imbottito

BAKED LASAGNE

Lasagne Tomato Sauce

¼ cup olive oil
1 small onion, chopped
1 garlic clove, chopped
1 6-ounce can tomato paste
1 14-ounce can peeled and crushed tomatoes
1 14-ounce can hot water
pinch of dried red pepper flakes, basil, and mint
salt and pepper to taste

1. Heat the olive oil. Add the onion and garlic and saute for about 3 minutes. Do not allow them to burn.

2. Add the tomato paste and stir until dissolved. Add the tomatoes and mix well. Add the hot water, stir well, and let the mixture come to a soft boil.

3. Add the seasonings, stir until they are blended, and let the sauce simmer while you prepare the lasagne. Or, if you wish, the sauce may be made as much as a day or two in advance and refrigerated before you finish the lasagne.

To Finish Preparation:

Lasagne can be prepared early in the day on which it will be served and then baked prior to serving.

2 tablespoons salt
1 tablespoon olive oil
1 pound lasagne noodles
2 pounds ricotta cheese
3 eggs
1 garlic clove, pressed (optional)
1¾ cups freshly grated Parmesan or Romano cheese
¼ cup fresh parsley, chopped
salt and pepper to taste
¾ pound mozzarella cheese, shredded

1. Combine the salt and olive oil with 8 quarts of rapidly boiling water. Add the noodles and cook about 15 minutes or until tender. Stir constantly with a wooden spoon to prevent sticking. Do not overcook. Drain and rinse under cold water and reserve.

2. Meanwhile, combine the ricotta cheese, eggs, garlic, ¾ cup grated cheese, parsley, salt, and pepper in a large bowl. Mix well.

3. Bring the tomato sauce, ricotta filling, and cooked noodles to a clean working surface. Set out a 9- x 13-inch baking dish.

4. Pour ½ cup of the tomato sauce into the bottom of the baking pan. Over this, place a layer of lasagne noodles (you may slightly overlap). Top with 1 cup tomato sauce. Spread one-third of the ricotta mixture here and there, reaching the edges of the pan. Sprinkle ⅓ of the Parmesan and mozzarella on the top. Start again with the noodles and repeat the layering process two more times until all the ingredients have been used. Now top with more tomato sauce and grated Parmesan cheese.

5. Bake in a preheated 350-degree oven for 40 minutes. Let rest for about 1 hour. Cut into 2-inch squares and serve with the remaining sauce, heated, and more grated cheese.

Serves 6–8

 Baked Stuffed Ziti

This dish can be varied according to the sauce you use in it. If you use my Marinara Sauce, you will have a very light dish, which will be almost pink in color. If you want a more filling dish, one that is practically a complete meal, use the Quick Meat Sauce (page 51) or the Sunday Gravy (page 47). It will then have a dark color.

1 pound ziti or any large macaroni
1 recipe for sauce or gravy (see introduction above)
1 pound ricotta cheese
8 ounces grated mozzarella cheese, plus more for topping
¼ cup freshly grated Parmesan cheese, plus more for topping
2 large eggs
salt and pepper to taste
2 tablespoons fresh parsley, chopped

1. Cook pasta according to directions, stirring often. Drain well and turn into a large bowl. Toss with a ladleful of sauce to keep it from sticking together.

2. Combine the ricotta, mozzarella, Parmesan, eggs, salt, and pepper. Using a whisk, mix until well blended. Add to the cooked, hot pasta. Toss lightly with a wooden spoon. Turn into a medium-size baking pan with a little sauce added to the bottom to prevent the pasta from scorching.

3. Spread a layer of sauce over the pasta. Top with mozzarella and Parmesan. Sprinkle with the chopped parsley. Cover with foil.

4. Bake in a preheated 350-degree oven on the middle rack for 25 minutes. Allow it to rest for 20 minutes before serving. Serve with the remaining hot sauce.

Serves 6–8

This dish should normally be prepared just prior to eating it, but it can be kept in the refrigerator after cooking for up to three days. To reheat, put 1 heaping tablespoon of water and ¼ cup of sauce in the bottom of a heavy skillet. Put baked ziti into the skillet, cover, and steam on low heat until thoroughly heated.

Spaghetti with Asparagus
and Lemon Sauce

salt
8 ounces spaghetti
6 tablespoons butter
8 fresh asparagus spears, snapped into 1-inch lengths
zest of 1 lemon
2 large eggs, beaten
½ cup heavy cream
2 tablespoons Parmesan cheese, freshly grated
4 grates of nutmeg
3 tablespoons fresh parsley, chopped
juice of 1 lemon
freshly ground pepper

1. Bring 3½ quarts of water to a rolling boil in a large pot. Stir in 1 tablespoon of salt. Add the spaghetti, stir, and cool it *al dente,* for about 6 minutes. Stir often.

2. While the pasta is cooking, melt the butter in a medium-sized frying pan. Add the asparagus pieces and cook them over medium heat for about 3 minutes. Meanwhile, finely grate the zest of 1 lemon.

3. Add the eggs, heavy cream, Parmesan cheese, nutmeg, parsley and half of the lemon juice; combine well. Taste the sauce. The lemon flavor should be subtle but not overpowering. Add more lemon juice as needed.

4. Drain the spaghetti well. Immediately return it to the pot it was cooked in and add the butter, asparagus, and the lemon sauce. Toss well.

5. Turn the heat to low and continue gently tossing the pasta over the heat for about 30 seconds, until the sauce thickens slightly and adheres to the pasta. Season to taste with salt and pepper and serve immediately.

Serves 4–6

 Frittata di Spaghetti

SPAGHETTI PIE

This is a good recipe for using up any leftover pasta to concoct a new dish! Excellent for lunch or a late-night snack.

> **¾ pound spaghetti (cooked)**
> **3 tablespoons melted butter**
> **1 cup Parmesan cheese, grated**
> **2 eggs (beaten)**
> **salt and pepper**
> **fresh parsley, chopped**
> **2–3 tablespoons olive oil**

You will need a good, heavy 12-inch skillet, preferably cast iron.

1. Cook the spaghetti according to the package directions, if not already cooked. Drain the spaghetti well and toss it with the butter, beaten eggs, Parmesan cheese, salt and pepper to taste, and chopped parsley. Mix thoroughly.

2. Put the olive oil in a heavy skillet. When the oil is hot, pour in the spaghetti mixture and shape it into a round pie.

3. Using medium heat, gently work the pasta so that it browns evenly, by gently turning it around in the same direction to avoid sticking.

4. When one side is brown, slide the omelette onto a large plate; return it to the skillet to allow other side to brown. Add another tablespoon of oil if needed.

5. Leave the pasta omelette to cool slightly before serving for a better flavor. Cut into wedges and serve with crusty Italian bread.

Serves 4

 # Fettuccine

Fettuccine is good with Quick Meat Sauce or Pesto Sauce (see the sauce chapter) or a mixture of butter, grated cheese, and chopped fresh parsley. The pasta can be made ahead and covered with lots of flour and a clean cloth before it is cooked. Uncooked fettuccine also freezes well when placed in a freezer in single layers on a cookie sheet and then placed in a plastic bag.

> **6 cups unbleached flour (King Arthur preferred)**
> **1 teaspoon salt**
> **3 eggs**
> **about ½ cup boiling water**

1. Pour 5 cups of flour on a smooth working surface. Make a well in the center. Sprinkle with the teaspoon of salt. Drop the eggs in the well, break the yolks with your fingers, and stir a bit. Then mix the flour and eggs together until they form a cornmeal texture. Gradually mix in boiling water, using as much as necessary to form a smooth, pliable dough. Be careful you don't burn your hands. Always throw the flour on the water before touching it with your hands. This will cool it off a bit.

2. Knead the dough for about 10 minutes, until it is shiny and smooth. Form it into a loaf shape, pat the top with some water, and cover with an inverted bowl for a half hour.

3. Divide the dough in half, keeping the remainder covered. Roll the dough into a large round, about ⅛ inch thick. Liberally sprinkle flour from the remaining cup of flour all over the dough to prepare for next step.

4. Starting at the top, gently fold over about 2 inches of dough. Continue to fold over dough so that the final width will be about 3 inches. The dough must be floured enough so that the layers do not stick together.

5. Beginning at one end of the roll, cut the dough into strips ¼ inch wide or a width you desire. (Be sure to use a sharp knife or the edges will be jagged.) Then sprinkle more flour on the cut pieces and gently toss them with your fingers until the noodles loosen and open to form long strands.

6. When you are ready to cook, boil the fettuccine in 6 quarts of water seasoned with 1 tablespoon salt. Boil gently, uncovered, stirring often, for about 5 to 7 minutes, or until tender.

7. Drain into a colander and then put in a large serving bowl. Cover with your chosen sauce and serve immediately.

Serves 8–10

 # Orange or Rosy Pasta

This colorful pasta is good with Marinara Sauce or Pesto Sauce (see the sauce chapter) or made "Alfredo" style. It also can be used for lasagne or manicotti. Experiment and make your own creation.

2 cups all-purpose flour (King Arthur unbleached preferred)
2 large eggs
3 tablespoons strained carrots or beets for babies, or tomato paste
boiling water

1. Mound 2 cups of flour on a work surface or in a large bowl and make a deep well in the center. Break the eggs into the well.

2. Beat the eggs lightly with a fork, and then stir in the carrots, beets, or tomato paste. Using a circular motion, mix the flour from the sides of the well into the eggs. If the dough is too crumbly to stick together, slowly add a few drops of boiling water.

3. Pat the dough into a ball and knead on a lightly floured surface for 10 minutes or until the dough is shiny-smooth and elastic. Cover and let rest for 20 minutes.

4. On a lightly floured surface, roll out one-fourth of the dough at a time to about ⅛-inch thickness. Keep the unrolled portions covered with a large inverted bowl.

5. Cut and cook as described for Fettuccine.

Yield: 4 cups fettuccine

 # Spinach Pasta

Spinach noodles are good with melted butter, plenty of grated cheese, and black pepper. Or be creative and use them with your favorite pasta sauce.

> **½ package (10-ounce size) frozen leaf spinach**
> **¼ cup water**
> **pinch of salt**
> **2 cups unbleached flour (King Arthur preferred)**
> **2 large eggs**

1. Cook the spinach in the salted water in a covered saucepan on medium heat for 5 minutes.

2. Meanwhile, mound the flour on a working surface or in a large bowl. Make a deep well in the center and break the eggs into the well.

3. Beat the eggs lightly with a fork. Using a circular motion, draw the flour from the sides of the well into the eggs. Gradually mix all the flour with the eggs.

4. Add the hot, undrained spinach (the juices will provide the water needed to make the dough). Being careful not to burn your hands, mix the spinach into the flour-egg mixture. If the dough is too crumbly to stick together, slowly add a few drops of hot, boiling water.

5. Pat the dough into a smooth ball and knead on a lightly floured surface for 10 minutes or until the dough is shiny-smooth and elastic. Cover and let rest for 20 minutes.

6. On a lightly floured surface, roll out one-fourth of the dough at a time to about 1/8-inch thickness. Keep the unrolled portions covered with a large inverted bowl.

7. Cut and cook as described for Fettuccine.

Yield: 4 cups of fettuccine

Sal's Linguini alla Vongole en Bianco

This white clam sauce can be made ahead and reheated. It refrigerates and freezes well. If you desire a more bountiful dish, add about ½ cup chopped mushrooms, canned or fresh, to the clams and continue cooking as directed. They work very well together.

6 tablespoons butter
1 garlic clove, chopped
1 shallot clove, chopped
3 scallions, sliced
4 shakes of Tabasco
½ large ripe tomato, quartered
squeeze of lemon
½ pound canned whole clams, or 12 fresh shucked clams (reserve juices)
2 pinches of chopped fresh parsley, plus more for garnish
⅓ cup dry white wine
½ pound thin linguine
freshly grated Romano cheese for garnish

1. Start heating a pot of salted water for the pasta, following package directions.

2. Heat 4 tablespoons of the butter in a small saucepan. Add the garlic, shallot, and scallions. Saute until transparent. Add the Tabasco, quartered tomato, and squeeze of lemon. Cook slowly for about 5 minutes. Add the reserved clam broth.

3. Raise the heat and let the mixture come to a boil. Then add the clams, chopped parsley, and white wine. Boil gently for a few minutes so that the clams are barely poached.

4. Put the pasta in the salted boiling water and cook for 7 minutes, or until al dente. Strain well by shaking the colander. Transfer to a deep serving dish, toss with the remaining 2 tablespoons of butter, and then pour the clam sauce on top. (Tossing the pasta with butter will prevent it from absorbing too much sauce.)

5. Sprinkle with chopped parsley and grated cheese and serve immediately.

Serves 2

Linguine with Red Clam Sauce

In this recipe we are cooking the clams together with the tomatoes and spices. The sauce in this recipe is lighter and more on the pink side.

3 10-ounce cans of clams
¼ cup olive oil
2 garlic cloves, minced
1 28-ounce can plum tomatoes, undrained
1 teaspoon each oregano and red pepper flakes
salt and pepper to taste
1 pound thin linguine
butter (optional)
grated Parmesan (optional)

1. Bring a large pan of salted water to boil for cooking the linguine.
2. Drain clams, reserving liquid.
3. Heat oil in a heavy, medium-sized skillet (preferably cast iron). Add garlic and saute until tender.
4. Place tomatoes in bowl and, with a fork, squeeze the pulp into the juice.
5. Add tomatoes and liquid to skillet and simmer over medium-high heat for 10 minutes.
6. Add salt and pepper, oregano, and red pepper flakes. Stir often with a wooden spoon.
7. Add clams and enough clam broth to make a pink sauce.
8. Adjust seasonings and cook for 5 minutes longer; remove from heat and reserve.
9. Cook linguine in boiling water, drain, and put in a warm bowl.
10. Toss with a pat of butter (optional).
11. Cover linguine with some of the clam sauce and toss gently, adding salt and pepper if needed.
12. Serve immediately and pass remaining sauce and grated cheese around table.

Serves 4–6

 Pasta with Broccoli  Sauce

This pasta dish can be eaten hot or cold, as a side dish or a main course. The total preparation time is approximately 45 minutes.

1 bunch of broccoli (about 1½ pounds)
½ cup olive oil
4 garlic cloves, chopped
salt and pepper to taste
¼ teaspoon dried red pepper flakes
3 cups warm water
½ pound pasta (ziti, gnocchi, or small shells)
⅓ cup freshly grated Romano or Parmesan cheese, plus more for garnish

1. Cut off and discard about ½ inch of the end of the broccoli stem. Cut the broccoli into flowerets. Trim the tough leaves, peel the stems, and cut them into 1½-inch lengths. Set all the pieces aside.

2. Heat the oil in a heavy skillet or medium-sized saucepan. Add the garlic, salt, pepper, and red pepper. Saute slowly on low heat until the garlic is lightly browned.

3. Remove the pan from the burner and gently pour in the 3 cups of warm water to start the sauce. Let the water-and-oil sauce boil briskly for a minute, then add the cut broccoli. Cook on medium heat to a soft boiling stage. Add more salt, pepper, and red pepper to taste.

4. Cook the pasta according to package directions, reserving some of the water before draining. (This can be added to sauce if more broth is desired.)

5. Put the drained pasta in a large skillet and pour the cooked broccoli sauce on top. Sprinkle with the grated cheese, cover, and simmer for 5 minutes or until the cheese is melted. Or to make it peasant-style (Ma's way), add the cooked pasta to the pan of broccoli, toss a couple of times until well mixed, then serve. Sprinkle each serving with more Parmesan or Romano cheese.

Serves 6

 Fettuccine alla
Carbonara

My brother, Dom Capossela, provided me with this recipe, which wins rave reviews in Dom's restaurant. You may use pancetta, an Italian ham, in place of the prosciutto for an even more authentically Italian flavor. For best results, have all ingredients at room temperature.

> **½ pound fettuccine**
> **¼ cup melted butter**
> **¼ cup heavy cream**
> **2 egg yolks**
> **⅔ cup grated Parmesan cheese**
> **3 slices prosciutto, chopped**
> **salt and pepper to taste**
> **¼ cup walnuts, finely chopped (optional)**

1. Using a large pot, bring 4 quarts of salted water to a boil, and add fettuccine.

2. While pasta cooks, warm melted butter and heavy cream in a small saucepan.

3. Remove from heat; allow to cool slightly.

4. When butter and cream have cooled somewhat (if mixture is too warm, the eggs will curdle), use a whisk to stir into it the 2 egg yolks.

5. Using a large, heavy skillet over medium heat, cook prosciutto until its fat is rendered and the meat is crisp.

6. Add cooked, well-drained fettuccine to skillet with prosciutto; pour butter and cream mixture over pasta and add ⅓ cup grated Parmesan cheese. Toss thoroughly over low heat, until the sauce coats every strand.

7. Season to taste with salt and freshly ground pepper.

8. Remove to serving platter and garnish with remaining cheese, ground walnuts, and more black pepper to taste.

Serves 2

 Pasta con Acciughe

A favorite tradition in our neighborhood, especially at Lent or on Christmas Eve, this pasta with anchovies is light, tasty, and easy to make. Eliminate the added water, and the sauce alone makes a delicious spread that can be used on any toasted bread.

> **6 quarts water for boiling pasta**
> **2 tablespoons salt**
> **1 pound thin spaghetti or thin linguine**
> **½ cup olive oil**
> **2 garlic cloves, minced**
> **2 cans (1¾-ounces) flat anchovies, undrained**
> **½ cup Sicilian dry-cured olives, pitted and chopped**
> **1 teaspoon capers**
> **¼ teaspoon red pepper flakes (optional)**
> **1 teaspoon fresh parsley, chopped**
> **Freshly grated Parmesan cheese**

1. Boil 6 quarts of water in a large pot, adding 2 tablespoons salt.

2. In medium-sized heavy skillet, heat olive oil on medium heat.

3. Add garlic, anchovies with their oil, olives, capers, and red pepper flakes. Saute 4–5 minutes, crushing with wooden spoon, until the anchovies dissolve and a sauce is formed. Remove from heat, but keep warm.

4. Add spaghetti to boiling water and cook about 10–15 minutes or until al dente.

5. Take one cup of the pasta water and add to warm anchovy sauce.

6. Drain the cooked pasta and place on a serving plate.

7. Heat the anchovy sauce until bubbling and immediately pour over pasta.

8. Gently lift pasta, allowing the sauce to spread evenly.

9. Sprinkle with fresh chopped parsley and grated Parmesan cheese.

10. Serve at once.

Serves 4–6

Pasta al Freddo

This cold pasta salad is a wonderful summer dish, especially good to have on hand when you need a quick bite to eat. It stores well in the refrigerator for several days.

6 quarts salted water
1 pound rigatoni or ziti pasta
½ cup olive oil
¼ cup red or white wine vinegar
4 garlic cloves, finely chopped
1 tablespoon fresh parsley, chopped
1 cup fresh basil leaves, chopped
½ teaspoon salt
freshly ground black pepper to taste
10 ripe tomatoes or 2 cups canned peeled plum tomatoes (juice reserved)
¼ cup black, Sicilian dry-cured olives, pitted (optional)
1 cup freshly grated Parmesan cheese for garnish

1. Bring 6 quarts of salted water to a boil and add the pasta.

2. Stirring often, bring pasta back to a soft boil, cooking about 7 minutes or until tender.

3. Strain, rinse under cold water, and drain well, tossing the colander lightly.

4. Transfer the pasta to a large serving platter. Reserve.

5. Combine the oil and vinegar in a large bowl and whisk until well blended.

6. Add the garlic, parsley, basil, salt, and pepper and stir well.

7. Peel the fresh tomatoes and slice them in small pieces. If you are using canned tomatoes, squeeze them slightly to remove as many seeds as possible and then dice.

8. Spoon the tomato mixture on top and gently lift the pasta without disturbing the tomatoes in order to allow some of the juices to pour into the pasta.

9. Add the olives to the pasta.

10. Cover with plastic wrap and marinate for a couple of hours. (Add the reserved tomato juice if this sauce looks too dry.) Refrigerate until ready to use.

11. Serve with Parmesan cheese.

Serves 4

# Linguini ai Tre Formaggi

LINGUINE WITH THREE CHEESES

Here is a good appetizer or side dish to serve with the meat of your choice. It will take a half hour to prepare and cook.

2 tablespoons olive oil
1 garlic clove
¼ cup chopped fresh Italian parsley
salt and freshly ground black pepper
1 pound linguine
½ cup crushed Gorgonzola cheese
¼ cup freshly grated Parmesan cheese
¼ cup freshly grated Romano or Pecorino cheese

1. Fill a large pot with 6 quarts of salted water and start heating it for the pasta.

2. Heat the oil in a large skillet, and push the garlic through a garlic press into the oil. Add part of the parsley and saute for a few minutes. Set the skillet aside until the pasta is cooked.

3. Add linguine to the rapidly boiling water. Cook the pasta until it is al dente. Reserve some pasta water, then drain the pasta, transfer it to the skillet, and toss with the garlic and oil mixture.

4. In a large bowl, add the 3 kinds of cheese. Immediately place pasta in cheese bowl, tossing quickly. Add hot pasta water if consistency is too thick. Add more salt and pepper to taste, if needed, and the remaining parsley.

5. Serve immediately.

Serves 4–6

 # Mom's Pasta and Ricotta alla Romana

Jacqueline Kennedy used to visit a certain now-defunct restaurant in our neighborhood just to order this peasant dish. The sauce may be made ahead, but the pasta should be cooked immediately before serving.

½ pound fine linguine or spaghettini
½ pound fresh plum tomatoes, or 1 cup canned plum tomatoes
2 tablespoons olive oil
1 garlic clove
3 tablespoons minced fresh basil
¼ cup chopped fresh Italian parsley
salt and freshly ground black pepper to taste
1 cup ricotta cheese
3 tablespoons freshly grated Parmesan cheese

1. Fill a large pot with 3 quarts of salted water and start heating it for the pasta.

2. Remove the hard portion of the fresh tomatoes near the stem. Chop the tomatoes until you have 1 cup. Reserve the juice in another cup. If you are using canned tomatoes, squeeze them to eliminate the seeds and reserve the juice.

3. When the water is rapidly boiling, add the pasta. Cook until tender or al dente, about 6 to 10 minutes.

4. While the pasta is cooking, heat the olive oil in a saucepan. Push the garlic through a garlic press into the oil, or mince it and add it to the oil. Saute for 1 minute on medium-low heat. Now add the chopped tomatoes, basil, parsley, salt, and pepper. Cook until the mixture is reduced to a sauce consistency. Add the reserved tomato juices if the sauce looks drier than you like.

5. Drain the cooked pasta thoroughly (reserve some cooking water). Return the pasta to the pot. Stir the ricotta into the hot pasta, tossing with a wooden spoon. Pour in the hot tomato sauce and toss again. Sprinkle with Parmesan cheese and serve at once. This produces a thick, cheesy dish. (If you prefer a moister consistency, use some of the reserved boiling water from the pasta and add as desired.)

Serves 2

 # Quick Primavera

This primavera can be kept in the refrigerator for several days to be used for lunch, an appetizer, or a main course. It can be served cold or at room temperature.

1 pound ziti, rotini, or tortellini
1 pound zucchini
1 pound ripe plum tomatoes
4 large mushrooms
3 tablespoons vegetable oil
6 shallots
6 parsley sprigs, chopped
2 tablespoons minced fresh basil, or 1 tablespoon dried basil
1 small garlic clove, crushed
½ cup chopped cooked broccoli
pinch of dried oregano, mint, and red pepper flakes
salt and freshly ground black pepper to taste
¼ cup grated fresh Parmesan, Pecorino, or Romano cheese

1. Fill a large pot with 6 quarts of water and start heating it for the pasta.

2. Wash and trim the zucchini, tomatoes, and mushrooms, but do not peel.

3. Pour the oil into a large skillet, but do not put the pan over the heat yet.

4. Dice the unpeeled zucchini and tomatoes into the oil and then dice the shallots. Slice the mushrooms into the mixture. Add the chopped parsley, basil, garlic, cooked broccoli, and pinch of oregano, mint, and red pepper flakes. Turn the heat to medium-high and cook, stirring often with a wooden spoon. After 5 minutes, add salt and pepper. Turn off the heat and reserve. By now, the water should be boiling for the pasta.

5. Cook the pasta according to the package directions, or for less time for a firmer pasta. Gently strain the pasta when it is cooked and shake it briskly to remove excess water.

6. Transfer the pasta to a large serving platter. Pour the sauce over it, a small amount at a time, and toss with two forks to mix before adding more. Add half the grated cheese and toss again. Taste, and add more salt and pepper if needed.

7. Serve immediately, with the remaining cheese in a separate bowl to be used according to individual taste. Or refrigerate, covered, up to several days if desired.

Serves 8

 # Potato Gnocchi

Gnocchi, also known as dumplings, are a great delicacy. They can be served with any tomato sauce (see the sauce chapter) or substituted for the pasta in the Pasta with Broccoli Sauce recipe (see page 79). Top with plenty of freshly grated Parmesan cheese, black pepper, and dried red pepper flakes, and watch your family's delight! A salad and light wine will complete the meal. They also can be served as a side dish or appetizer.

> **1 pound potatoes**
> **2 cups unbleached flour (King Arthur preferred)**

1. Wash, pare, and cube the potatoes. Cover them completely with boiling salted water, cover the pot, and cook about 20 minutes or until tender when pierced with a fork. Drain the potatoes, but do not rinse them with cold water; they should remain boiling hot. Reserve some hot water for further use.

2. Put the cooked potatoes on a flat working surface and mash. Immediately measure the flour on top of the potatoes and mix well to make a soft elastic dough.

3. Knead the dough well until it is pliable, adding some of the reserved hot water if needed. To knead the dough, fold the opposite side over toward you. Using the heel of your hand, gently push the dough away from you. Give it a quarter turn, always turning in the same direction. Repeat the process rhythmically until the dough is smooth and elastic (5 to 8 minutes), using as little additional flour as possible.

4. To make gnocchi, break off small pieces of dough. Using the palm of your hand, roll the pieces to pencil thickness. Cut them into pieces about ¾ inch long. Curl each piece by pressing lightly with your index finger and pulling your finger along the piece of dough toward you. Gnocchi may also be shaped by pressing each piece lightly with a floured fork to form an indentation.

5. Bring 3 quarts of salted water to a boil. Add gnocchi gradually, a few pieces at a time. Boil rapidly, uncovered, for about 8 to 10 minutes, or until tender. Drain. Top with sauce of your choice and serve.

Serves 6–8

 # Gnocchi alla Modenese

GNOCCHI WITH HAM AND EGGS

You will surely impress your guests when you try this very unusual style of making gnocchi—good for testing your pasta-making skills.

3 cups all-purpose flour
5 ounces bread crumbs
1 egg
1/8 teaspoon nutmeg
1/4 pound boiled ham, chopped
1 cup milk
6 quarts water
salt
6 tablespoons butter
5 ounces freshly grated Parmesan cheese

1. Using a wooden spoon, thoroughly mix the flour, bread crumbs, egg, nutmeg, ham, and milk until the gnocchi dough is formed.

2. Let the dough mixture rest for about 10 minutes in a warm place.

3. Divide gnocchi dough into orange-sized balls, then roll into 1/2-inch-thick strands.

4. Cut strands into 1-inch pieces and set aside.

5. Boil 6 quarts of salted water.

6. Add all the gnocchi pieces to boiling water, a few at a time. Allow water to return to boil and allow gnocchi to cook 2 to 3 minutes more.

7. Remove the gnocchi and place in a serving bowl. Add butter and cheese. Toss thoroughly and serve.

Serves 4–6

TO FREEZE GNOCCHI, FETTUCCINE, OR RAVIOLI

Place freshly made pasta on a tray and put in freezer. When frozen, transfer to plastic bags and store in freezer until needed.

Ricotta Gnocchi a la Louise

1 pound ricotta cheese
1 egg, slightly beaten
1 teaspoon salt
2½ cups unbleached flour (King Arthur preferred)
4 quarts boiling salted water

1. In a large bowl, mix the ricotta, salt, and egg.

2. Add the flour and work mixture with your hands until a soft dough is formed.

3. Turn onto a floured board and knead lightly until the dough is firm and smooth. The dough should be soft, but not sticky; if sticky, keep flouring hands until it feels comfortable to handle.

4. Break off small pieces of dough. Using the palm of your hand, roll the pieces to a double pencil thickness, about 10 inches long.

5. Cut into 1-inch pieces. Press each piece lightly with a floured fork to form an indentation.

6. Set pieces aside and sprinkle with additional flour to keep pieces from sticking to each other or to their surface.

7. Continue until all the dough has been used up, then drop the gnocchi into 4 quarts of salted boiling water.

8. When the gnocchi floats to the top, drain immediately and transfer to a bowl.

9. Serve immediately with my Marinara (page 46) or Creamy Broccoli Sauce (page 61) tossed with freshly grated Parmesan cheese.

Serves 4–6

My friend Louise bakes the gnocchi and sauce in a foil-covered pan in a preheated 375-degree oven for 15–20 minutes.

Pasta con Piselli e Formaggio

PASTA WITH PEAS AND CHEESE SAUCE

The Romans made much of this especially delicate preparation that unites homemade pasta, green peas, cream, and cheese. This dish is a delightful appetizer for a simple roast, or it can be the main course for supper or lunch.

> **1 pound fresh egg noodles (like tagliarini)**
> **4 quarts boiling salted water**
> **3 cups fresh shelled peas (or thawed, frozen petite peas)**
> **2 tablespoons butter**
> **⅛ teaspoon nutmeg**
> **2 cups whipping cream**
> **1 egg, beaten**
> **1 cup freshly grated Parmesan cheese, plus additional for topping**

1. Drop noodles into rapidly boiling water over high heat.

2. When water again comes to a boil, cook noodles for 2 minutes, then add the fresh peas and cook 5 minutes longer. If you are using frozen peas, cook only 2 minutes.

3. Drain noodles and peas.

4. Using a wide, heavy skillet over medium heat, melt butter.

5. Add nutmeg and 1½ cups cream; stir using a wooden spoon.

6. When cream is warm, add pasta and peas and bring to a boiling point.

7. Remove pan from heat and stir in the beaten egg.

8. Add the 1 cup grated cheese and stir mixture until well blended. Add more cream if sauce seems too thick.

9. Sprinkle with more grated cheese and an extra dash of nutmeg.

10. Serve immediately.

Serves 4–6

 # Paglia e Fieno

"STRAW AND HAY"

If I had to choose among the many old-world dishes, this would be a strong favorite. It is so quick and easy and very popular in our local Italian restaurants.

> **salted boiling water**
> **1 pound wide egg noodles**
> **4 tablespoons butter**
> **¼ pound pancetta, cut in small cubes**
> **1 cup light cream**
> **1 cup frozen peas, defrosted**
> **1½ cups grated Parmesan cheese**
> **½ teaspoon freshly grated black pepper**

1. Cook noodles in salted boiling water until al dente.

2. Drain; toss with 2 tablespoons of the butter; reserve.

3. In a small saucepan, warm light cream (do not boil). Reserve.

4. Using a large, heavy skillet, saute remaining 2 tablespoons butter and the pancetta until the meat is fairly crisp.

5. Drain off fat; add the warmed cream, peas, 1 cup grated cheese, and pepper.

6. Stir thoroughly on medium heat, using a wooden spoon, until cream is fairly bubbly and sauce thickens slightly.

7. Add reserved noodles to skillet and, over medium-high heat, toss mixture until pasta is well coated with sauce.

8. Add remaining ½ cup grated cheese and serve immediately.

Serves 4–6

 Ziti with White
Cream Sauce

We always counted on pasta to get us through the day. There was always plenty of it, and lots of different, inexpensive ways to prepare it. Here we have a simple departure from the red sauce recipe. Simply, it is flour, butter, and cheese—the same ingredients that appear in many of our foods of yesteryear.

> **salted boiling water**
> **1 pound ziti (with no lines)**
> **4 tablespoons butter**
> **2 tablespoons flour**
> **1 cup milk**
> **salt and pepper to taste**
> **Romano or Parmesan cheese**

1. Cook ziti in salted boiling water until tender.

2. Drain and put in a serving platter.

3. Toss with 2 tablespoons butter and keep warm.

4. Melt remaining butter over very low heat, stir in flour until well blended, then add milk slowly, turning constantly with wooden spoon.

5. When mixture is well blended, bring to a soft boil and cook for 10 minutes or until sauce has thickened, stirring often.

6. Add salt and pepper to taste and stir well.

7. Pour immediately over warm, cooked ziti.

8. Sprinkle ziti with grated cheese and serve immediately.

Serves 4

If a looser sauce is desired, add more milk to flour mixture.

Pasta con Uovo e Formaggio

PASTA WITH EGGS AND CHEESE

When I used to come home from school, and my mother had all her chores completed, she would make this wonderful snack for me. I would always top it with plenty of black pepper and lots of Parmesan cheese. In those days there was no such product as grated cheese. We always had a big chunk of this cheese sitting in the fridge and the cheese grater hanging nearby. We ground our own pepper from a wonderful pepper mill. My father would sit at the kitchen table when he came home from work and just crank away until we had enough for the evening meal. We can recapture those days by using only fresh ingredients, such as pure olive oil and fresh eggs. In this dish, rice may be substituted for the pasta. It will taste just as wonderful.

boiling salted water
½ pound small pasta shells or ½ pound rice, cooked
2–3 tablespoons pure olive oil
2 eggs, slightly beaten
freshly grated cheese (Romano or Parmesan)
freshly grated black pepper

1. Cook shells in boiling salted water until al dente.

2. Drain some of the water until you have only enough to cover the pasta, with a little extra to spare.

3. Return to medium heat and slowly drizzle in the olive oil, enough only to barely cover the top of the pasta.

4. Using a fork, work the beaten eggs into the mixture; stir well.

5. Add 3 tablespoons of grated cheese and black pepper to taste.

6. Serve immediately in deep dishes or bowls.

7. Cover with additional cheese and pepper to taste. If desired, drizzle more olive oil over pasta and cheese.

Serves 2–4

Pizza, Calzone, Polenta, and Bread

 # Pizza

Pizza is certainly the most perfect food. When I was a young girl, my mother would give me my allowance of 35 cents every Friday, and I would visit the pizza parlor to order a pizza to go. A whole pizza (they really made them much smaller then) for myself! I always loved my mother, but never as much as when I bit into my Friday treat. To this day I feel like a little girl whenever I sit down to my own pizza pie.

Basic Pizza Dough

> ¾ **cup lukewarm water**
> 1 **package dry yeast**
> ⅛ **teaspoon sugar**
> 3 **cups unbleached flour (King Arthur brand gives a quality lift)**
> 1 **teaspoon salt**
> ¼ **cup olive oil**
> **vegetable oil**

1. Place the lukewarm water in a small bowl and sprinkle the yeast and sugar over it. Let stand in a warm, draft-free place for 10 to 15 minutes, until a foam forms on top.

2. In a large bowl, combine 1 cup of the flour and the teaspoon of salt.

3. Add the olive oil to the yeast mixture. Pour the mixture into the bowl of flour.

4. Gradually add the second cup of flour, stirring with a wooden spoon. When the dough begins to pull away from the sides of the bowl, turn it out onto a floured board.

5. Gradually knead the rest of the flour into the dough until the dough is smooth, elastic, and no longer sticky (about 10 minutes). The amount of flour needed will vary, depending on how moist the dough is and on the weather; a damp or humid day will cause excess moisture.

6. Coat a medium-size bowl with vegetable oil and place the ball of dough in it, rolling to coat it on all sides. Cover it tightly with plastic wrap and set in a warm place until it has doubled in bulk, about 45 to 60 minutes. To test if the dough has doubled, gently press two fingers into it; if they leave impressions, the dough is ready. While the dough is rising, prepare the sauce.

Basic Pizza Sauce

¼ cup olive oil
1 garlic clove, crushed
1 tablespoon tomato paste
1 8-ounce can peeled and crushed tomatoes
pinch of dried oregano, red pepper flakes, basil, and mint
salt and freshly ground black pepper to taste

The sauce can be made ahead and then reheated when it is needed. The recipe makes about 1½ cups of sauce.

1. Heat the oil in a saucepan and add the garlic. Simmer on low heat until the garlic is golden brown, but not burned.

2. Add the tomato paste and stir to mix well. Add the tomatoes with their juice, herbs, salt, and pepper. Bring to a soft boil, stirring often, and let simmer 10 to 20 minutes.

To finish pizza:

Use any or all of these ingredients:

olive oil
3 Italian sausages, fried until lightly browned and sliced (optional)
¼ pound pepperoni, sliced (optional)
1 medium-size green bell pepper, seeded and sliced in thin rings (optional)
¼ pound thinly sliced mushrooms (optional)
½ to 1 can anchovy fillets, drained (optional)
1 medium Bermuda onion, thinly sliced (optional)
½ pound shredded mozzarella cheese
½ cup freshly grated Parmesan or Romano cheese

1. Preheat the oven to 450 degrees. (To produce a heavenly, crispy pizza, the first thing to remember is that a very hot oven is very important! This will brown the crust and cook the sauce quickly so it will not seep through the dough.)

2. Lightly flour a clean flat surface, enough so that the dough does not stick. Flatten the dough with your hands until it forms a circle. Start punching it all around with the back of a clenched

fist to shape it into a large 14- to 15-inch circle, sprinkling it with flour as needed. Make a rim all around the circle, using your fingertips.

3. Rub 1 tablespoon of olive oil onto the surface of a large pizza pan. Arrange the circle of dough on the pan.

4. Add the pizza sauce to the center of the dough and spread it almost to the edges. Scatter over the entire dough, as desired, the sausages, pepperoni, pepper, mushrooms, anchovies, and onion slices. Top with the mozzarella and Parmesan or Romano cheeses.

5. Drizzle olive oil evenly over the entire pizza. Put the pizza on the top rack of the 450-degree oven. Let it cook for 20 minutes. This will seal the crust and tomatoes immediately and heat the oil on the bottom of the pan to cook the dough. When the dough is golden, move the pizza to the middle rack, lower the oven temperature a little, and cook 10 to 15 minutes.

Serves 2–6

 # Calzone

This is a delicious warm lunch, or it can be served cold on a summer's day. When I serve it warm, I sometimes top it with a dab of marinara sauce for a scrumptious taste. All that is needed to complete the meal is a tossed salad.

1 1-pound chunk of prosciutto or boiled ham, cubed
2 pounds ricotta cheese, drained if very wet
1 cup freshly grated Parmesan or Romano cheese
3 eggs
salt and pepper to taste
Basic Pizza Dough (page 94) or 1 pound store-bought pizza dough
olive oil
½ pound mozzarella, cubed
1 cup homemade or canned tomato sauce

1. Using a large bowl, mix ham or prosciutto, ricotta, grated cheese, eggs, salt, and pepper (the cheese will produce a salty taste, so test carefully). Set this filling aside.

2. Stretch the dough to make a 12- to 14-inch round. Leave dough slightly thick so that the filling will not ooze out.

3. Put the dough on a lightly oiled pizza pan, avoiding the edges. Gently spoon the filling onto half the pizza round. Fold the other half of dough over to form a large turnover. Use your fingertips to press the edges tightly together until all the dough is sealed.

4. Moisten the top and sides of the calzone with olive oil, using a pastry brush or the palm of your hand to spread it evenly. Cut a few slits in the middle of the calzone. Place some cubes of mozzarella and a ladleful or two of tomato sauce in each of these slits. Use all the cheese and sauce.

5. Bake the calzone in a preheated 350-degree oven for 40 to 45 minutes or until golden brown. It is best to use the medium rack of the oven.

6. Let the calzone rest for at least 20 minutes to allow the cheese mixture to set. Cut in slices and serve as an appetizer or as a lunch dish, topped with additional tomato sauce if desired.

Serves 4–6

Calzone with
Spinach-Ricotta Filling

Calzone is great with a variety of ingredients. Many of my friends layer it with salami, baked ham, Provolone cheese—sort of an Italian sub. It is good with any vegetables, such as broccoli, mushrooms, or spinach. Once you become accustomed to preparing this wonderful food, you will become more creative with it.

1 cup firmly packed spinach leaves, washed and dried
1 cup ricotta cheese
½ cup freshly grated Parmesan cheese
1 egg yolk
1 garlic clove, pressed
salt and freshly grated black pepper to taste
Basic Pizza Dough (page 94) or 1 pound store-bought pizza dough
olive oil
½ pound mozzarella, cubed

1. Finely mince the spinach leaves and blend with the ricotta cheese, Parmesan cheese, egg yolk, garlic clove, and salt and pepper.

2. Before adding the filling, remember to put dough on pan you will be using. Then prepare and fill the dough as directed on the previous calzone recipe. Brush the top and sides of the calzone with olive oil. Cut a few slits in the middle of the calzone. Place the cubes of mozzarella in each of these slits.

3. Bake the calzone in a preheated 350-degree oven on the middle rack for 40 to 45 minutes, or until golden brown.

4. Let the calzone rest for at least 20 minutes before serving to allow the cheese mixture to set.

Serves 4–6

 Claire's Pepperoni Pie

My high-school friend Claire would serve Pepperoni Pie as an appetizer when we had one of our gatherings at her house. It is also good as a one-step meal, similar to a quiche.

¾ cup pepperoni, diced
¾ cup Muenster cheese, cubed
¾ cup flour
2 eggs
1 cup milk

1. Place all the ingredients in a small bowl in the order given.

2. Stir with a slotted spoon until the batter is smooth. The mixture should be lumpy only because of the pepperoni and cheese.

3. Pour the batter into a greased 9-inch pie plate.

4. Bake in a preheated 400-degree oven for 30–35 minutes or until the center is firm (test with a toothpick).

5. Cut into wedges and serve.

Serves 6–8

Digging for Gold

My grandparents had a clever way of turning a humble and inexpensive meal into a treasure hunt. When nonna served polenta to her twelve children, she would pour it onto a wooden board and then pour sauce into several deep indentations that she made in the polenta. My grandfather would then hide a penny or two in the polenta. Each child was given a section of the board from which they could eat. The anticipation of finding the coins was so exciting, it was almost like digging for gold. Little did they all know that the real gold was the memories that were being created.

A staple of northern Italy and most Italian homes in the North End of Boston, polenta is a sort of mush made from cornmeal. It can be cooked to the consistency of cream of wheat and eaten with milk and honey or butter and cheese. Leftovers can be cut into slices that are fried, broiled, baked, or toasted and served with a variety of sauces and fillings. Like pasta or rice, polenta accents and absorbs any flavor it is matched with. It can be used in appetizers, side dishes, or main courses. For example, try this hors d'oeuvre: On skewers, alternate cubes of leftover polenta and fontina cheese that have been dipped in beaten egg and rolled in seasoned bread crumbs; deep-fry and serve hot. Or, for a hearty inexpensive meal on a cold winter night, serve polenta the old-fashioned Italian way. Spread it on a large board in the middle of the table and top it with cacciatore sauce and freshly grated Parmesan cheese. Seat your family or guests around the table, pour the wine, and have each person pick a corner and start eating.

> **1¾ cups yellow cornmeal**
> **2 cups cold water**
> **1 teaspoon salt**
> **5 cups water**
> **3 tablespoons olive oil**
> **melted butter or fontina cheese**

1. In a bowl, combine the cornmeal, cold water, and salt. Mix and set aside.

2. In a large heavy pot, bring the 5 cups of water to a boil. Add the oil and stir in the cornmeal mixture. Always stir clockwise. With a wire whisk, beat the cornmeal until it thickens, about 5 minutes. This will keep the polenta smooth and free of lumps. Cook it over medium heat, stirring *constantly* with a wooden spoon for 30 minutes. Use a wooden spoon with the longest handle you can find and wear long

sleeves, for polenta will bubble and can splatter. If the batter gets too thick, add a ladleful of water and continue stirring.

3. When the polenta is the consistency of cream of wheat, cover the pot and leave it on the heat for 3 minutes more without stirring. Shake the pot a little; this will allow some steam to get under the polenta so it will detach itself from the bottom of the pot easily. Then turn the polenta onto a smooth surface or into a lightly oiled round bowl. The polenta should be allowed to set and become firm enough to cut, but it should still be warm when it is served.

4. Cover the polenta with melted butter or fontina cheese. To cut it, use a wooden spatula if you have one, or a piece of string or dental floss. It is customary to avoid anything metal, however, because the taste of metal will destroy the taste of polenta.

5. Serve with additional salt and pepper to pass around, dried red pepper flakes, and grated Romano or Pecorino cheese.

Serves 6–8

Sausage Gravy for Polenta

1½ pounds Italian sausages, cut in chunks
½ cup water
olive oil
3 garlic cloves, chopped
1 small onion, chopped
2½ cups plum tomatoes
1 28-ounce can kitchen-ready tomatoes*
salt and pepper to taste
pinch of red pepper flakes
pinch of sweet basil
pinch of mint

1. In a wide, medium-size saucepan saute sausages with water, simmering on medium heat until water evaporates.

2. Add enough olive oil to cover bottom of pan; allow sausages to brown. Remove with a slotted spoon and reserve.

3. Add chopped garlic and onion; brown slightly.

4. Squeeze the plum tomatoes into the pan and stir well.

5. Add large can of kitchen-ready tomatoes*; stir until mixture comes to a soft boil.

6. Add salt and pepper, red pepper flakes, sweet basil, and mint to taste.

7. Stir sauce, and add reserved sausages.

8. Simmer gently for 20 minutes, stirring frequently with a wooden spoon.

9. Adjust seasonings and serve as sauce for polenta or homemade pasta.

*Peeled and ground, such as Pastene brand.

Serves 4–6

 # Fried Polenta

During my childhood we ate polenta so often that there was always some left over in the refrigerator. My grandfather, who was the cook of cooks, often fried the leftover polenta. He faithfully stood by the stove and diligently pressed and arranged the polenta until it was cooked to his liking. This he would use in place of bread. It was served with greens, such as sauteed spinach, escarole, or brocci di rape. To us, leftover polenta was better than the fresh version of the day before. Tastier than bread, it was filling also. Remember to use only wooden objects when touching the polenta.

4–6 cups cooked polenta, at room temperature
olive oil
string (for cutting)

1. Place cooked polenta on a wooden board that is covered with a sheet of waxed paper.

2. With a wooden spoon, press down on the polenta until it is in a pie shape, but still thick.

3. Heat enough olive oil to cover bottom of a medium-size cast-iron skillet. Cook oil until smoking, using medium-high heat.

4. Remove skillet from heat and place near board with polenta.

5. Lift wax paper and polenta from board and carefully place the polenta in the sizzling skillet, using the paper as a shield.

6. Return skillet to heat and fry the polenta, constantly pressing down with a wooden spoon until of even thickness all around and touching the pan on all sides.

7. Cook on medium heat without turning until polenta is crusty and golden brown at bottom.

8. Invert polenta pie onto a large platter.

9. Heat more olive oil to cover bottom of skillet.

10. Return polenta to pan and brown on reverse side.

11. Transfer completed pie to same platter, cut into wedges using the string, and serve with vegetables of your choice.

Serves 2–4

You may also top fried polenta with tomato sauce and grated cheese and serve as a main course.

 Focaccia

There are so many ingredients that you can use to top the flat, usually round bread called focaccia. In this recipe I give you my favorites, but you can experiment with any leftovers or seasonings of your choice. Focaccia is a wonderful snack or appetizer and makes a tasty and satisfying lunch.

1 pound pizza dough
1 small onion, thinly sliced
olive oil
salt and pepper to taste
1 cup shredded mozzarella
1 can anchovies, chopped
1 garlic clove, chopped
1 tablespoon crushed rosemary
oregano (optional)
1 teaspoon red pepper flakes
dry-cured olives, pitted and chopped
grated cheese

1. Stretch dough in a rectangular shape onto pizza tray.

2. Saute onions in 2 tablespoons olive oil, until tender.

3. Season with salt and pepper to taste.

4. Spread onion mixture over dough and sprinkle with mozzarella, chopped anchovies (and oil), chopped garlic, rosemary, oregano, red pepper flakes, olives, and lots of grated cheese.

5. Bake in a hot oven, preheated to 450 degrees, for about 20 minutes or until almost browned.

6. Cut in squares and serve hot or cold.

Serves 4

 Zeppole con Baccalà

You may know this traditional favorite as carnivale fritters or pizza fritta. Called zeppole in Italian, this treat can be made in many ways. My recipe uses baccalà (salted cod), but zeppole can also be filled with anchovies or any vegetable, such as cooked cauliflower or broccoli. I hope you enjoy this version, which comes straight from my grandmother and is cooked in the same fashion as the old-time zeppole. Watch the directions for an important step that the Italians believe is necessary for a successful dough. (Hint: If you know why the Christians believe in Easter, you will recognize its connection to dough.)

> **2 pounds boneless baccalà, soaked and boiled**
> **1 square fresh yeast or 1 packet dry**
> **2¼ cups warm water**
> **1½ teaspoons salt or to taste**
> **8 cups unbleached flour (King Arthur preferred)**
> **1 tablespoon black pepper, or to taste**
> **olive oil**
> **vegetable oil with olive oil added**

1. Baccalà should be soaked in cold water the night before, then boiled about 15 minutes (or until tender), drained, and refreshed under cold water until cooled.

2. Tear cooked baccalà into bite-size chunks; reserve.

3. In a large bowl, dissolve yeast in ¼ cup of the warm water, using fingertips.

4. Let stand 5–10 minutes or until it is bubbly and creamy. (If yeast does not activate, starter must be repeated. Check the expiration date on your package of yeast to be sure it is still good.)

5. Add salt and 2 tablespoons olive oil.

6. Pour starter dough into a very large stainless bowl. Slowly whisk in flour and remaining warm water until dough is thicker than pancake batter, using more water if needed. Dough should be heavy and sticky.

7. Wet hands and knead dough until smooth and shiny. Do this by loosening dough from edge of bowl and gently folding dough over and over, from top to bottom, always staying in one direction, until well mixed.

8. Stir in black pepper and cooked fish chunks and, with wooden spoon or even wet hands, mix until fish is well coated with the batter, again folding in one direction.

9. Rub dough lightly with olive oil on all sides.

10. Bless the dough (make a cross sign with hands) and cover tightly with plastic wrap; then place a heavy towel on top to keep warm. Let rise in a warm place about 1½–2 hours or until doubled in size.

11. When dough has doubled, stir with a wooden spoon and reserve.

12. Fill a large, heavy fry pan with 2 inches of vegetable and olive oil. Heat oil over medium heat.

13. Bring bowl with zeppole and baccalà to stove and add ½ cup of batter with fish to hot oil for small zeppoles or 1 cup batter for large zeppole. Dip the spoon you are using in oil, then in batter to enable dough to slide off into the oil without sticking; continue this step each time.

14. Fry zeppole, uncrowded, until deep golden-brown and crisp on both sides. Bear down slightly with your spoon on the dough to cook well.

15. Add more oil as needed, removing any burnt particles in pan.

16. Remove cooked zeppole using a slotted spoon and drain on paper towels.

17. Sprinkle with salt and serve warm or at room temperature with lemon wedges.

Yield: 2½ dozen large or 4–5 dozen small zeppole.

Unused batter may be covered and refrigerated until needed. Stir dough well before using.

 # Black Pepper Taralli

These taralli were made by one of our own senior citizens from the North End of Boston. They are crispy and great for dipping in your morning coffee. These are found hanging in our pastry and bread shops on long strings, enabling them to dry out after being cooked in boiling water. You may add more or less black pepper than the recipe calls for.

> **6 eggs**
> **½ cup vegetable oil**
> **1 packet dry yeast**
> **4 cups unbleached flour, divided (King Arthur preferred)**
> **1 heaping teaspoon black pepper**
> **1½ teaspoon fennel seed**

1. In large mixing bowl, beat eggs thoroughly.

2. Add oil and beat again.

3. Mix yeast with 1 cup flour, then beat this mixture into the first mixture.

4. Add remaining flour gradually, along with black pepper and fennel seed. Stir well.

5. Place dough on wooden board or counter. Knead dough until smooth, about 10 minutes.

6. Break off 24 small pieces and roll each one into a pencil shape.

7. Bend the "pencils" to form a circle, and secure edges by pinching ends together.

8. Place in a pot of boiling water a few at a time and cook until they float to the surface.

9. Remove from the water and allow to cool on a wire rack.

10. When cool, bake on ungreased cookie sheets in a 350-degree oven for 25–30 minutes or until golden brown and dry.

Yield: 24 taralli

 # Pizza Giena

ITALIAN EASTER PIE

Many thanks to my aunt, Lucy Baldassare, who generously shared her mother's glorious recipe with our family. I now pass this recipe on to you, with my aunt's blessing, so that you may share this wonderful Easter tradition with your family. The dough is so manageable, you could cry. The secret is to allow it to rest, covered, for at least half an hour. This recipe makes a large amount, so you may want to share a piece or two with a friend. You will need a heavy, rectangular baking pan, 13 inches long by 9 inches wide by 3 inches deep.

Crust

> **5 cups unbleached flour, unsifted (King Arthur preferred)**
> **2 tablespoons freshly ground black pepper**
> **½ cup vegetable shortening**
> **4 eggs, slightly beaten**
> **¾ cup warm water**
> **egg wash (2 eggs and 3 tablespoons milk)**

1. Using a large bowl, add measured flour and black pepper, mixing slightly with a fork.

2. Add shortening and, working fast, press together, using your fingertips to blend evenly.

3. Make a well in the flour and add the beaten eggs and warm water (use ¼ cup water at a time until you have a soft and pliable but firm dough).

4. Press dough firmly together, adding more water if needed.

5. Turn onto a slightly floured surface and knead thoroughly, at least 5–7 minutes.

6. Cover with a bowl and let rest ½ hour or more.

7. Cut ⅔ of the dough and roll it out, turning often, to fit the bottom and up the sides of the ungreased baking pan.

8. Roll out the remaining dough for the top crust and set aside (make a few slits).

This recipe keeps 5 days or more in the refrigerator. It requires no yeast (therefore no waiting for the dough to rise), yet the finished product is of no comparison to other styles of preparation. You will surely pass this one on to your children.

Filling

2 pounds ricotta cheese
1 large pepperoni (about 1 pound)
1 double Abbruzese salami (about ⅓ pound)
1 large supresata (about ¾- to 1-pound piece)
¼ pound Genoa salami
½ pound mozzarella cheese, cubed
1 dozen medium-size whole eggs
½ cup freshly grated Romano cheese
1 tablespoon black pepper
2 pounds fresh cheese (such as formaggio or fresco)
1 pound prosciutto, thinly sliced

Have your butcher slice the meats in thick strips. Be sure to remove the skin before chopping the cold-cut meat into small cubes.

1. Using a large bowl or deep pan, combine all ingredients except fresh cheese and prosciutto.

2. When mixture is thoroughly blended, use your fingertips to break the fresh cheese into large pieces and toss gently with the cold-cut meats mixture. Try not to crush this delicate cheese when tossing. Reserve.

3. Line bottom crust with half of the prosciutto slices.

4. Gently pour ricotta mixture into prosciutto-lined baking pan or pans, and cover top with remaining prosciutto slices.

5. Cover entire mixture with reserved dough.

6. Take the edges of the top and bottom dough, press together, and roll inward.

7. Continue around the edges of the pan to form a decorative edge similar to a pie.

8. Crimp edges, then press gently with the tines of a fork.

9. Take any remaining scraps of dough, roll together, and cut into two lattice strips to form a cross and place in the middle of top crust.

10. Brush all over with egg wash and prick the dough in three or four scattered places on the top to allow steam to escape.

11. Place in a preheated 400-degree oven for ½ hour, then lower heat to 350 degrees. If you are using 10-inch round pans (you will need 3 or 4 of them), bake at 350 degrees for 30 minutes and lower heat to 300 degrees.

12. Continue cooking for 30 to 40 minutes or until golden brown.

13. Let cool 4 to 6 hours in refridgerator.

14. Cut in wedges and serve.

Serves 15–20

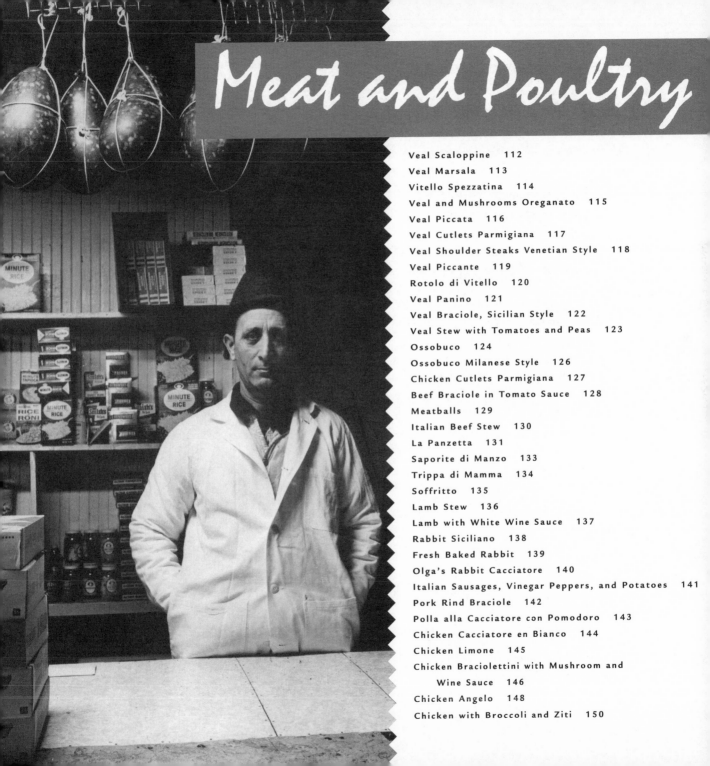

Meat and Poultry

 Veal Scaloppine

This is a favorite in most Italian restaurants, including my brother's restaurant, Dom's, in the North End. A very quick, simple recipe if all the ingredients are on hand.

6 tablespoons unsalted butter
6 2-ounce veal scallops
flour to coat veal
salt and pepper to taste
chopped fresh parsley for garnish

1. Using a medium-high heat, melt the butter in a saute pan.

2. Lightly dredge the veal with flour, shaking off the excess.

3. When the butter is hot but not burning, place the veal in the saute pan. Lightly brown the slices on one side, turn them over, and cook quickly, 1 minute or so, on the other side. You must work fast to produce a tender veal.

4. Transfer the veal slices to a warm platter. Stir the sauce well, scraping up any bits that may be stuck to the pan. Pour it over the veal.

5. Season with salt and pepper and sprinkle with fresh parsley. Serve immediately with buttered pasta or rice.

Serves 2

◆◆◆◆◆◆◆◆ Veal Marsala ◆◆◆◆◆◆◆

Have all the ingredients nearby and ready. Work quickly! Once you are prepared, this dish can be cooked and served in less than 10 minutes.

6 tablespoons unsalted butter
6 2-ounce veal scallops
flour to coat veal
salt and pepper to taste
2 shallots, chopped
3 or 4 ounces Marsala wine
6 fresh mushrooms, thinly sliced
chopped fresh parsley for garnish

1. Using a medium-high heat, melt the butter in a saute pan.

2. Lightly dredge the veal with flour, shaking off any excess.

3. Place the veal in the saute pan and lightly brown on one side. Sprinkle with salt and pepper, turn over, and add chopped shallots. Cook 1 minute more.

4. On high heat, add the Marsala and boil rapidly to burn off the excess alcohol. Add the mushrooms and cook briefly to blend flavors.

5. Transfer the veal to a warm platter. Pour the sauce over the veal, sprinkle with chopped parsley, and serve immediately.

Serves 2

 # Vitello Spezzatina

VEAL AND PEPPERS SAUTE

For this recipe it is important not to overcook the vegetables; they should be crisp. The tender meat and crunchy vegetables recapture the grand old custom of keeping food as close as possible to its natural state.

> **1½ pounds lean veal**
> **olive oil**
> **3 large cloves garlic, peeled**
> **3 large bell peppers, chopped**
> **2 large white onions, chopped**
> **salt and pepper**
> **red pepper flakes (optional)**
> **fresh parsley, chopped**

1. Have butcher slice the veal ¼ inch thick as for cutlets. Cut into ¼ inch slices.

2. Cover the bottom of a 12-inch frying pan with olive oil to a depth of ¼ inch. Slice garlic cloves lengthwise into thirds and saute slowly over low heat until translucent. Do not burn. Remove the garlic.

3. Add the veal; turn heat to medium-high and immediately add the peppers and onions; cover.

4. Cook for 1½ minutes; turn the veal, lower heat, and continue to cook until done (approximately another 3 minutes).

5. Season to taste with salt, pepper, and red pepper flakes if desired. Sprinkle with fresh parsley.

Serves 2–4

 Veal and Mushrooms  Oreganato

6 veal shoulder steaks
½ cup flour seasoned with oregano and parsley
3 tablespoons olive oil
2 cloves garlic, crushed
1 can whole tomatoes
salt and pepper
2 tablespoons oregano
1 15-ounce can mushrooms, drained, or ¼ pound fresh mushrooms
¼ cup dry white wine

1. Dredge the steaks in the seasoned flour. Shake off the excess flour.

2. Heat the oil in a heavy skillet; cook the crushed garlic in the oil gently until golden brown.

3. Add the steaks and cook until brown on both sides.

4. Add the mushrooms to the meat and saute, uncovered, for 5 minutes. Sprinkle with the oregano and salt and pepper to taste.

5. Add the tomatoes, with their juice, and the wine; simmer gently until steaks are tender. Adjust seasonings and serve hot with tomato mixture over meat.

Serves 4–6

 # Veal Piccata

VEAL WITH PROSCIUTTO

¼ cup unsalted butter
1 pound veal scallops
2 tablespoons flour
salt and freshly ground black pepper
⅛ pound prosciutto, sliced very thin and slivered
2 tablespoons stock
1 tablespoon butter
1 teaspoon chopped fresh parsley
2 teaspoons lemon juice

1. Heat the butter in a frying pan.

2. Dredge the meat in flour, salt, and pepper.

3. Place the meat in the frying pan and cook over high heat for 2 minutes on each side. Transfer the meat to a warm platter and keep it in a warm place.

4. Place the prosciutto in the frying pan and cook it 3 minutes, stirring quickly. Remove it from the pan and place it over the veal.

5. Add the stock, butter, and parsley to the pan gravy. Scrape the pan well, cook for 2 minutes, and add the lemon juice.

6. Pour the sauce over the meat. Serve immediately with sauteed sliced zucchini or squash.

Serves 4

 Veal Cutlets Parmigiana

Truly a favorite for all times, this dish has been in my family forever. It is simple to make and is so appealing that there is no doubt you will win praises. Cutlets may be prepared in advance, such as early in the day. You also can cook and refrigerate them for a couple of days. For this recipe you will need at least 2 cups of my meatless marinara. Spaghetti is a wonderful accompaniment, along with a fresh salad. (Chicken may be substituted for the veal.)

6 boneless veal cutlets (4 ounces each)
2 eggs
3 tablespoons milk
3 cups dry bread crumbs or more, if needed
Parmesan cheese, freshly grated
¼ cup fresh parsley, chopped
salt and pepper to taste
2 cups olive oil
2 cups meatless tomato sauce (see page 46)
8 ounces shredded mozzarella cheese

FRESH BREAD CRUMBS

To make fresh bread crumbs, use day-old Italian bread. Cut any leftover pieces into small chunks. Put in the blender a few chunks at a time. Blend just until you have light and fluffy crumbs. Use for coating meats or fish, for making meatballs, or for using as stuffing for peppers and artichokes.

1. Place veal between sheets of waxed paper. With smooth surface side of mallet or rolling pin, pound to ¼-inch thickness.

2. In a medium-sized shallow dish, beat eggs with milk. Place bread crumbs in another dish and mix with ¼ cup Parmesan, chopped parsley, and salt and pepper to taste.

3. Coat cutlets with egg, then bread crumbs, pressing down slightly so that crumbs will adhere to both sides. Place on wax paper to set.

4. Heat olive oil in medium-sized heavy skillet, using medium-high heat. Add cutlets, a few at a time, and fry about 1 minute on each side until golden brown and crisp. Drain on paper towels.

5. Place cutlets on heavy baking sheet and cover each cutlet with tomato sauce. Sprinkle with ½ cup grated Parmesan and mozzarella. Bake in a hot 375-degree oven for 10 to 15 minutes or until cheese is melted and tops are golden brown.

Serves 4

Veal Shoulder Steaks Venetian Style

Our family loved meat that was still attached to the bone. Veal was easily available and was reasonably priced, so there was always plenty to go around. This recipe is typical of the style we remember coming home to.

veal shoulder steaks
½ cup flour
salt and pepper to taste
3 tablespoons olive oil
2 garlic cloves, chopped
3 ripe fresh tomatoes, chopped
pinch of red pepper flakes
¼ cup white wine
¼ pound fresh button mushrooms
2 tablespoons fresh parsley, chopped

1. Dip veal steaks in flour to which ½ teaspoon salt and pepper has been added.

2. Heat olive oil in heavy skillet.

3. Add veal and, using medium heat, fry till golden brown on both sides.

4. Add garlic and saute with meat until golden brown.

5. Add chopped tomatoes, red pepper flakes, and salt and pepper to taste.

6. Stir well until a nice sauce is formed.

7. Add wine, mushrooms, and chopped parsley; mix well.

8. Simmer gently until veal is tender.

Serves 4–6

Veal Piccante

VEAL WITH ANCHOVIES

2 ounces unsalted butter
6 2-ounce veal scallops
flour to dredge veal
6 flat anchovies, drained and
  chopped
12 capers (in water), drained
½ lemon
freshly ground black pepper
chopped fresh parsley

1. Heat the butter in a saute pan over medium-high heat.

2. Dredge the veal in flour and shake off the excess.

3. Place the veal in the pan and lightly brown on one side. Turn it over, raise the heat to high, and add the anchovies and capers. Let the mixture get red hot.

4. Squeeze the half lemon (juice only) over the veal. Add pepper to taste. Shake pan vigorously, sprinkle the veal with parsley, and serve immediately.

Serves 2

If It's Tuesday, This Must Be...

Italian families in the North End used to have the same basic menu schedule for each day of the week. On Sundays we had tomato gravy with meat, either meatballs, sausages, pork, or braciole (rolled stuffed beef). Monday was soup day, usually beef or chicken, with a salad. On Tuesdays and Thursdays we ate the leftover tomato gravy and meat from Sunday (my mother would also drop some eggs into the sauce). Wednesday was variety night. We would have either chicken cacciatore, sausages and potatoes with vinegar peppers, pork chops, minestra (cabbage and beans), or rice and beans in tomato sauce with lots of grated cheese. Of course, on Fridays no meat was allowed, so my mother would make stuffed calamari with spaghetti, fried fish, or sometimes deep-dish pizza—my favorite. On Saturdays my mother economized with dishes like tripe with tomato sauce or, you guessed it, franks and beans, but on some occasions we would have steak, which my grandfather would grill over the flame of our gas stove. It smelled wonderful, but my mother didn't appreciate all the grease on her shiny stove! All these meals stand out in my memory with gratitude for the love and care my mother gave her family through this good food.

Rotolo di Vitello

ROLLED BREAST OF VEAL

1¼ pound boned breast of veal
¼ cup olive oil
6–7 sage leaves
salt and pepper to taste
¼ boiled ham (not smoked), chopped
⅓ cup fresh or canned peas
¼ pound freshly grated Parmesan cheese
1 whole egg
juice of a lemon

1. Preheat oven to 375 degrees.

2. Rub the veal with 1 tablespoon oil and sprinkle with salt and pepper.

3. Combine the sage leaves, ham, peas, cheese, and egg. Spread mixture over veal.

4. Roll up the meat tightly and fasten with string.

5. Place the meat in a baking dish and pour remaining oil and lemon juice over veal.

6. Bake for 1 hour or until meat is tender at the touch of a fork.

Serves 4–6

 # Veal Panino

My brother, Dom Capossela, put himself through college and law school working as a waiter and then decided to open his own restaurant. The original Dom's was located on Commercial Street in the North End and has since relocated to Bartlett Place on the corner of Salem and Parmenter streets. Dom's was one of the first restaurants in Boston to make its own pasta, antipasti, and desserts and to explore regional Italian cooking.

> **4 3-ounce veal cutlets, pounded very thin**
> **2 thin slices prosciutto**
> **2 thin slices fontina cheese**
> **1 small garlic clove, pressed**
> **chopped fresh parsley**
> **few drops olive oil**
> **1 teaspoon freshly grated Parmesan cheese**
> **egg wash of 2 eggs, 4 tablespoons milk, and 1 tablespoon chopped fresh parsley**
> **½ cup olive oil**
> **1 lemon**
> **1 tablespoon melted butter**

1. Pound the cutlets very thin. Sandwich between them the thin slices of prosciutto, fontina cheese, bits of pressed garlic, chopped parsley (about 1 teaspoon per sandwich), few drops of olive oil, and grated cheese.

2. Using two serving forks or tongs, gently dip the veal sandwich in the egg wash. Then fry the sandwich in the hot olive oil. If the oil is not hot enough when you add the cutlet, the egg will slither into the oil and leave the cutlets bare and unattractive; if the oil is really sizzling, the egg will puff into a protective shell and seal in the juice of the meat and cheeses.

3. Once the egg has adhered and the meat is cooking nicely, lower the heat and cook for at least 15 minutes on one side and 5 minutes more on the other side.

Serves 2–4

 # Veal Braciole Sicilian Style

For this recipe you will need a prepared tomato sauce in which to add the braciole. Serve with pasta and salad for a complete meal.

7 large scallops of veal, thinly sliced
1 cup fresh bread crumbs
1 egg, slightly beaten
1 tablespoon parsley
2 small garlic cloves, chopped
¼ cup Romano or Pecorino cheese, grated
¼ cup pignoli nuts, slightly crushed
salt and pepper to taste
olive oil

1. Spread veal slices on counter, pounding slightly to flatten.

2. Put bread crumbs in a medium-size bowl and add beaten egg, parsley, garlic, grated cheese, pignoli nuts, salt, and pepper to taste.

3. Mix together to form a soft paste.

4. Spread this paste evenly over veal slices, leaving edges bare.

5. Roll each veal slice tightly and tie with string or secure with toothpicks.

6. Using a heavy skillet, brown veal braciole in enough olive oil to cover bottom of pan.

7. When meat is nicely browned, add to hot cooked tomato sauce. Use a pan large enough to keep meat from crowding.

8. When ready to serve veal, place in a serving platter, remove string or toothpicks, and cut in thin slices.

9. Pour some hot sauce over braciole and serve with pasta.

Serves 4–6

Veal Stew with Tomatoes and Peas

The aroma of this meal will make your neighbors come knocking. Don't be surprised if they linger until dinnertime. A good loaf of Italian bread will complement this hearty winter meal.

1½ pounds boned shoulder of veal, cut into cubes
½ cup olive oil
2 garlic cloves, mashed
¾ cup flour
½ teaspoon dried marjoram
salt and pepper to taste
1 cup dry white wine
1 tablespoon chopped fresh parsley
1 bay leaf
1 14-ounce can tomatoes, or 2 large ripe tomatoes, seeded and chopped
1 cup fresh peas, or 1 10-ounce package of frozen small peas, thawed

1. Heat the oil in a large stew pan; add the garlic and brown gently. Discard the garlic.

2. Spread the flour on waxed paper. Dip the pieces of veal in the flour, coating them on all sides. Shake off the excess flour.

3. Add the veal to the pan with the marjoram, salt, and pepper. Over medium-high heat, brown the veal thoroughly on all sides. When the meat is well browned, add the wine, parsley, and bay leaf. Cook slowly until the wine evaporates.

4. Add the tomatoes, enough warm water to cover the meat, and more seasonings as needed. Stir gently, scraping up any residue on the bottom of the pan. When the tomato sauce begins to boil, cover the pot and set the heat to simmer. Cook slowly until the veal is very tender, about ½ to ¾ of an hour.

5. When the veal has been cooking for about 45 minutes, add the peas, toss well, and adjust seasonings. More water may be added during cooking time if necessary. Remove the bay leaf before serving.

Serves 4

 # Ossobuco

Ossobuco *means, literally, "bone with a hole," and refers to the fact that the veal shanks are sawed crosswise, exposing the marrow-filled hole through the middle of the bone. This is the way my brother Dom serves Ossobuco in Dom's Restaurant.*

3 veal shanks, cut in half
½ cup butter
½ cup chopped onions
½ cup chopped celery
½ cup chopped carrots
1 garlic clove, minced
1 heaping tablespoon fresh parsley, chopped
about ½ cup flour
salt and pepper to taste
½ cup olive oil
½ cup white wine
½ cup chicken broth
1 bay leaf
2 cups canned chopped Italian plum tomatoes, strain juices

1. Melt the butter in a large Dutch oven over medium heat. When it is hot, but not burning, add the onions, celery, and carrots. Stir often. When the onions are transparent, turn off the heat. Add the garlic and parsley and stir for a few minutes.

2. Put about ½ cup of flour in a paper bag. Add salt and pepper and the veal shanks. Shake the bag vigorously. Shake the excess flour from the shanks.

3. In a separate skillet, brown the shanks in the olive oil. Remove them from the skillet and place them on top of the vegetables in the Dutch oven.

4. Use the drippings in the skillet as a base for your sauce. Start by pouring out any excess fat. Add the wine to the remaining drippings and cook rapidly, until the mixture thickens.

5. Now add the broth, bay leaf, and tomatoes. Bring the sauce to a boil. Then, pour it over the veal and vegetables in the Dutch oven.

6. Cover the Dutch oven and bake in a preheated 350-degree oven for 1½ hours. Baste often. Add more broth if it starts to dry out, but do not drown the veal shanks. The sauce should be fairly thick.

7. Remove the bay leaf. Serve as is or over noodles. Don't forget to provide a spoon for each person to scoop out that wonderful, tasty marrow.

Serves 4

Ossobuco may be prepared in advance, refrigerated for 2 or 3 days, and reheated before serving.

Ossobuco Milanese Style

This dish has been showing up on a lot of restaurant menus lately, although it frequently requires advance notice. The meat is succulent, and don't forget to eat the marrow in the bones. It is both nutritious and delicious!

1 tablespoon butter
4 veal shin bones, 4 inches long, with meat
2 tablespoons flour
salt and pepper to taste
½ cup dry white wine
1 cup water
1 teaspoon fresh parsley, chopped
½ garlic clove, chopped
4 strips lemon peel, 1 inch long
1 anchovy fillet, chopped
1 tablespoon broth
1 tablespoon butter

1. Heat the tablespoon of butter in a deep heavy skillet.

2. Roll the bones in the flour. Place them in the skillet, add salt and pepper, and cook over medium heat until browned. Turn the bones occasionally.

3. Add the wine and continue cooking until the wine evaporates. Add the cup of water, lower the heat, cover the skillet, and cook 1 hour. Add more water, if necessary.

4. Five minutes before serving, add the parsley, garlic, lemon peel, and anchovy. Cook 2 minutes longer, turning the bones over once.

5. Place the bones on a serving dish. Add the stock and butter to the pan gravy, mix well until the sauce thickens, and pour it over the bones.

Serves 4

Chicken Cutlets Parmigiana

For this recipe you will need to make my marinara sauce (page 46) first. Veal may be substituted for the chicken.

> **1 pound chicken cutlets**
> **2 eggs**
> **salt and pepper to taste**
> **3 cups bread crumbs or more, if needed**
> **2 tablespoons grated cheese**
> **¼ cup fresh parsley, chopped**
> **olive oil**
> **marinara sauce (see recipe page 46)**
> **sliced mozzarella cheese**

1. Have your butcher pound boneless chicken breasts into thin cutlets.

2. In a medium-size bowl, beat eggs with salt and pepper to taste.

3. In a semi-flat dish, mix bread crumbs, grated cheese, and parsley.

4. Dip cutlets in egg wash and roll in bread crumbs, bearing down to allow bread to stick to chicken.

5. Place on a platter and let rest about 10 minutes.

6. Heat the olive oil on medium heat using a large, heavy skillet.

7. When oil is good and hot, add the chicken cutlets without crowding. Lower heat and cook until well browned on both sides, turning only once. Continue until all the chicken pieces are cooked, adjusting the heat so that chicken is always sizzling, but not burning.

8. Place the chicken cutlets, in one layer, on a shallow baking pan. Top each cutlet with a scoop of marinara and a thin slice of mozzarella cheese.

9. Bake in a 350-degree oven for 15 minutes or until mozzarella turns golden brown and cutlets are cooked.

10. Serve immediately with extra sauce.

Serves 4

 # Beef Braciole in Tomato Sauce

ROLLED STUFFED BEEF

You'd better make a couple—this will be a big favorite!

> **1½ pounds flank, skirt, or top of the round steak**
> **2 garlic cloves, finely chopped**
> **½ cup fresh parsley, chopped**
> **¾ cup freshly grated Parmesan cheese**
> **½ teaspoon salt**
> **1 teaspoon freshly ground black pepper**
> **⅓ cup olive oil**
> **2½ cups canned peeled and crushed tomatoes**
> **pinch of dried basil, red pepper flakes, and mint**
> **salt and freshly ground black pepper to taste**

1. Lay the meat out flat on a smooth working surface. Flatten it to ½-inch thickness, pounding it lightly with the dull edge of a meat cleaver, or use a meat mallet. Keep the meat in one piece.

2. Cover the steak with the garlic, parsley, cheese, salt, and pepper.

3. Roll up the steak, jellyroll fashion, and tie it securely with cotton string or several toothpicks.

4. Heat the oil in a large heavy skillet and brown the meat thoroughly on all sides. This should take 10 minutes.

5. Add the tomatoes and seasonings to the browned braciole. Cover the skillet. Simmer the meat for about 1 hour or until it is tender. Do not overcook, or it will fall apart.

6. When the meat is ready, place it on a large serving platter, cut the string, slice, and serve with the sauce poured over it. This may be accompanied by cooked pasta.

Serves 4

Braciole can be made in advance. It can be refrigerated for 3 to 5 days after cooking and it freezes well if it is covered with the sauce.

 # Meatballs

For a soft, moist meatball, add uncrowded to a light tomato sauce; keep sauce gently boiling to allow meatballs to float to the surface.

1½ pounds ground meat (1 pound beef; ½ pound pork)
2 medium eggs
2 cups soft bread crumbs, or enough to hold mixture together
½ cup chopped fresh parsley
½ cup freshly grated Parmesan or Romano cheese
1 large garlic clove, finely chopped
salt and pepper to taste

TO FREEZE MEATBALLS

Put uncooked meatballs on large trays and place in freezer. When completely frozen, remove from trays and put in plastic freezer bags, a few in each bag. Defrost as needed or put bags in boiling water and cook until soft. Add to sauce.

1. Combine all the ingredients in a large bowl. Toss gently with your hands until the meat has become thoroughly blended with all the seasonings. The mixture should be fairly moist.

2. To form the meatballs, wet your hands in a small bowl of lukewarm water and then pick up about ⅓ cup of the meatball mixture. Roll it in the palm of your hands to form a smooth ball about 2½ inches in diameter.

3. Drop the meatballs directly into your basic tomato sauce recipe. Or, if you prefer a crusty meatball, fry in approximately 3 tablespoons of olive oil on medium heat for about 5 minutes, turning to brown evenly. Then drop them into gently boiling tomato sauce as they are browned. Meatballs take 20 minutes to cook well. (Remember to scrape the bottom of the skillet and pour any crusty meat particles into the meat sauce.)

Yield: 10–15 medium meatballs

 # Italian Beef Stew

Experiment with different kinds of wine in this stew. Burgundy will keep it on the sweet side, while a dry white wine will keep it light.

2 pounds cubed lean beef
flour
4 tablespoons olive oil
2 ounces salt pork, diced into small pieces
3 large onions, thickly sliced
salt and freshly ground black pepper to taste
3 garlic cloves, slivered
10 sprigs parsley, leaves only, chopped
1 bay leaf, crumbled
½ teaspoon red pepper flakes
½ cup wine
3 large potatoes, cut in chunks
3 celery stalks, sliced
3 or 4 carrots, sliced in chunks
2 medium-size fresh tomatoes, diced, or 1 14-ounce can plum tomatoes with their juice
½ pound mushrooms, thickly sliced
½ cup hot water

1. Dredge the meat in flour. Shake off the excess.

2. Heat the olive oil and salt pork in a heavy pot or Dutch oven. Remove the salt pork when it is slightly browned. Add the onions, beef, salt, and pepper. Cook for 10 minutes, stirring often.

3. Add the garlic, chopped parsley, bay leaf, and red pepper flakes. Let the mixture heat thoroughly. Sprinkle the wine into the pot. Stir and simmer, covered, for 10 minutes.

4. Add the potatoes, celery, carrots, tomatoes with their juice, and mushrooms. Stir and cook for 10 minutes longer.

5. Add the hot water, cover, and simmer for 40 minutes, stirring at least twice to prevent sticking.

6. Uncover the stew and simmer 10 minutes more or until the meat is tender. Taste for salt and pepper and add more if needed.

This stew refrigerates well for several days.

Serves 4–6

 # La Panzetta

STUFFED VEAL FLANK

This is an old recipe, and one that should be treasured. Serve it on special occasions because it is a "fussy" dish. The combination of the fatty meat, the very rich, custardlike cheese and eggs, and the gravy makes it succulent and delicious. The meat will need to be ordered in advance from your butcher, as it is not easily available. Have him cut a pocket all the way through the meaty end of the flank. For the gravy, you will be following the Sunday Gravy recipe, substituting this meat for the meat in that recipe.

> **1 4½- to 5-pound veal flank, with pocket cut**
> **¼ pound ricotta cheese**
> **5 eggs**
> **1½ cups freshly grated Romano cheese**
> **½ cup chopped fresh parsley**
> **4 garlic cloves, chopped**
> **salt and pepper**
> **olive oil**
> **Tomato Sauce from Sunday Gravy recipe, doubled (page 47)**

1. Blend the ricotta and eggs with the grated cheese, parsley, garlic, salt, and pepper.

2. Pour a little of this mixture into the cavity of the veal. If any of it leaks out because of a slight

tear in the meat, pour mixture back into the bowl and sew up that tear with a large needle and thread. Place your stitches very close together. Pour the mixture back into the opening. When the opening is filled, sew it up with the needle and thread. Again, place the stitches very close together to keep the filling from seeping through. You may need to lay the veal flat as you are preparing it. (Don't worry if you lose a little filling.)

3. Heat the oil in a roasting pan large enough for the veal to lie flat. Gently lift veal and place in pan. Sprinkle the veal all over with about 1 tablespoon of salt and 1 tablespoon of pepper. Fry the meat until it is very brown and crisp on both sides, turning gently with a large, strong spatula or a large fork (do not pierce the meat). Remove it from the pan and set it aside in a warm place. This will set the egg and seal the meat openings.

4. Start cooking your tomato sauce in the same pan, using the drippings from the veal. When the sauce comes to a boil, add the veal, lower the heat to medium, and cook for at least 3½ hours. (You can also bake the veal and sauce in a 350-degree oven for the same amount of time, if you wish.) Adjust the heat as necessary to keep the sauce from drying out. The meat is cooked through when it gently lifts from the bone without falling apart.

5. Lift the meat onto a large platter and let it rest while you serve a first course of pasta (about 1 to 2 pounds), spooning the gravy from the panzetta over the pasta.

6. Slice the veal between the bones as you would a prime rib. Serve with the sauce.

Serves 6–8

 # Saporite di Manzo

BEEF PATTIES WITH BALSAMIC VINEGAR AND PARMESAN CHEESE

1 pound beef round, chopped
1 cup freshly grated Parmesan cheese
2 egg yolks
salt and pepper to taste
3 tablespoons butter
¼ onion, thinly sliced
1 tablespoon vegetable oil
½ cup cream
1 tablespoon balsamic vinegar

1. Combine the beef, cheese, and the egg yolks.

2. Mix thoroughly, add salt and pepper, and shape into six patties.

3. Brown patties in a heavy skillet with 2 tablespoons butter. Remove when cooked and keep warm.

4. In same skillet, saute the onion in the oil and 1 tablespoon butter, using medium heat.

5. When onion is golden brown, add the cream, salt and pepper, and balsamic vinegar; stir thoroughly.

6. Cook gently until cream has thickened and is slightly reduced.

7. Shut off the heat and allow the sauce to set for 1 to 2 minutes.

8. Pour sauce over patties and serve with noodles and a vegetable of your choice.

Serves 4–6

 Trippa di Mamma

When people refer to "Italian soul food," this has to be one of the things they have in mind. Tripe is both a peasant's dish and a delicacy. It is a Saturday afternoon favorite in local Italian neighborhood restaurants. Honeycomb tripe can be purchased at the local butcher and often at the supermarket as well.

This can be prepared a day or two ahead of serving. It refrigerates well and can be frozen.

3 pounds honeycomb tripe
½ cup olive oil
1 garlic clove, chopped
½ large onion, chopped
1 tablespoon dried red pepper flakes
3 bay leaves
a pinch each of dried basil, mint, and oregano
dash Tabasco
3 ounces canned tomato paste
1 28-ounce can peeled and crushed tomatoes
salt and pepper to taste
½ cup freshly grated Parmesan cheese, plus more for serving
freshly chopped parsley

1. Rinse the tripe under cold running water and scrub it with salt until it is white and clean.

2. Place the tripe in a deep pot filled with about 5 quarts of cold water. Cover and let it come to a soft boil. Continue cooking for about 1 hour or until tender. Drain and rinse under cold water until it is cool enough to handle. Cut it into pieces about 3 inches long and 1 inch wide. Reserve.

3. Heat the oil in a large pot. Saute the chopped garlic, onion, red pepper flakes, bay leaves, basil, mint, oregano, and Tabasco. Add the tomato paste and stir briskly. Add the can of tomatoes, salt, and pepper. Stir constantly until all the ingredients are blended and gently boiling.

4. Add the tripe and simmer, covered, for about ½ hour, adding hot water if sauce is too thick. Adjust seasonings.

5. Now add the grated cheese and parsley. Simmer again for about 15 more minutes. Remove the bay leaves. Shut off the heat and wait about ½ hour before serving.

6. Serve with plenty of grated cheese and additional salt and pepper.

Serves 6

 # Soffritto

What wonderful images this recipe brings to mind! Days of peasant cooking that would delight even a hunter's appetite—enough so that I know he would leave his fireside to follow the exciting aromas from my mother's Italian kitchen in the North End! This dish is deliciously nutritious! Serve with crusty, hot bread and a nice salad.

3 beef hearts (approximately 2 pounds total)
olive oil
1 large onion, thinly sliced
2 garlic cloves, chopped
1 small can tomato paste
1 teaspoon each salt and pepper
1 teaspoon red pepper flakes
1 teaspoon dried basil
½ teaspoon oregano
½ cup white wine

You can fry small hot fresh peppers along with the garlic and onion for a pungent flavor, but omit the crushed pepper flakes.

1. Wash beef hearts, place in a stainless steel pot, and cover with water.

2. Simmer until cooked, about 20–30 minutes.

3. Drain, allow to cool, and wipe each heart with a damp cloth.

4. Cut away all the fat and membranes, and dice the meaty part into bite-size pieces. Reserve.

5. In a medium-size heavy skillet, heat enough olive oil to cover bottom of pan.

6. Fry hearts with the onion and garlic until the vegetables are tender but not limp.

7. Using a wooden spoon, gently stir in the tomato paste and salt and pepper until mixture is well blended.

8. Add the red pepper flakes, dry basil, oregano, and additional salt and pepper if needed. Stir until meat is nicely coated.

9. Add wine and simmer uncovered for 30 minutes or until a nice sauce forms, adding more wine if needed.

10. Allow to set at least 30 minutes before serving to better capture the flavors.

Serves 3–4

 # Lamb Stew

SPEZZATINO DI AGNELLO

Nothing can beat a bowl of stew. It is warm and nourishing and full of love.

3 pounds lamb chunks
flour
½ cup oil
2 garlic cloves, crushed
4 carrots, thickly sliced
3 or 4 celery stalks, sliced
3 large onions, thickly sliced
2 large potatoes, thickly sliced
1 heaping tablespoon tomato paste
1 14-ounce can whole tomatoes, or 2 cups Marinara Sauce (see page 46)
salt and pepper to taste
pinch of dried red pepper flakes, mint, oregano, and basil
1 cup dry white wine

Cutting onions with a very sharp knife helps keep your eyes from tearing.

This stew freezes and refrigerates well.

1. Put the meat in a large bowl and sprinkle with flour, turning often until all sides are coated.

2. Put the oil and garlic in a large heavy pot. Saute on low heat for about 20 minutes so that the oil absorbs all the flavor of the garlic without burning.

3. Meanwhile, start cleaning and preparing the vegetables. Reserve.

4. After the garlic has been cooking for 20 minutes, remove it from the oil. Raise the heat to high and fry the lamb and onions until they are well browned, turning often.

5. Lower the heat to medium. Add the tomato paste and stir well. Now add the tomatoes or Marinara Sauce and seasonings. Stir until mixed thoroughly. Saute for about 5 minutes, turning often.

6. Sprinkle the cup of wine all over and simmer, covered, for 20 minutes. Stir several times during cooking.

7. After 20 minutes, add the carrots, celery, potatoes, and more of the seasonings. Stir well and cover. Cook for another ½ hour or until the meat is tender. Turn off the heat and let the mixture rest (covered) for about 20 minutes.

Serves 6–8

 # Lamb with White Wine Sauce

3 pounds leg of lamb, boned and cut in cubes
½ cup flour
1 garlic clove, chopped
1 teaspoon dried rosemary
¼ cup olive oil
salt and pepper to taste
1 cup dry white wine
1 teaspoon tomato paste
¼ cup warm water
1 cup canned peeled plum tomatoes, squeezed to break into small pieces
1 8-ounce can of peas (optional)

1. Put the lamb cubes and flour in a paper bag. Shake the bag to coat the meat evenly with flour.

2. Chop the garlic and rosemary together into tiny bits. Heat the olive oil in a Dutch oven over high heat. Saute the garlic and rosemary until golden.

3. Add the lamb to the Dutch oven. Brown it thoroughly by turning it over and over on all sides. Add salt, a few grinds of pepper, and the wine. Stir gently and cook for about 5 minutes. Reduce the heat to medium.

4. Dilute the tomato paste in the warm water. Add it to the Dutch oven, stir gently, then add the tomatoes. Bring all the ingredients to a soft boil, reduce heat, and simmer 1 hour, stirring occasionally. Remove the lamb from the heat.

5. I like to throw a can of peas in the pot after the lamb has completed cooking. Stir gently, cover the pot, and let the meat rest for about 10 minutes.

6. Serve with buttered noodles or garlic bread.

Serves 6

This dish can be made in advance and refrigerated or frozen.

Rabbit Siciliano

Chicken can be substituted for the rabbit in this recipe, but since we don't often find a good rabbit recipe, why not give it a try in its authentic version?

1 small rabbit (about 3 pounds), cut in small pieces
⅔ cup olive oil
2 celery stalks, sliced
1 6-ounce jar black, dry-cured, Sicilian olives, pitted and halved
2 garlic cloves, chopped
¼ teaspoon dried oregano
pinch of dried red pepper flakes
freshly ground black pepper to taste
1 teaspoon salt
1 teaspoon capers in water, drained
½ cup white vinegar

1. Wash the rabbit well. Soak it in cold salted water for several hours. Dry with paper towels and reserve.

2. Heat the oil in a large heavy skillet and saute the sliced celery for 5 minutes. Remove the celery from the pan and reserve.

3. Raise the heat and fry the rabbit a few pieces at a time until nicely browned.

4. Lower the heat to medium and add the celery, olives, garlic, seasonings, and capers. Stir gently until the rabbit and seasonings are well blended. Sprinkle with the vinegar, and simmer, covered, for about ½ hour or until the rabbit is tender. Add more of the above seasonings if needed.

5. Remove the pan from the heat and let it rest, covered, for about 10 minutes to combine flavors. Serve with noodles and a salad.

This dish can be refrigerated for several days.

Serves 4

138

 # Fresh Baked Rabbit

This is one of my favorite recipes. After months of experimenting and combining different vegetables, I feel it is the best-tasting rabbit dinner ever—a five-star meal. Polenta makes a good accompaniment.

2½ **pounds fresh whole rabbit, cut in serving size pieces**
1 large onion, cut in large chunks
3 carrots, cut in chunks
6–8 stalks young celery, cut in chunks
salt and pepper to taste
turmeric
½ **pound salt pork, diced in small pieces**
1 whole bud garlic (separate cloves and leave skin on)
2 large shallots, coarsely chopped
1 cup chopped fresh fennel or 1 tablespoon fennel seeds
¾ **cup white wine**
½ **cup Marsala wine**

The addition of salt pork distinguishes this recipe from all others. The total cooking time is 1 hour, 15 minutes.

1. Preheat oven to 550 degrees.
2. Wash rabbit with coarse salt and wipe dry with paper towel.
3. Spread onion, carrots, and celery on bottom of large baking pan.
4. Spread rabbit pieces over vegetables.
5. Sprinkle rabbit and vegetables generously with salt and pepper and turmeric.
6. Add diced salt pork evenly on rabbit pieces.
7. Scatter garlic cloves, chopped shallots, and fennel over rabbit.
8. Bake in hot oven for 30 minutes.
9. Turn pieces around, lower heat to 350 degrees, and continue baking 15 minutes more.
10. Raise heat again to 550 degrees, and pour in white wine. Bake 10 minutes longer.
11. Add Marsala and bake 10 more minutes or until golden brown.
12. Place rabbit on large platter and top with vegetables and wine sauce from bottom of pan.

Serves 4–6

 Olga's Rabbit Cacciatore

When I was a child, my grandfather would often come over to our house and request that my mother prepare this recipe. Since he always asked for it in Italian, my brothers, sisters, and I always thought we were eating chicken, and my mother didn't tell us any differently since she thought we might be a little sensitive to eating a rabbit. We used to get a bunny each Easter and raise it as our pet. When it became grown we were told it had to be given away. Little did we know it was to become a Sunday dinner. Only in later years did we find out how lucky we were to have such delicacies as Rabbit Cacciatore as part of our ethnic tradition.

1 small rabbit (about 3 pounds), cut in small pieces
⅔ cup olive oil
2 large green peppers, sliced
3 medium onions, sliced lengthwise
½ pound button mushrooms, cut in chunks
6 garlic cloves, halved
salt and pepper to taste
3 red, ripe tomatoes, peeled and chopped
dried red pepper flakes to taste
1 6-ounce can small peas (reserve juice)

1. Wash the rabbit well and soak it in cold salted water for several hours. Dry with paper towels and reserve.

2. Put the oil in a large heavy skillet and saute the peppers until tender. Remove them from the oil and set aside. Saute the onions until tender and remove them from the oil. Add to the peppers. Saute the mushrooms and 3 garlic cloves until slightly browned. Add to the peppers and onions.

3. Now put the rabbit and the remaining garlic cloves in the skillet and fry until browned. Salt and pepper the meat. Add the tomatoes, stirring gently. Cover.

4. Let the rabbit boil slightly to dry out any remaining water. Add red pepper flakes, more salt and pepper, and other seasonings, if desired. If the mixture becomes too dry, add juice from the can of peas.

5. Remove the cover after 20 minutes and add the pepper and onion mixture. Let simmer 10 minutes, then add the peas. Remove the skillet from the heat and let rest for a few minutes to allow flavors to combine.

This dish may be refrigerated for a couple of days.

Serves 4–6

Italian Sausages, Vinegar Peppers, and Potatoes

My mother made this meal at least once every two weeks, alternating the sausages with pork chops. We would follow the heavenly aroma all the way up three flights of stairs and patiently sit at the kitchen table with fork and crusty bread in hand. Pork chops may be substituted for the sausages in this recipe.

2 pounds sweet, all-pork Italian sausages
¼ cup olive oil
6 large potatoes, peeled, thickly sliced, and wiped dry
6–8 spicy or hot vinegar peppers (purchase at supermarket or make them your-
  self; see page 219)
salt and pepper to taste

1. In a large heavy skillet, over medium heat, fry the sausages in hot oil until well browned. Pierce them gently with a fork as they cook. Using a slotted spoon, transfer the sausages to a large platter.

2. In the same skillet, on high heat, add the clean, dried potatoes. (To prevent the potatoes from sticking, add a little salt to hot oil.) Cook until crispy, turning them often with a spatula.

3. Keep the heat on high and add the cooked sausages, stirring gently.

4. When all the ingredients are well heated, add the vinegar peppers, one at a time. Tear them into bite-size pieces over the skillet, allowing the juices to fall over the sausages and potatoes. Toss gently. The pepper juices will cause the mixture to steam, so be careful. Saute for about 3 minutes and add more salt if needed.

5. Remove the skillet from the heat and let rest for 5 minutes. Serve with Italian bread and a salad.

Serves 4–6

If you are on a busy schedule, fry the sausages and prepare all of the ingredients early in the day. Keep the sliced, uncooked potatoes in water, however, or they will brown. Then assemble and cook the dish just prior to serving. It is best eaten the same day it is prepared because the potatoes, in particular, will not taste the same after refrigeration.

 # Pork Rind Braciole

Pork rind is the skin of the pig. It is considered a treat in an Italian home, but a lot of people don't know how to prepare it. This recipe was made mainly by the Sicilian people and, unfortunately, was never written down. It will be lost forever if it is not recorded. I have tried to recreate the traditional recipe to the best of my knowledge. Like other braciole meats, this is added to tomato sauce.

> **2 pounds pork rind, thinly sliced**
> **¼ cup fresh parsley, chopped**
> **¼ cup grated Romano cheese**
> **2 small garlic cloves, chopped**
> **salt and pepper to taste**
> **2-ounce chunk of Romano cheese, cut in pieces**
> **¼ cup Sicilian dry-cured olives, pitted and halved**

1. Boil some hot water, shut off the heat, and wash rind by dipping it in the boiled water for a minute. Remove to cool.
2. Spread rind on table and cover with parsley, grated cheese, garlic, salt and pepper, and small pieces of Romano cheese.
3. Roll pork rind and tie with a string or toothpicks.
4. Fry in large, heavy skillet, over low heat, until browned on all sides.
5. Pour tomato sauce into the skillet and cook until rind is tender.
6. Place on a serving platter, remove string or toothpicks, and carve into thin slices.
7. Serve with more sauce and pitted dry-cured olives on top.

Serves 4

 # Polla alla Cacciatore con Pomodoro

CHICKEN PEASANT STYLE WITH TOMATOES

1 2½-pound whole chicken
¾ cup olive oil
3 cloves garlic, crushed
salt and pepper to taste
2 green peppers, cut into strips
2 red peppers, cut into strips
4 medium onions, sliced thick
¼ cup tomato paste
1 28-ounce can plum tomatoes
½ teaspoon red pepper flakes (optional)
1 cup whole button mushrooms or sliced larger mushrooms
chopped fresh parsley

This may be eaten as a main course or alongside spaghetti with crusty Italian bread.

1. Wash and pat dry chicken. Cut into bite-size pieces.

2. Using a large, heavy skillet with cover, add the olive oil and crushed garlic and saute until garlic is golden brown. Remove the garlic.

3. When the oil is fairly hot, add the chicken pieces and saute until the chicken is nice browned, turning as needed, adding salt and pepper to taste. Cover the chicken and let it simmer over a low flame until it is tender, about 5 minutes.

4. Add the sliced peppers and onions; cook until they are tender—crisp, not limp.

5. Using a medium-high heat, add the tomato paste and blend in well. Then add the tomatoes with their juices. Season to taste, adding red pepper flakes if desired.

6. When the tomatoes have cooked to a sauce consistency, add the mushrooms and sprinkle with fresh parsley. Toss the mixture in the pan to allow the flavors to blend. Cover and let rest ½ hour before serving. Serve at room temperature, or reheat if preferred.

Serves 4–6

 # Chicken Cacciatore en Bianco

CHICKEN WITH WHITE WINE SAUCE

I often make this recipe when I have guests over for dinner. Needless to say, it is a hit. Let the mixture rest for about five minutes before serving it and you will have a luscious sauce with the chicken. Any cacciatore recipe is tastier after it has set for a while. Try serving some buttered noodles topped with the chicken and vegetables.

> olive oil
> 3 green or red bell peppers, sliced
> 1 onion, sliced
> ¼ pound unsalted butter
> 6 boneless, skinless chicken breasts, cut in bite-size pieces
> salt and pepper to taste
> 1 shallot, chopped
> pinch tarragon
> ½ pound mushrooms, sliced
> 2 tomatoes, blanched, skin removed
> ½ cup dry white wine
> fresh chopped parsley

1. In a large heavy skillet heat enough oil to cover bottom of pan.
2. Add peppers and saute a few minutes; then add onions and cook until slightly transparent. Cook quickly but carefully so that the vegetables retain their color and crispness. Remove from skillet and reserve.
3. Remove oil from skillet; heat 1 stick unsalted butter.
4. Add boneless chicken chunks, and saute until lightly browned. While chicken is cooking, add salt and pepper, chopped shallot, tarragon, and mushrooms.
5. When meat is cooked, add drained vegetables, tomatoes, and white wine.
6. Boil briefly to evaporate alcohol. Garnish with fresh parsley.

Serves 6

Chicken Limone

This dish is best made right before serving. Be sure to have all your ingredients prepared and on hand. As with most breast of chicken dishes, veal may be substituted for the chicken.

6 boneless chicken breasts
2 eggs
¼ cup milk
1 cup flour
¼ cup butter
¼ cup olive oil
4 tablespoons unsalted butter
2 lemons
salt and pepper to taste
1 tablespoon chopped fresh parsley

1. Slice the chicken breasts into very thin medallions (or buy small chicken cutlets).

2. In a large bowl, beat the eggs with the milk. Put the flour on a shallow plate.

3. Heat the ¼ cup of butter and oil in a heavy skillet on medium temperature. At the same time, dredge the chicken in the flour, then dip it quickly in the egg wash.

4. Saute the chicken for a few minutes on each side until golden brown.

5. Transfer the chicken to a serving platter and keep warm. Pour off any oils that remain in the skillet.

6. Add the 4 tablespoons of unsalted butter to the skillet. With a wooden spoon, loosen all the particles on the bottom of the pan.

7. Raise the heat under the skillet. Squeeze the juice of one lemon into the skillet. Add salt, pepper, and chopped parsley.

8. Slice the second lemon. Overlap the chicken and the lemon slices on the serving platter. Pour the sauce on top and serve immediately with hot buttered linguine or noodles.

Serves 6

Chicken Braciolettini with Mushroom and Wine Sauce

6 large boneless chicken breasts
1 large garlic clove
freshly ground black pepper
¼ cup freshly grated Parmesan or Romano cheese
¼ pound shredded mozzarella or fontina cheese
¼ bunch fresh parsley, chopped (reserve 1 tablespoon for garnish)
6 thin slices prosciutto or ham
1 stick unsalted butter
¼ cup olive oil
1 cup Madeira or Marsala wine
½ pound whole button mushrooms or thinly sliced mushrooms

1. Have butcher pound the meat slightly to break the tendons, or use the flat side of a heavy meat cleaver to do so yourself.

2. Lay the flat pieces of chicken on a smooth clean surface. Using a garlic press, squeeze the garlic clove. With your fingertips, transfer these particles to the cutlet pieces. Sprinkle black pepper, grated cheese, shredded cheese, and parsley all over the chicken. Cover each breast with a slice of prosciutto or ham. Roll each breast jellyroll style, carefully tucking in all loose ends. Secure with toothpicks (the same number for each breast).

3. Heat the oil and butter in a large skillet over medium heat. Add the chicken breasts and brown well all over. With a slotted spoon, transfer the chicken to a baking pan. Bake for 20 minutes in a preheated 350-degree oven or until the chicken is cooked moist-tender.

4. To make sauce, drain the fat from the skillet and return unwashed pan to stove on medium heat, scraping all browned bits from bottom of pan with a wooden spoon.

5. Raise the heat to high and pour in the wine, stirring well. Add the mushrooms and cook 1 more minute, shaking skillet. If the sauce appears too thin, sprinkle with some flour and cook, stirring well, until it reaches your desired thickness. If more sauce is desired, add some chicken broth and more wine.

6. Remove the chicken from the oven, carefully remove all toothpicks, and transfer to a warm serving platter. Pour the hot sauce on top. Sprinkle with the reserved tablespoon of chopped parsley. To serve cut meat in thick slices and coat with sauce and mushrooms.

Note: If using small pieces of chicken breasts, it will not be necessary to bake the chicken. Simply cook in skillet as directed, transfer to a warm platter, and prepare sauce.

Serves 6

It's a goood idea to put the same number of toothpicks in each breast. This way, when it's time to remove them, you'll be sure not to miss any.

 # Chicken Angelo

During a fund-raising luncheon at the North End Union (a settlement house), I salvaged all the leftovers, added chicken and sausages with the correct seasonings, and produced this unusual and hearty meal. I still get raves from friends who make it at home. Add your own leftovers and enjoy!

> **2 chickens**
> **1 pound sweet Italian sausages**
> **½ cup olive or vegetable oil**
> **salt and pepper to taste**
> **1 cup butter or margarine**
> **4 garlic cloves, chopped**
> **2 large onions, sliced**
> **2 shallots, crushed**
> **12 medium-size ripe tomatoes (6 cut in chunks, 6 cut in large slices)**
> **pinch of dried oregano**
> **½ cup plus 2 tablespoons of chopped fresh parsley, and more for garnish**
> **2 cups homemade or canned chicken stock**
> **flour**
> **2 cups dry white wine**
> **1 pound whole button mushrooms**
> **1 8-ounce can artichoke hearts in water (reserve water and cut hearts in fours)**
> **1 pound large shells or ziti**
> **1 bunch broccoli, cut into flowerets (save the stems for another use)**

1. Cut the chickens into small pieces. Cut the sausages into bite-size pieces.

2. Heat the oil in a large skillet. Fry the chicken and sausages until nicely browned. Sprinkle generously with salt and pepper. Place all the fried pieces in a large baking pan.

3. In the same skillet, melt half of the butter or margarine. Add 2 garlic cloves, the sliced onions, and the crushed shallots. Saute gently. Add the 6 chopped tomatoes, salt, pepper, oregano, and ½ cup of chopped fresh parsley. Toss lightly a few times, then pour over the meat in the baking pan.

4. In a large jar, shake the chicken stock with enough flour to make a thin paste. Pour into a small saucepan and cook over medium heat until slightly thickened. Add salt and pepper to taste.

5. Reserve ½ cup of the thickened stock. Pour the remainder over the chicken and sausages, tossing lightly to coat all the pieces. Bake in a preheated 350-degree oven for about 25 minutes. Sprinkle with 1 cup of white wine and continue baking for another 15 minutes.

6. In a large skillet, melt the remaining butter. Add the mushrooms, the 6 sliced tomatoes, the quartered and drained artichoke hearts, 2 tablespoons of fresh parsley, salt, and pepper. Saute for 3 minutes and add the reserved ½ cup of thickened stock. When heated through, add more wine as needed to keep the sauce from thickening too much. Simmer gently for about 10 minutes.

7. Meanwhile, boil the pasta according to package directions. Drain, then toss in a little butter so that it will not stick.

8. At the same time, saute the broccoli with 2 garlic cloves in enough oil to cover the bottom of the pan, mixed with the juice from the artichokes. Combine the broccoli and the cooked pasta. Sprinkle with salt and pepper.

9. Put the broccoli and pasta on a large platter. Spoon the baked chicken and sausages on top. Cover with the sauce. Sprinkle chopped parsley over all and serve.

Serves 12

You can make this recipe through step 6 early in the day. Cook the pasta and saute the broccoli immediately before serving

Chicken with Broccoli and Ziti

A really quick, easy, and delicious meal. The combination of milk and grated Parmesan renders a light, creamy sauce. The broccoli should remain crisp and green during cooking.

2 large boneless chicken breasts, cut into strips
2 cups broccoli flowerets
¼ cup olive oil
1-2 garlic cloves, slivered
salt and pepper to taste
¼ cup milk
2 tablespoons unsalted butter
½ cup freshly grated Parmesan cheese
½ pound ziti
red pepper flakes (optional)

1. Heat ¼ cup oil in a large skillet over medium heat. Saute the chicken with the garlic, salt, and pepper until lightly browned.

2. Add the broccoli flowerets. Toss with the chicken and adjust seasonings. Cook and stir for 1 minute.

3. Add ¼ cup milk and ¼ cup grated Parmesan cheese. Using high heat, quickly toss all ingredients until a nice milky sauce has formed (1 or 2 minutes).

4. Cook the ziti according to package directions. Drain, but do not rinse.

5. Toss the ziti with the butter. Add to the chicken and broccoli and toss gently. Sprinkle with the grated Parmesan cheese, red pepper flakes, and more salt and pepper to taste. Serve.

Serves 4

If you wish, this dish can be refrigerated for 1 or 2 days and then reheated gently before serving.

Fish and Shellfish

 # Shrimp Scampi Aglio e Olio

SHRIMP WITH OIL AND GARLIC SAUCE

Whenever I see shrimp on sale, I know immediately how I will cook them. I buy a nice, crusty loaf of Italian bread, get out my cast-iron skillet, and fire away. Of course I will use plenty of garlic and never remove the shells from the shrimp. Leave them on to keep the shrimp from shrinking when cooking and to preserve those wonderful juices. Great served over thin spaghetti or linguine fini.

> **1 pound large shrimp, shell on**
> **½ cup olive oil**
> **¼ cup butter or margarine**
> **3 garlic cloves, chopped**
> **pinch of red pepper flakes**
> **salt and freshly grated pepper to taste**
> **3 tablespoons fresh lemon juice**
> **1 tablespoon grated lemon zest**
> **¼ cup fresh parsley, chopped**

1. Rinse shrimp and set aside.

2. Melt olive oil and butter in a heavy skillet.

3. Add garlic and red pepper flakes and saute on low heat, about 5 minutes.

4. Raise heat to high, and when oil is hot, immediately add shrimp in shell. Toss the shrimp around constantly, until they turn pink.

5. Remove pan from heat. Add salt and pepper to taste, lemon juice, lemon zest, and fresh chopped parsley.

6. Return pan to high heat and saute for a minute or two until butter sauce has slightly thickened.

7. Serve immediately in bowls with the juices poured over the shrimp.

Serves 4

 # Quick Scampi with Cream Sauce

We use a lot of shrimp during the holidays and this is one recipe we all enjoy. It may be served over fresh, thin noodles (about ½ pound) and accompanied by garlic bread.

8 large red scampi, peeled
flour
olive oil
1 garlic clove, crushed
1 shallot clove, chopped
salt and freshly ground black pepper to taste
1 heaping tablespoon lemon juice
dash of Tabasco
dash of white wine
½ cup heavy cream

1. Dust the scampi with flour. Shake off the excess.
2. Pour the oil into a heavy skillet, just enough to cover the bottom of the pan. Add the crushed garlic and shallot and cook until tender.
3. Over medium heat, cook the scampi with salt, pepper, lemon juice, and Tabasco for 5 minutes.
4. Add wine. Bring the mixture to a boil and remove from heat. Slowly add the cream. Return the skillet to the burner and let the mixture boil for a minute or two. Serve bubbling hot.

Serves 2

Baked Stuffed Shrimp Italian Style

I have been making this recipe for years, and I think it is one of the best ever. Try this stuffing also with lobsters or clams. It is excellent!

> 1½ *pounds large shrimp, unpeeled*
> 2½ *cups coarse bread crumbs*
> 12 *salted crackers, crumbled*
> 3 *ounces canned crabmeat (optional)*
> ½ *cup freshly grated Parmesan cheese*
> ½ *cup chopped fresh parsley*
> 4 *tablespoons butter, melted*
> ¼ *cup lemon juice*
> *few drops of Tabasco*
> 1 *garlic clove, chopped*
> *pinch of dried tarragon*
> *salt and freshly ground black pepper to taste*
> 1 *tablespoon olive oil*
> *lemon slices for garnish*

1. Leave the shell on the shrimp. Remove all tentacles. Lay each shrimp flat on the counter. Slice open, devein, and spread open butterfly style.

2. In a large bowl, mix the bread crumbs, crackers, crabmeat (optional), grated cheese, parsley, melted butter, lemon juice, Tabasco, garlic, and tarragon. Add salt and pepper to taste. At this point, stuffing should be moist. Add extra melted butter and lemon juice if needed.

3. Stuff each shrimp until it is well packed. Place the stuffed shrimp on a cookie sheet, each one nestled into another, in a half-moon curve, so the stuffing will stay secure.

4. Drizzle olive oil lightly over the shrimp. Bake the shrimp in a preheated 400-degree oven on the middle rack for about 20 minutes, or until golden brown. Serve with plenty of lemon slices.

Serves 4–6

 # Quick Seafood Diavolo

This fish medley is a feast in itself. You need only some hot garlic bread and maybe a salad. Use any or all the shellfish listed in this recipe, and the results will still be pleasing.

> ½ cup olive oil
> 1 garlic clove, chopped
> 1 bunch scallions, chopped
> pinch of dried red pepper flakes and oregano
> a few drops of Tabasco
> ¼ pound mushrooms, chopped
> 2 cups canned tomatoes, or 3 peeled tomatoes, chopped, with juices
> ¼ cup dry white wine
> 12 littleneck clams, scrubbed clean
> 12 mussels, scrubbed clean and debearded
> 6 fresh shrimp, or 1 can any size shrimp
> ½ pound baby scallops, or large scallops, quartered
> ½ cup bottled clam juice
> salt and pepper to taste
> ½ pound of any firm white fish (sole, haddock, etc.)
> 1 pound linguine or thin spaghetti
> 2 tablespoons butter or margarine
> chopped fresh parsley

1. Heat the oil in a large kettle over medium heat. Add the garlic, scallions, red pepper flakes, oregano, Tabasco, and mushrooms.

2. When the mixture starts to brown, add the tomatoes and their juices. Simmer for 2 minutes. Raise the heat to high. Add the white wine and let the sauce come to a boil. Add the clams, mussels, shrimp, scallops, and clam juice. Sprinkle with salt and pepper to taste.

3. Cook, covered, on medium-low heat until the clams start to open. At this point, add the white fish. Salt and pepper again to taste, if desired. Cover again and cook for 3 minutes.

4. Meanwhile, cook linguine or thin spaghetti according to package directions. Drain well and toss

with the butter. Put onto a large serving platter.

5. Cover the pasta with half of the sauce. Sprinkle with parsley. Place the shellfish around the outside of the platter. Pour the remaining sauce into a serving bowl for use by the family as desired.

Serves 4–6

 # Cioppino

This is not exactly a soup, and not exactly a stew. It is a combination of flavors that are light and nutritious.

⅓ cup olive or vegetable oil
3 garlic cloves, chopped
1¼ cups chopped onion
¾ cup sliced scallions
½ cup chopped green pepper
1 6-ounce can tomato paste
1 28-ounce can plum tomatoes
½ bunch parsley, chopped
1 teaspoon dried oregano
1 teaspoon dried basil
1 teaspoon dried red pepper flakes
1 teaspoon dried tarragon
salt and pepper to taste
1¼ cups Burgundy wine
1 11½-ounce jar whole clams, undrained
1½ pounds haddock, sole, or halibut (no bones)
1½ pounds medium-size shrimp, unpeeled
3 6½-ounce cans crabmeat, drained

1. Heat the oil in a 6-quart kettle. Saute the garlic, onions, scallions, and green peppers until tender (about 10 minutes), stirring often.

2. Add the tomato paste and stir until well blended. Add the can of tomatoes, including the juice.

Stir gently until the mixture comes to a boil. Add parsley, oregano, basil, pepper flakes, tarragon, salt, and pepper to taste.

3. Simmer for about 5 minutes, then add the wine. Simmer for 10 minutes, and then add the clams, fish of your choice, shrimp, and crabmeat. (You may cut the fish into chunks if the pieces are too large but they are likely to break apart in the cooking process.) At this point you may need more salt and pepper.

4. Simmer, covered, for about 15 minutes, then uncovered for 15 minutes more.

5. Remove the kettle from the heat and let it rest for about 10 minutes.

6. Serve in large bowls, accompanied by garlic bread and salad. Put a large empty bowl in the middle of the table to receive the shells. Have plenty of napkins available.

Cioppino can be refrigerated, but it is best served the same day that it is made.

Serves 6

 # Scallops Marinara

½ cup butter or margarine
1 pound fresh sea scallops
2 cloves garlic, chopped
3 scallions, chopped
1 small onion, chopped
1 16-ounce can whole tomatoes, chopped (reserve juice)
¼ pound fresh button mushrooms, quartered
¼ cup dry white wine
1 tablespoon lemon juice
salt and freshly ground pepper to taste
pinch tarragon
¼ cup chopped fresh parsley

1. In a large heavy skillet, melt the butter or margarine. Add the scallops, garlic, scallions, and onion. Saute for about 3 minutes, stirring gently.

2. Add the tomatoes and mushrooms and saute about 2 minutes.

3. Add the wine and lemon juice, salt, pepper, and tarragon. Cook briskly on medium-high heat for about 2 to 3 minutes.

4. Add the reserved tomato juice and cook on high heat for about 5 minutes. Add the parsley and serve immediately. You may wish to serve spaghetti or linguine on the side.

Serves 2–3

Italian-Style Steamed Mussels

Once you prepare this tried-and true recipe, you will find it hard to cook mussels differently ever again.

3 quarts mussels
12 shallots, thinly sliced
1 onion, thinly sliced
2 tablespoons olive oil
2 tablespoons unsalted butter
4 garlic cloves, chopped
½ cup bottled clam juice
½ cup dry white wine
1 bay leaf
3 heaping tablespoons chopped Italian parsley
1 teaspoon dried thyme
1 teaspoon freshly ground black pepper

These mussels are great served as an appetizer

1. Clean the mussels carefully and pull off the beards. Discard any mussels with open shells. Keep refrigerated until ready to use.

2. In a large heavy pot, saute the shallots and onions in the oil and butter over low heat until translucent, not brown. Add the garlic during the last 2 minutes of sauteing.

3. Add the clam juice, white wine, bay leaf, parsley, thyme, and pepper. Cook, covered, over low heat, 10 to 15 minutes.

4. Raise the heat and add the mussels. Cook, covered, just until all the shells are opened. Discard any unopened mussels. Remove the bay leaf.

5. Serve hot in soup bowls, accompanied by crusty Italian bread. Provide extra plates for the empty shells.

Serves 6–8

 # Baked Stuffed Clams

This is our basic style of baking clams —simple but so tasty that I know you will enjoy them.

12 large clams
1 cup Italian-style dry bread crumbs
2 garlic cloves, chopped
1 tablespoon finely chopped fresh parsley
salt and pepper to taste
olive oil (just enough to cover the bottom of the pan)
1 whole lemon plus lemon wedges for garnish
paprika

I like to add a dash or two of Tabasco sauce to the stuffing mixture. As another option, I pour enough water or wine in the bottom of the pan before baking to keep clams on the moist side.

1. Scrub the clams thoroughly. Open them carefully and pour the juices into a bowl. Chop the clams into small pieces and add to the juices. Reserve 12 shells on a baking sheet.

2. Saute the garlic, parsley, salt, and pepper in the olive oil for about 2 minutes, stirring constantly. Put bread crumbs in a medium-sized bowl. Add garlic mixture and the clams and their juices. Toss lightly until mixture becomes soft and moist but not soaked with juices.

3. Spoon the mixture into the clam shells until they are filled. Sprinkle lightly with the juice of the lemon and top with a light dusting of paprika.

4. Bake the clams in a preheated 375-degree oven for 20–25 minutes or until a crust forms on the stuffing. Serve with lemon wedges.

Serves 6

 Steamed Clams in  Garlic Sauce

This is the only way to make perfect and delicious steamed clams. Instead of using plain water, I make a savory sauce that can be poured over linguine or spaghetti, making it a double treat. You can also put the clams in a bowl and serve them with the flavorful sauce. Either way, you will be pleased with the results.

> **5 pounds clams (littlenecks or steamers)**
> **1 stick butter**
> **½ cup olive oil**
> **3 cloves garlic, chopped**
> **½ bunch fresh parsley, chopped**
> **1–2 bunches scallions, chopped**
> **3 shots Tabasco (optional)**
> **pinch of tarragon**
> **1 lemon, halved**
> **1–2 cups white wine**

1. To remove any sand, soak clams in cold, salted water.

2. Using a medium-size pot with cover, heat butter and olive oil together.

3. Add garlic, parsley, scallions, Tabasco, and tarragon.

4. Squeeze lemon halves into butter mixture, then toss the halves into the pot.

5. Saute sauce on medium heat for 5 minutes.

6. Add whole clams (in shell) and toss gently until clams are covered with spices.

7. Put heat on high, cover the pot, and add wine when mixture starts to boil.

8. Lower heat to medium-high and let clams cook, covered, until all clams have opened, about 10 minutes. Discard any unopened clams after cooking time is over.

9. Serve immediately in individual bowls or pour garlic sauce and opened clams over pasta.

Serves 4–6

 Quick Mussels  Marinara

This is an appealing appetizer in which the fish and tomatoes combine to produce a light, traditional flavor.

> **4 quarts mussels**
> **olive oil (enough to cover the bottom of the pan)**
> **2 garlic cloves, finely chopped**
> **¼ teaspoon dried oregano**
> **1 tablespoon dried basil (use fresh if available)**
> **¼ teaspoon dried tarragon**
> **¼ teaspoon dried red pepper flakes**
> **2 teaspoons chopped fresh parsley**
> **1 14-ounce can peeled and crushed tomatoes**
> **salt and pepper to taste**
> **1 cup dry white wine**

1. Scrub the mussels well. Scrape off the beards, using your fingers or a rough brush. Rinse under cold running water and drain. Discard any mussels with shells that remain open when tapped. Keep the mussels refrigerated until ready to use.

2. In a pot large enough to hold the mussels, combine the olive oil, garlic, oregano, basil, tarragon, red pepper, and parsley. Saute on low heat for about 5 minutes.

3. Add the tomatoes, salt, and pepper. Let the mixture come to a gentle boil, and cook on low heat for about 15 minutes to blend the flavors. Add the wine and mussels. Cover and cook 5 to 8 minutes, shaking the pan so the mussels cook evenly. Discard any unopened mussels.

4. Serve in heated soup bowls with crusty Italian bread or pour over linguine.

Serves 4–6

 # Stuffed Calamari in Tomato Sauce

In classical times, inkfish were thought to be the finest "fish" of the sea. Today, Italians still feel that way. We prepare squid (calamari) in a great many ways, as appetizers, with pasta, as meatballs, marinated, fried in olive oil, and more. It is a "must" for us to have some in our freezers at all times. Squid freezes well, uncooked or cooked, so they are always available when we want a quick, exciting meal. Stuffed Calamari, made with one of two stuffings, is a favorite.

Calamari Sauce

> *½ cup olive oil*
> *2 medium onions, chopped*
> *2 large garlic cloves, chopped*
> *pinch of dried basil, oregano, and red pepper flakes*
> *3 ounces tomato paste*
> *1 28-ounce can crushed and peeled tomatoes*
> *salt and pepper to taste*

1. In a large heavy saucepan, combine the oil, chopped onions, garlic, basil, oregano, and red pepper flakes. Saute until the onions are golden brown (do not burn).

2. Add the tomato paste and stir gently until the mixture is well blended. Add the can of tomatoes and stir until the sauce comes to a light boil. Add salt and pepper to taste and a pinch more of red pepper, basil, and oregano. Let the sauce simmer on lowest heat while you prepare the squid. Stir the sauce often as it cooks.

To Clean Squid

To clean the squid, separate the head and tentacles from the body. Cut the tentacles apart from the body at the eyes. Discard the head and eyes. Remove the quill and ink sac from the body. Wash out the body; it should be completely empty. Peel off the skin as you wash the body and tentacles under running water. Reserve the tentacles (they may be chopped and added to the stuffing mixture). Drain well and pat dry with paper towels.

 # Bread Stuffing for Calamari

3 pounds medium-sized whole squid, cleaned (see page 162)
3 cups soft fresh bread crumbs (use day-old Italian bread)
½ cup freshly grated Parmesan cheese
½ cup chopped fresh parsley
1 teaspoon salt
1 teaspoon pepper
2 small garlic cloves, pressed
½ cup olive oil, or enough to coat bread crumbs evenly without soaking them
1 pound thin spaghetti or linguine
freshly grated Parmesan cheese for garnish (optional)

1. Toss the first seven ingredients to mix well.

2. Stuff the squid bodies very loosely with the stuffing, about ⅔ full or less, as the squid will shrink when cooked. Secure the top of each squid with a toothpick. Gently drop the stuffed squid into the sauce, which is at a soft boiling stage. They will take about 20 minutes to cook.

3. Bring 6 quarts of salted water to a boil to cook the pasta. When the water is rapidly boiling, add the pasta and cook according to package directions. Drain and place on a large serving platter. Cover with some sauce. Place the stuffed calamari around the pasta (be sure to remove the toothpicks). Put extra sauce and grated cheese on the table and serve.

Serves 6–8

Ricotta-Stuffed Calamari

We have a famous restaurant in Boston's North End, Trattoria Il Panino, that is noted especially for this style of cooking calamari. They can be baked as directed or dropped in a meatless tomato sauce. Either way, they are just as delicious. Choose only fresh, young calamari for better flavor. You will need my fresh marinara sauce (page 46) for this recipe. You can serve this alone or as a sauce for linguine.

2 pounds medium-size whole calamari, cleaned (see page 162)
1 pound ricotta cream cheese, firm
2 eggs (yolks only), slightly beaten
1 garlic clove, chopped
½ cup grated mozzarella cheese
¼ cup grated Parmesan cheese
1 tablespoon chopped parsley
salt and pepper to taste
½ cup freshly ground bread crumbs
½ cup olive oil
2 cups marinara sauce
1 cup white wine

1. In a wide, medium bowl, mix ricotta with egg yolks, garlic, mozzarella, grated cheese, parsley, salt and pepper to taste, and bread crumbs.

2. Using a teaspoon, loosely stuff bodies of calamari until ½ full. Secure edges with toothpicks.

3. Brown quickly, uncrowded, in hot olive oil, until the calamari start to turn pink. Some stuffing may ooze out, but that's normal.

4. Using a slotted spoon, carefully lift calamari from pan. Drop them into the prepared tomato sauce and cook slowly over medium-low heat until cooked, about 20 to 30 minutes. Calamari can also be cooked by placing them in a deep baking dish or pan in one layer. Cover with marinara sauce and white wine. Season with salt and pepper to taste and fresh parsley.

5. Cover with foil and bake in a preheated 350-degree oven until tender, about 20 minutes.

6. Remove from oven and allow to rest at least 15 minutes for better flavor.

Serves 6

Risotto e Calamari

RICE WITH SQUID

Squid is one of the tastiest species to be found in our seas and can be used in a variety of preparations. For this recipe, I have combined squid with rice, but you can feel free to add any other shellfish without altering the delicious flavor. Of course, you will need to adjust the amount of liquid and seasonings accordingly.

1 pound long-grain rice
1¼ pounds of whole, cleaned baby squid
½ tablespoon olive oil
1 tablespoon fresh parsley, chopped
2 garlic cloves, chopped
¼ cup sweet white wine
½ teaspoon turmeric
2 cups (or more if needed) chicken broth, heated
1 tablespoon butter

1. Wash rice, carefully removing any stones. Reserve.

2. Wash and drain squid.

3. In a heavy skillet, saute parsley, tossing gently, and garlic in olive oil until garlic is golden brown.

4. Add squid and, tossing gently, cook over a low flame for about 5 minutes.

5. Add wine and slowly simmer, allowing liquid to be slightly absorbed.

6. Add rice to the squid mixture and sprinkle with turmeric. Toss mixture gently.

7. Add boiling chicken broth one ladle at a time, stirring constantly so that the rice absorbs the broth gradually. Broth should cover risotto no more than ½ inch over the surface.

8. Cook approximately 25 minutes, using a low heat. Add more boiling broth if mixture appears too dry.

9. Sample the risotto for doneness, then add butter to risotto 1 minute before it is ready and mix well.

10. Remove from heat and allow to rest at least 20 minutes before serving.

Serves 4

 # Calamari Freddo

COLD STUFFED SQUID

In my childhood we always ate calamari, so it was necessary to design different ways of preparing it to keep everyone interested. This is an exciting favorite. My brother Dom Capossela successfully serves it in his restaurant. The requests for this recipe have been so overwhelming that we are happy to release our family secret.

> **3 pounds baby squid, cleaned (see page 162)**
> **1 pound tentacles**
> **¾ cup olive oil**
> **2 garlic cloves, chopped**
> **salt and pepper to taste**
> **3 tablespoons fresh parsley, chopped**
> **2 cups soft bread crumbs**
> **⅓ cup fresh grated Romano cheese**
> **toothpicks**
> **2 lemons**

1. Rinse squid and tentacles; pat dry with paper towels.

2. Using a heavy skillet, saute tentacles in ¼ cup warm olive oil until tentacles are slightly pink.

3. Add chopped garlic, a pinch of salt and pepper, and 2 tablespoons fresh chopped parsley. Saute until garlic is translucent.

4. In a medium bowl, add bread crumbs, Romano cheese, and tentacle mixture. Toss well.

5. Lightly stuff baby squid with this mixture, securing edges with toothpicks.

6. Poach in soft boiling water about 3–5 minutes until tender.

7. Using a slotted spoon, remove squid from water and place in a decorative bowl.

8. Drizzle with ½ cup olive oil and ¼ cup freshly squeezed lemon juice. Sprinkle with 1 tablespoon fresh chopped parsley. Refrigerate overnight.

9. Serve on a small plate with half of a fresh lemon and sprig of parsley.

Serves 4–6

 # Calamari Fritti

FRIED CALAMARI

During our festivals, fried calamari are sold off pushcarts. The lines of people waiting to buy these calamari are usually longer than those at other stands. There are many styles in which to prepare fried calamari, but I think you will like my way just fine.

1 pound calamari, cleaned (see page 162), with tentacles
½ cup milk
½ cup King Arthur unbleached flour
½ cup fine cornmeal
pinch of paprika
sprinkle of garlic powder
salt and pepper to taste
3 cups vegetable oil
1 teaspoon freshly squeezed lemon juice
lemon wedges

This calamari also tastes great with a few drops of Tobasco sprinkled on it.

1. Score diagonal slashes in a diamond pattern on squid bodies, do not cut through. Cut calamari into 1-inch rings; leave tentacles whole.

2. Using a wide, deep bowl, mix the flour and cornmeal together. Add paprika, garlic powder, and salt and pepper to taste.

3. Put milk in a deep, small bowl and add lemon juice.

4. Dip the rings and tentacles in the milk a few pieces at a time. Toss pieces around in the flour thoroughly until all moisture is absorbed.

5. Put floured pieces in a sieve and shake them well over the flour bowl until all excess flour is removed.

6. Place on wax paper and continue the process until all the rings and tentacles are used up.

7. Put oil in a pot and bring it to a boil. Fry the calamari in batches, without crowding, until golden brown and crisp.

8. Drain on paper towels, salt to taste, and serve immediately with lemon wedges.

Serves 4

167

 Calamari con Vino

SQUID WITH WINE

1 pound cleaned squid (see page 162), cut into 2-inch rings
2 tablespoons olive oil
2 cloves garlic, chopped
¼ cup dry white wine
salt and pepper to taste
1 tablespoon chopped fresh parsley
pinch of dried tarragon
pinch of red pepper flakes (optional)

1. Using a heavy skillet, heat the olive oil and lightly brown the garlic.

2. Add the squid and saute 3 minutes, tossing frequently.

3. Add the wine, salt, pepper, parsley, and tarragon. Cook over a high flame until the wine has slightly evaporated.

4. Turn off the heat and let the mixture rest 5 minutes. Serve as an appetizer or over cooked thin spaghetti.

Serves 3–4

 Calamari with Fresh
Tomatoes Saute

This recipe will give you a light, delicate meal. It is a spicier, short-cut version of stuffed calamari. As with all calamari dishes, this recipe may be made in advance and refrigerated or frozen.

1½ pounds squid, cleaned (see page 162)
¼ cup plus 1 tablespoon olive oil
1 bunch scallions, chopped
1 shallot, chopped
2 garlic cloves, chopped
¼ teaspoon dried red pepper flakes
Tabasco
3½ cups peeled and diced fresh tomatoes (seeds discarded)
fresh or dried basil, tarragon, mint, and oregano to taste
salt and freshly ground black pepper to taste
½ cup finely chopped fresh parsley
6 black olives, pitted and sliced
lemon wedges for garnish

1. Wash squid and pat dry with paper towels. Cut the bodies into rings about ½ inch wide. Cut the tentacles into bite-size pieces. There should be about 2½ cups. Set aside.

2. Heat the ¼ cup of oil in a heavy skillet and saute the scallions, shallot, garlic, and red pepper flakes for about 5 minutes on low heat. When the scallions are cooked, raise the heat to high and add the cut squid. Toss lightly and quickly, sprinkling with a dash or two of Tabasco. Cook 2 minutes. With a slotted spoon, take the squid out of the pan and set aside.

3. Dry out all the water from the skillet by boiling rapidly for a few minutes. Then add the tablespoon of olive oil and the fresh tomatoes. Saute the tomatoes, adding basil, more red pepper flakes, tarragon, mint, oregano, salt, and pepper to taste. Cook 5 minutes.

4. Add the cooked calamari, chopped parsley, and sliced olives. Simmer for 5 minutes, adding more seasonings if needed. Let the mixture rest for 10 minutes so the flavors can meld. Serve with lemon wedges, alone or with spaghetti.

Serves 4

 Marinated Baby  Squid Salad

Many of our seafood restaurants specialize in calamari salad, and all have their own style. This recipe is a standard one, which allows you to add a few ingredients you may remember your mother using when you were a child.

> **1 pound whole baby squid, cleaned and rinsed (see page 162)**
> **3 stalks celery hearts, chopped**
> **2 garlic cloves, chopped**
> **2 tablespoon fresh chopped parsley**
> **pinch of red pepper flakes**
> **1 tablespoon olive oil**
> **3 tablespoons vegetable oil**
> **3 tablespoons red-wine vinegar**
> **salt and freshly ground black pepper to taste**

1. Cut cleaned squid in thin rings.

2. Put in cold water (enough to cover it) and softly boil, about 5 minutes, or until tender.

3. Drain well and put in a medium-size serving bowl.

4. Add remaining ingredients and toss gently.

5. Refrigerate at least a day or two to allow flavors to blend.

6. Serve as an appetizer with wonderful round Italian bread.

Serves 4

 # Baked Razor Clams

Razor clams are not easily available at all times. They can usually be found at our local fish store at Eastertime, but you must be there on the spot, for the supply is limited and they disappear quickly. My mother prepared them this wonderful, tasty way. I remember biting on the shell to scrape off the delicious crusty tomato and cheese mixture. You must be careful not to overcook the clams or they will be tough.

> **2 dozen razor clams**
> **1 cup white wine**
> **½ cup olive oil**
> **1 16-ounce can plum tomatoes**
> **1 cup grated Parmesan cheese**
> **salt and pepper to taste**
> **1½ tablespoon oregano**
> **5 garlic cloves, chopped**
> **1 tablespoon red pepper flakes**
> **2 tablespoons fresh parsley, chopped**
> **1 bunch scallions (with chive ends), chopped**
> **½ pound linguine or thin spaghetti**
> **1 tablespoon butter**

1. Preheat oven to 500 degrees.

2. Wash clams thoroughly in several changes of cold water until all the grit is gone.

3. Put clams in large baking pan, allowing them to form one layer.

4. Add the white wine to the bottom of the pan, plus enough water to submerge the clam flesh as it cooks. Do not submerge the top shell.

5. Sprinkle clams with ¼ cup of the oil.

6. Squeeze the plum tomatoes and their juice generously over the clams.

7. Add grated Parmesan cheese, salt and pepper to taste, oregano, garlic, red pepper flakes, parsley, and scallions.

8. Drizzle with remaining oil and sprinkle with additional salt and pepper if desired.

9. Bake for 20 minutes, adding additional wine if needed to keep clams from drying out.

10. Serve immediately over linguine or spaghetti that has been tossed with butter.

Serves 2–4

 # Anna B.'s Polpi

OCTOPUS SICILIAN STYLE

My mother-in-law claims this is the best! Octopus has a rich, sweet flavor, similar to that of squid. This dish is wonderful for Christmas Eve or during Lent. It can be served warm or cold as an appetizer or as a side dish with thin linguine and butter sauce.

> **2 2½- to 3-pound fresh octopus**
> **4 garlic cloves, chopped**
> **½ cup olive oil**
> **1 small onion, chopped**
> **1 small bunch celery, chopped**
> **1 8-ounce jar unsalted capers, drained**
> **1 6-ounce jar Sicilian, black, dry-cured olives (soaked and pitted)**
> **2–3 hot vinegar peppers, sliced (optional)**
> **1 6-ounce can tomato paste**
> **¾ cup red wine vinegar**
> **salt and pepper to taste**
> **½ cup chopped fresh parsley for garnish**

1. Clean each octopus body by continuously pouring salt on it and scrubbing with both hands in a back-and-forth motion. Using your fingers, reach inside the opening in the head and remove any loose particles. Invert the head and wash it inside and out with more salt. Pull out the inner sac. Cut away the eyes. Leave the octopus in one piece.

2. Put the cleaned octopus in a large bowl filled with cold salted water to soak for 30 minutes.

3. Fill a large pan with enough water to be able to cover the octopus. Bring the water to a boil. When it reaches the boiling point, add 6 tablespoons of salt.

This can be refrigerated for one week, if necessary

4. Pick up the octopus with a fork in the back of the neck. Dip the tentacles into the briskly boiling water three times. (Ma B. says this is an old custom and a very important step to prevent shock to the fish, which would immediately toughen it.) On the third time, slide the octopus off the fork into the water. Cover the pan after both octopuses have been added.

5. Cook until tender, using a fork to determine doneness. Figure on 45 minutes or more, according to their size. Do not overcook. Drain in a large colander and cool to room temperature. Using a sharp, thin knife, cut the meat into 2-inch or bite-size pieces, being very careful not to let the meat tear. Reserve.

6. In a large skillet, fry the garlic in the olive oil until tender. Add the onion, celery, capers, olives, vinegar peppers, and chopped octopus. Simmer for about 15 minutes at a very low temperature. Add the tomato paste and mix well. Simmer for 5 more minutes. Sprinkle wine vinegar over the mixture, stir well, and cover. Simmer at the lowest temperature for 20 minutes more. Add salt and pepper, if needed.

7. Transfer to a large serving platter and sprinkle with chopped parsley.

Serves 8–12

Festivale!

Each weekend in the summer the North End comes alive with religious street festivals. During this period of celebration, Italian food and novelty vendors line the streets, filling the air with aromas of fresh fried calamari, oven-baked pizza and calzone, Italian sausage with peppers and onions, and other regional treats. Italian symphonic marches and religious hymns can be heard from the marching bands parading through the streets, and classic Neapolitan love songs and Sicilian folk music resound from the bandstands.

During the festivals statues representing the different patron saints from various towns in Italy and Sicily are carried in procession through the narrow winding streets. But the highlight of the entire season is the spectacular "flight of the angel," which takes place at the feast of the Madonna del Soccorso (Our Lady of Perpetual Help). Also known as the Fisherman's Feast, this event

1 whole salmon (about 5 pounds)
soy sauce
15 Saltine crackers, crushed
½ cup fresh bread crumbs
¾ stick butter
2 bunches scallions, chopped
1 large shallot, chopped
2 garlic cloves, chopped
¼ cup parsley, chopped
1 teaspoon tarragon
salt and pepper to taste
2 lemons
large piece fresh ginger, slivered
thick stalks of carrots and celery (to use as a rack)
1 large onion, thickly sliced
dry white wine
olive oil
turmeric
Tabasco

1. Preheat oven to 450 degrees.

2. Cover salmon generously with soy sauce, inside and out.

3. In medium-size bowl, add crushed crackers and bread crumbs. Set aside.

4. In small skillet, melt butter and saute scallions, shallot, garlic, parsley, and tarragon.

5. Add to crumb mixture and toss well.

6. Squeeze with lemon juice until bread mixture is moist and add salt and pepper to taste.

7. Line bottom of baking pan with stalks of carrots, celery, and onion.

8. Place salmon on top of vegetables and stuff cavity with crumb mixture.

9. Tuck slivers of ginger inside the fish. Scatter more under and around fish.

10. Rub fish with olive oil and sprinkle with turmeric and salt and pepper. Decorate with slices of lemon and smother with ginger slivers.

11. Throw the used lemon halves into the bottom of the pan and add white wine.

12. Bake 20 minutes, then add more wine, a few shots of Tabasco, and some soy sauce to bottom of pan.

13. Bake about 20 minutes more, until golden brown.

Serves 4–6

originated in the fishing village of Sciacca, Sicily, and takes place the third weekend in August. The Madonna is the patroness of the fishermen, who pray to her for their safety at sea both in Boston and in Sicily.

The "flight of the angel" happens at the conclusion of the procession on the Sunday of the feast. A little girl dressed as an angel is lowered from a third-floor window via a block-and-tackle pulley system erected by the fishermen. She descends to the statue of the Madonna, where she recites a litany of prayers in honor of the Madonna and presents the statue with a bouquet of flowers. Then the angel is hoisted back up to the window amid a blizzard of paper confetti being thrown from the rooftops, while the marching bands play and thousands of people cheer wildly. This is truly one of Boston's most exciting and unique events of the summer season and shouldn't be missed by anyone!

—Jimmy (Bono) Geany, Fisherman's Feast Chairman, 1986–1991

 # How to Steam Fresh  Live Lobsters

This recipe explains the most perfect and best way to steam lobsters. Placing the lobster in cold water prevents it from being shocked, and leaves the meat tender and juicy soft. You may use the cooked lobsters for lobster diavolo, lobster casserole, or any other lobster favorite.

> 4 live whole lobsters, about 1–1½ pounds each
> 1 cup beer
> 1 bunch scallions, trimmed
> 8 sprigs parsley
> ½ large onion, thickly sliced
> 2 lemon halves
> salt and pepper to taste
> 1–2 shots Tabasco

1. Using a large pot with a cover, add cold water to fill pot at least 4 inches.

2. Place live lobsters in pan with cold water.

3. Add beer, whole scallions, parsley sprigs, sliced onion, lemon halves, salt and pepper to taste, and Tabasco sauce.

4. Place covered pot on medium-high heat and bring to a boil. Lower heat and steam lobsters approximately 25–30 minutes, or until all the lobsters are bright red.

5. Turn lobsters around a few times while steaming, alternating the top ones to the bottom for even cooking. Check liquid for evaporation, and add more beer or water if needed.

6. Place on platter and serve immediately with melted butter to which Tabasco and freshly squeezed lemon juice has been added.

Serves 4

 # Baked Lobster
Imbottito

STUFFED LOBSTER

I have devised this perfect way to cook baked stuffed lobster using garlic and fresh bread crumbs. The lobster is so succulent and tasty, you will hesitate to prepare it any other way. All ovens vary, so you might have to watch that the crumbs do not burn before the lobster is cooked. If they begin to brown, cover with a foil tent. We do not remove anything from the lobster, such as the tomalley or the sac. Fresh live lobster is best for this recipe, but squeamish cooks may want to boil the lobsters in advance.

> **2 large lobsters (about 1½ pounds each), live or boiled**
> **1½ sticks butter or margarine, melted**
> **2 cloves garlic, finely chopped**
> **1 clove shallot, finely chopped**
> **1 bunch scallion, finely chopped**
> **pinch of tarragon**
> **shot or two Tabasco (optional)**
> **2 lemon halves**
> **2 cups freshly grated bread crumbs**
> **½ strip (a single rolled package) of Ritz crackers, crumbled**
> **¼ cup chopped parsley**
> **1 bottle of clam juice**
> **salt and pepper to taste**
> **paprika**

1. Cut lobster down middle and spread open widely.

2. Place in baking pan, to accommodate comfortably.

3. Melt 1 stick butter in small saucepan; add garlic, shallots, scallions, tarragon, Tabasco, and the juice of one lemon half.

4. Add a few pieces of lemon peel and saute about 5 minutes.

5. In a large bowl, combine bread crumbs, crumbled crackers, chopped parsley, and the juice of a fresh lemon. Toss well. Add melted butter and mix thoroughly.

6. Slowly, pour clam juice into bread crumb mixture until stuffing is well moistened but not soaked. Add salt and pepper to taste.

7. Stuff lobster from cavity to tail until well filled.

8. Drizzle lobster with ½ stick melted butter or margarine and enough paprika to lightly color.

9. Pour remaining clam juice to bottom of pan and bake lobster, uncovered, in a 450-degree oven on middle shelf for 20 minutes.

10. Lower heat to 350 degrees and cook for about 30 minutes more for live lobster or 15 minutes for boiled ones.

11. When lobsters are cooked and stuffing is crusty brown, remove from oven and baste with remaining juices from the bottom of the pan.

12. Cover tightly with foil and allow to set for about 20 minutes (I also like to put a heavy towel over the foil) to keep the steam in, thus making for a juicier lobster. Serve with melted butter that has been seasoned with fresh lemon juice and Tabasco.

Serves 2

 # Lobster fra Diavolo

Traditionally, this recipe was prepared in our home using only the lobster bodies and not the whole lobster. The bodies were less expensive and were sold by the bagful, so there was plenty for all the family to enjoy. We developed a taste for the innards of the lobster body, particularly the tomalley, or "green stuff," in the middle. You can use either the bodies alone or whole lobsters cut up, whichever your budget and taste buds prefer.

8–10 cooked lobster bodies or 2 1¼-pound steamed lobsters
¾ cup olive oil
1 large onion, chopped
2 garlic cloves, chopped
2 shallots cloves, chopped
pinch each of red pepper flakes, dried tarragon flakes, fresh parsley,
**   and dried basil**
1 can chopped mushrooms (reserve liquid)
2 dashes Tabasco sauce
reserved tomalley
salt and pepper to taste
1 6-ounce can tomato paste
1 28-ounce can crushed tomatoes
water
1 pound linguine, cooked according to package directions

1. Cut live lobsters in segments and reserve tomalley from bodies.

2. Cover bottom of deep, heavy sauce pan with olive oil.

3. Saute onion, garlic, and shallots in oil and gently simmer until golden.

4. Add red pepper flakes, tarragon, parsley, and basil. Stir well.

5. Add drained mushrooms and Tabasco. Simmer until vegetables are slightly crisp.

6. Add the reserved tomalley and stir until it melts down.

7. Add the tomato paste and blend well.

8. Add the crushed tomatoes and stir until blended with the tomato paste and oil.

9. Add salt and pepper to taste and a pinch more of any of the dry seasonings, stirring well.

10. When the sauce starts to boil slightly, add the reserved mushroom juice and enough water to equal ½ can of the tomatoes.

11. Let sauce come to a boil and add the lobsters.

12. Gently mix sauce with lobsters, and bring the mixture to another boil, stirring often. Adjust seasonings.

13. Simmer uncovered for ½ hour, turning the lobsters 4 to 5 times during the cooking period.

14. Serve over 1 pound of cooked linguine that has been tossed with butter.

Serves 4–6

 # Tonno and Noodles, Sicilian Style

½ pound fresh noodles, cooked and tossed with 1 tablespoon butter
1 large can tonno (tuna)
4 tablespoons olive oil
1 garlic clove, slivered
1 8-ounce can whole tomatoes, squeezed
1 small can peas, drained
1 small can ripe pitted olives (or ¼ pound pitted dry-cured Sicilian olives), sliced

1. Drain canned tuna; reserve.

2. Heat the oil in a heavy skillet and cook the slivered garlic until golden brown.

3. Remove the garlic and add the tomatoes and juice to the oil, cooking over low heat for 10 minutes to thicken.

4. Add the peas, flaked tuna, and slivers of ripe olives and heat thoroughly. Be careful not to crush the tuna.

5. Serve over warm cooked noodles and top with a little Parmesan cheese.

Serves 2–4

 # Spaghetti and Crabs

What fun we had going to the fish market for crabs and crab bodies when I was a child. At that time you could buy them so cheaply. There was also a man who drove a pick-up truck and went around the North End shouting, "cawadi, cawadi," which meant you could buy wonderful boiled crabs, cooked right in the pots on the truck, for maybe five cents each. We would eat them while sitting on our doorsteps and put the empty shells in the paper bags they came in. Besides boiling them, here is a special way my mother cooked fresh, raw crabs.

**⅓ cup olive oil
3 garlic cloves, chopped
1 medium onion, chopped
1 tablespoon red pepper flakes
1 tablespoon oregano
1 6-ounce can tomato paste
1 28-ounce can ground peeled tomatoes
salt and pepper to taste
8 fresh, whole crabs, rinsed slightly
½ cup dry white wine or water
1 pound spaghetti or thin linguine (linguine fini)
grated Parmesan or Romano cheese**

1. Heat oil in a large saucepan over medium heat.

2. Add chopped garlic, onion, 1 teaspoon of red pepper flakes, and 1 teaspoon of oregano; saute for about 5 minutes.

3. Add tomato paste and blend in well, stirring constantly with a wooden spoon.

4. Add tomatoes and stir constantly until mixture is blended well.

5. Sprinkle with additional red pepper flakes, oregano, and salt and pepper to taste.

6. Bring sauce to a soft boil, and add whole, rinsed crabs. Stir gently, tossing crabs around sauce.

7. Put heat on medium-high and add white wine or water. Bring sauce to a soft boil and adjust seasonings.

8. Simmer covered for about 15 minutes, then remove cover and simmer at least until pasta is cooked.

9. While crab sauce cooks, prepare pasta al dente in a large pot of boiling water. Drain well.

10. Place pasta on a very large platter and spoon some of the crab sauce on top.

11. Toss pasta lightly to coat well with sauce (to stop pasta from sticking).

12. Surround the pasta with crabs and sprinkle with grated cheese.

13. Serve immediately with lots of napkins and additional sauce. Have some empty bowls available for shells.

Serves 4–6

 # Eels Marinara

Serve this dish as an appetizer, or as a main course with pasta and vegetables.

> **2 pounds fresh eels**
> **⅓ cup olive oil**
> **1 small onion, minced**
> **2 garlic cloves**
> **1 small piece lemon peel**
> **⅛ teaspoon dried sage**
> **2 tablespoons tomato paste, diluted in ½ cup water**
> **½ cup dry white wine**
> **salt and pepper to taste**

1. Have the eels cleaned by the fish merchant and the heads removed and discarded. Rinse thoroughly in cold, salted water, and dry. Cut eels into 3-inch pieces.

2. Pour the oil into a large, deep skillet. Add the onion, garlic, lemon peel, and sage. Saute gently until the garlic is golden brown. Discard the garlic.

Refrigerates well for 2 or 3 days.

3. Add the pieces of eel and fry over medium heat for about 5 minutes. Turn often, gently, using a spatula.

4. Add the diluted tomato paste and wine. Simmer, uncovered, for 10 minutes. Add salt and pepper and simmer for 8 to 10 minutes more.

5. When the liquid is almost evaporated, transfer to a warm serving platter.

Serves 2–4

Eels with Peas alla Romana

1½ pounds fresh small eels
3 tablespoons olive oil
½ garlic clove, minced
4 scallions, sliced
salt and pepper to taste
pinch of dried red pepper flakes
½ cup dry white wine
1 tablespoon tomato sauce
2 cups shelled fresh or frozen peas
2 tablespoons warm water or clam broth

1. Have the eels cleaned by the fish merchant and the heads removed and discarded. Rinse thoroughly in cold, salted water, and dry. Cut the eels into 3-inch pieces.

2. Pour the oil into a heavy saucepan. Saute the garlic and scallions until slightly browned.

3. Add the eels, salt, black pepper, and red pepper flakes. Cook on medium-high heat until the liquid from the eels has evaporated, turning only once or twice.

4. Add the wine, tomato sauce, and peas. Mix well. Add the water or stock and lower the heat to medium. Cook, uncovered for 15 to 20 minutes or until the peas are tender. Stir gently a couple of times only. Taste for more salt and pepper.

5. Serve in soup bowls with crusty bread.

Serves 4

Fried Small Eels

Another Christmas Eve favorite.

> **3 pounds fresh small eels**
> **1 cup flour**
> **1 teaspoon paprika**
> **salt and pepper to taste**
> **1 cup olive oil (use more as needed)**
> **1 lemon, quartered, for garnish**

1. Have the eels cleaned by the fish merchant and the heads removed and discarded. Rinse thoroughly in cold, salted water and pat dry with paper towels. Cut them into 2-inch pieces.

2. Season the flour with paprika, salt, and pepper. Put the flour in a brown paper bag. Shake the pieces of eel in the bag, a few at a time, to evenly distribute the flour mixture. Set aside.

3. Heat the olive oil in a medium-size heavy skillet over medium-high heat. When the oil is hot, add some of the pieces of eel so they can fry uncrowded until brown on both sides. The frying time will be about 10 to 15 minutes on each side. Drain on paper towels. Add more oil to the skillet as needed. When all the pieces have been cooked, transfer them to a warm platter.

4. Sprinkle with more salt and pepper, if desired, and serve with lemon quarters.

Serves 4

 # Olga's Fish Cakes

My mother never had any idea that this recipe would follow her granddaughter to Georgia, where it would become a big hit with all of her friends.

> **3 large boiling potatoes, peeled**
> **3 pounds fish fillets or other skinless pieces (pollock, scrod, or any inexpensive boneless fish will do)**
> **½ cup freshly grated Parmesan cheese**
> **2 garlic cloves, finely chopped**
> **1 cup chopped fresh parsley**
> **3 eggs**
> **salt and freshly ground black pepper to taste**
> **fresh bread crumbs**
> **flour**
> **1 cup olive oil**
> **lemon slices, parsley, and tartar sauce (optional)**

1. Cut the potatoes into large cubes and boil for 20 minutes. Drain them thoroughly by shaking the colander well. Then put the potatoes in a large bowl and mash until fluffy.

2. Put the fish in a saucepan (cut it to fit, if necessary). Add water to cover the fish. Boil gently for 5 minutes.

3. Drain the fish and add to the potatoes. Add the grated cheese, garlic, parsley, eggs, salt, and pepper. Gently toss the mixture until well blended.

4. Add bread crumbs a little at a time until the mixture becomes firm to the touch but not dry. Keep the potato-fish mixture light and not laden with crumbs.

5. Bring the mixture to the stove area along with a dish of bread crumbs and a small bowl of water to moisten your hands when rolling the fish cakes. Take a fistful of the fish mixture and roll it into a round ball. When the ball is smooth, gently flatten it to form a patty. Use the water to keep your hands moist (this will prevent the fish cakes from sticking to your palms and help keep a smooth shape). Lightly dust the fish cake with bread crumbs or flour to dry excess moisture (this will also stop it from sticking to the skillet). Place the fish cake on a large tray and let set for 5 minutes. Repeat with the rest of the mixture.

6. Heat the olive oil in a large heavy skillet on medium-high heat. Gently add the fish cakes to the hot oil without crowding. Fry on both sides until golden brown or until a nice crust forms. Use a spatula to turn the cakes over gently. Transfer to a paper-lined dish to absorb excess oil. Continue until all the mixture has been used.

7. When all the fish cakes have cooked and drained, arrange on a platter with lemon slices, parsley, and tartar sauce. Serve.

Yield: 15 cakes

 # Haddock alla Pizzaiola

A thick piece of sole may be substituted for the haddock in this recipe.

>**2 pounds haddock fillets**
>**1 pound fresh tomatoes, seeds removed, chopped**
>**1 tablespoon chopped fresh parsley**
>**1 large garlic clove, finely chopped**
>**pinch of dried tarragon and mint**
>**salt and freshly ground black pepper to taste**
>**5 tablespoons olive oil**
>**¼ cup freshly grated Parmesan cheese**
>**lemon wedges for garnish (optional)**

1. Place the fish in a buttered baking dish.

2. Mix together the tomatoes, parsley, garlic, seasonings, olive oil, and cheese. Toss gently until well mixed. Spread evenly over fish fillets.

3. Bake the fish in a preheated 350-degree oven for 20 minutes, until cheese is nicely melted and tomatoes are soft.

4. Serve very hot with lemon wedges and pan drippings.

Serves 4

Mackerel in Tomato Sauce

3 pounds mackerel
2 tablespoons olive oil
1 small onion, sliced
1 garlic clove, chopped
1 tablespoon chopped fresh parsley
1 14-ounce can peeled and crushed tomatoes
salt and pepper to taste
½ teaspoon dried red pepper flakes
½ teaspoon dried basil
½ teaspoon dried oregano
2 tablespoons water

1. Remove the bones from the mackerel. Cut the mackerel into 4 pieces.

2. Heat the olive oil in a large heavy skillet. Add the onion, garlic, and parsley, and cook until the onions become translucent.

3. Add the tomatoes and seasonings. Cook for 5 minutes on medium heat, stirring often.

4. Add the water and let it come to a boil. Add the mackerel and cook for 5 minutes, uncovered. Turn the fish over and cook an additional 10 minutes.

5. Serve the mackerel in flat plates with the sauce, or serve over spaghetti.

Serves 4

This may be refrigerated for 2 to 3 days.

Pan-Fried Smelts or Sardines

A quick and easy Lenten favorite. We like to cook our smelts whole for easier handling. Cooked this way, they look very appealing when served on a decorative platter, accompanied by lemon and parsley. When ready to eat, simply lift the meat off the bone; it will come off very easily.

2 pounds fresh whole smelts or sardines (small size if possible)
semolina flour
paprika
salt and pepper
olive oil
lemon wedges and chopped fresh parsley for garnish

1. Rinse the smelts or sardines under cold water and dry with paper towels.

2. Put 1 cup of flour in a paper bag (adding more as you go along, if needed) along with a sprinkle of paprika, salt, and pepper. Shake 3 or 4 fish at a time in the bag to coat them with flour. When all the fish have been floured, quickly fry in hot olive oil until golden brown. Be careful not to crowd the fish in the pan. Continue until all the fish are used. Drain on paper towels.

These are best eaten the same day they are made.

3. Serve immediately, garnished with lemon wedges and parsley.

Serves 6–8

 # Baccalà with Vinegar Peppers

This is another of my mother's delicacies. How I enjoy her talents! This recipe should be prepared from several hours to 24 hours in advance to enhance the flavors. Serve with crusty Italian bread as an appetizer or with other main dishes for dinner during Lent.

>   **2 pounds dried salt cod (baccalà)**
>   **6 large vinegar peppers, hot or sweet**
>   **olive oil**
>   **salt and freshly ground black pepper to taste**
>   **3 large garlic cloves, chopped**
>   **chopped fresh parsley**
>   **about 10 black, Sicilian, dry-cured olives, pitted and sliced**

1. Soak the salt cod in enough cold water to cover for 24 hours. Change the water at least six times to remove the salt. Keep refrigerated. When you are ready to cook, drain and rinse well in cold water.

2. Put the fish in a large pot and cover with water. Gently boil on medium heat until the fish is tender. (The fish should not become so soft that it breaks apart in the water.) Rinse under cold running water and drain well.

3. With your fingers, tear the fish into bite-size pieces. Spread them attractively on a large serving platter. Tear the vinegar peppers over the fish, letting the juices fall on the cod.

4. Sprinkle the cod and peppers with a drizzle of olive oil. Use salt only if it is needed, and pepper. Sprinkle the cod and peppers with the chopped garlic, chopped parsley, and black pitted olives. Gently lift the fish with a spatula to let the other ingredients fall through so everything marinates evenly. Do this several times before serving but try not to disturb the arrangement.

5. Refrigerate, covered, for at least a few hours.

Serves 6–8

 # Baccalà and Potatoes

Codfish, dried in the sun and wind, was once considered a poor man's fish. The poor man always knew what a tasty food he had.

> 1½ *pounds dried salt cod (baccalà)*
> *olive oil*
> *3 garlic cloves, chopped*
> *1 tablespoon dried oregano*
> *1 teaspoon dried red pepper flakes*
> *4 fresh basil leaves, or a huge pinch of dry basil*
> *1 14-ounce can plum tomatoes*
> *5 medium potatoes, peeled and quartered*
> ¼ *pound Spanish green olives, pitted*
> *salt and pepper to taste*
> *1 tablespoon chopped fresh parsley*
> *10 Sicilian dry-cured, black olives, pitted*

1. Soak the salt cod in enough cold water to cover for 24 hours. Change the water at least six times to remove the salt. Keep refrigerated. When you are ready to cook, drain and rinse well in cold water. Cut into 3- or 4-inch squares.

2. Heat enough oil to cover the bottom of a heavy saucepan, and saute garlic, oregano, red pepper flakes, and basil. After the garlic has slightly browned, add the plum tomatoes and cook for 15 minutes. Gently crush the tomatoes with a large fork and stir often.

3. Add the fish, potatoes, and green olives. Stir well, using a wooden spoon. Add salt and pepper to taste, and more red pepper if desired.

This dish refrigerates well.

4. Cover and simmer on low heat for 45 minutes or until the potatoes are tender and the fish is cooked. Remove from the heat. Sprinkle with chopped parsley and black olives. Let rest for 10 minutes. Serve with Italian bread.

Serves 4

 Baccalà Fritto

FRIED SALT COD

This salt cod dish is best eaten the day it is cooked. Serve it as an appetizer or a side dish.

> **1 pound dried salt cod, cut into 3x5-inch pieces**
> **¼ cup olive oil**
> **2 tablespoons vegetable oil**
> **3 garlic cloves, crushed**
> **¼ cup diced salt pork**
> **flour (enough to coat fish)**
> **¼ teaspoon freshly ground black pepper**
> **3 tablespoons fresh lemon juice**
> **chopped fresh parsley and lemon wedges for garnish**

1. Soak the fish in enough cold water to cover for 24 hours. Change the water at least six times to remove the salt. Keep refrigerated. When you are ready to cook, drain and rinse well in cold water. Pat dry with paper towels.

2. Heat both oils in a large heavy skillet over medium-low heat. Add the garlic and salt pork. Cook about 10 minutes or until the garlic is lightly browned and the fat has melted.

3. Using a slotted spoon, remove the garlic and any unmelted fat. Discard. Raise the heat to medium-high.

4. Combine the flour and pepper on a plate. Dip the fish in the flour to coat lightly.

5. Using tongs, add the fish to the skillet. Cook until the fish is golden on both sides or until it begins to flake, about 10 minutes. Turn it only once.

6. Using a spatula, gently transfer the fish to a heated serving platter.

7. Discard all but ¼ cup of the drippings in the pan. Stir the lemon juice into the skillet. When hot and bubbly, pour it over the fish. Garnish the platter with parsley and lemon wedges.

Serves 4–6

 # Merluzzi in White Sauce

SICILIAN-STYLE WHITING

My Uncle Tony, now deceased, taught me how to cook this wonderful "poor man's repast." Because whiting is a bony fish, we usually strain the juices and discard the fish unless it has previously been de-boned.

2 pounds whiting, cleaned and dressed
⅓ cup olive oil
1 large onion, sliced
1 garlic clove, chopped
1 shallot, chopped
3 scallions, sliced
1 tablespoon chopped fresh parsley, plus more for garnish
pinch of dried tarragon, red pepper flakes, and oregano
salt and pepper to taste
water (enough to cover the fish)
⅓ cup dry white wine

1. Heat the olive oil in a medium-size heavy saucepan over medium heat. Saute the onion, garlic, shallot, scallions, parsley, tarragon, red pepper flakes, and oregano.

2. When the onion is transparent, add the fish and salt and pepper to taste. Brown lightly for a few minutes, turning often. Raise the heat to high and add enough water to cover the fish. Add the white wine. Let the mixture come to a rapid boil. Boil for 5 minutes, or until the fish is cooked and the sauce turns milky white. Taste for more salt and pepper. Check the fish carefully in order to remove all bones.

Can be refrigerated for 1 or 2 days.

3. Serve very hot in soup bowls with more fresh parsley on top and accompanied by garlic bread. Or use as a sauce for ½ pound spaghettini.

Serves 4–6

 Fish Salad a la Papa

My beautiful friend Jeannete Bennett, now deceased, contributed this recipe many years ago for our fund-raising North End Italian cookbook. She said it was brought here from Italy by one of her Sicilian friends.

It was customary to soak storebought fish in milk to refreshen it before cooking. You may want to try this yourself. For added flavor you should precook the mushrooms the day before. Boil them for a couple of minutes and marinate them in enough red wine to cover. It is not necessary to refrigerate them. Marinating the mushrooms gives a wonderful zip to the salad.

> **2 pounds cod or haddock fillets**
> **1 cup milk**
> **½ cup water**
> **1 head Boston lettuce**
> **1 garlic clove, chopped**
> **1 cup Sicilian dry-cured olives, pitted**
> **½ cup sliced almonds**
> **1 large red onion, sliced in rings**
> **¼ cup olive oil**
> **juice of 2 lemons**
> **salt and pepper to taste**
> **1 cup button mushrooms, marinated in red wine**
> **1 teaspoon fresh parsley, chopped**

1. Boil fish in a mixture of the milk and water for 5–8 minutes, or until the fish is flaky.

2. Cool the fish and cut it into 2-inch squares.

3. Carefully place on a decorative platter garnished with lettuce leaves.

4. Add chopped garlic, olives, almonds, and top with onion rings.

5. Pour olive oil and lemon juice evenly over fish.

6. Sprinkle with salt and pepper to taste.

7. Arrange mushrooms around fish and sprinkle the whole dish with parsley.

Serves 4

 Periwinkles alla
Palermo

PERIWINKLES IN SAUCE

This is an old, rare recipe, one that has been in our family for quite some time. This recipe is adaptable to any shellfish but is especially complementary when using periwinkles, or snails. You will likely find these critters in old fish markets, climbing in huge barrels, especially around holiday time. Buy only live snails with the heads out of the shell. When I was very young, we used to buy our periwinkles freshly boiled and served in paper bags. Of course, we always had our safety pins with us to pry them from their shells. This dish is served as an appetizer and will keep everyone busy while you're preparing other foods.

> **3 pounds fresh periwinkles (or snails)**
> **salt**
> **olive oil**
> **1 small onion, chopped**
> **1 garlic clove, chopped**
> **½ cup tomato paste**
> **1 pint hot water**
> **pepper to taste**
> **pinch of red pepper flakes**
> **1 tablespoon fresh parsley, chopped**

1. Place snails in a medium-size deep pot and cover with water.

2. Rub salt around inside of pot above the water line to keep snails from crawling out.

3. Soak for ½ hour, then wash thoroughly several times in fresh water.

4. Drain well in a plastic colander to prevent shells from cracking.

5. Using the same deep pot, heat enough oil to cover bottom.

6. Add chopped onions and garlic and cook on low heat for 5 minutes.

7. Add tomato paste, stirring constantly with a wooden spoon.

8. Add pint of hot water and mix well.

9. Gently add snails to sauce and simmer for 10 minutes.

10. Add salt and pepper to taste, a pinch of red pepper flakes, and parsley; stir well and cover.

11. Simmer for another 20 minutes.

12. Remove to deep bowls and serve hot with sauce. To remove meat from shells, use toothpicks or oyster forks.

Serves 6

 # Scungilli en Bianco

SCUNGILLI SALAD

Scungilli are usually prepared at Lent or at other times that a meatless meal is desired. Simply serve them as an appetizer or atop an antipasto. All you need is some delicious Italian bread and a fine wine to complete the menu. Don't forget that the meat has to be removed from the shell. Simply pull it out with a large safety pin or other pointed utensil. You may use canned scungilli (sometimes labeled as conch) if you prefer.

> **8 scungilli, in shells or 2 8-ounce cans conch**
> **2 garlic cloves**
> **2 stalks celery, thinly sliced**
> **2 teaspoons fresh parsley, chopped**
> **½ cup olive oil**
> **¼ cup lemon juice**
> **sprinkle of paprika**
> **pinch of red pepper flakes**
> **10 Sicilian dry-cured olives, pitted and halved**
> **salt and pepper to taste**
> **2 vinegar peppers**
> **lettuce**

1. Scrub conch shells thoroughly with a stiff brush under hot water.

2. Place in large pot of boiling water, enough to cover, and cook on medium heat for about 1 hour,

adding more water if needed.

3. Remove pan from heat and rinse shells with cold water until cooled.

4. Pull meat from shells with a large pin, pointed knife, or fork.

5. Slice fish meat lengthwise, using a small sharp knife or razor blade.

6. Place in a bowl and toss with remaining ingredients, adjusting seasonings if needed.

7. Cover and refrigerate overnight.

8. Arrange salad on serving platter lined with lettuce, and drizzle with additional olive oil if needed.

Serves 4–6

Vegetables

 # Cauliflower with Anchovy Sauce

When you shop for cauliflower, avoid loose, spread-out heads. That is a sign of overmaturation. Choose compact white heads with fresh-looking green leaves and creamy white or purple curd. This recipe is a Sicilian dish—very popular and very economical. It is customary to undercook cauliflower to enhance its unique flavor.

1 head cauliflower, rinsed, trimmed, and left whole
fresh lemon juice
½ cup unsalted butter
1 small garlic clove, crushed
3 anchovy fillets, well drained and patted dry
1 hard-cooked egg
1 teaspoon small capers, rinsed and drained
1 teaspoon fresh parsley, finely chopped

1. Using a deep pot with a cover, steam whole cauliflower in 1 inch of boiling water. Add 1 tablespoon lemon juice to water to help keep cauliflower white. When water comes to a boil, simmer 10 minutes uncovered, then cover and simmer about 15 minutes more. Drain well and reserve to a deep serving dish.

2. Heat butter in a small saucepan over medium-low heat. When foam subsides, add garlic and saute for 1 minute.

3. Stir in anchovy fillets and mash with wooden spoon until dissolved. Remove from heat and drain. Reserve.

4. Separate yolk from white of hard-cooked egg. Finely chop white, and set aside. Press yolk through sieve with wooden spoon, and reserve.

5. Just before serving cauliflower, quickly reheat anchovy sauce over low heat. Stir in chopped egg white, 1 teaspoon lemon juice, and capers.

6. Pour hot anchovy sauce over top of reserved cauliflower. Sprinkle with egg yolk and parsley.

7. Serve immediately. For individual servings, cut flowers down to stem, put on plates, and spoon with sauce.

Serves 4–6

 # Baked Stuffed Finger Peppers

DITIELLI

Serve with lasagne or manicotti, chicken or turkey. These peppers also make a delicious sandwich the next day when served with white poultry meat or leftover pork.

6 green Italian finger peppers
1 cup fresh soft bread crumbs
2 garlic cloves, chopped
1 tablespoon chopped fresh parsley
¼ cup freshly grated Parmesan cheese
salt and pepper to taste
olive oil

> **TO MAKE BREAD CRUMBS**
>
> *Use day-old Italian bread cut into small pieces and ground in a blender. Make coarse crumbs for stuffings and fine crumbs for coatings. The crumbs can be frozen in a plastic bag. Fresh or frozen-fresh bread crumbs make all the difference in the world to a recipe.*

1. Remove the stems and seeds from the peppers, leaving a small opening.

2. Mix together the bread crumbs, garlic, parsley, cheese, salt, and pepper. Slowly drizzle olive oil over the mixture until crumbs are slightly glistening.

3. Push the bread stuffing into the pepper cavity loosely; do not pack.

4. Place the peppers on a baking sheet. Drizzle very lightly with more olive oil and sprinkle with salt.

5. Bake in a preheated 450-degree oven (use the middle rack) for about 20 minutes or until dark and almost burned. This gives them a tasty flavor.

6. Let the peppers rest at least ½ hour before transferring them to a serving platter. They will keep 2 to 3 days in the refrigerator.

Serves 2–3

 # Baked Stuffed Bell Peppers, Sicilian Style

This recipe makes a substantial meal for lunch or an appetizer for company. The addition of anchovies and olives makes them quite spicy, so adjust the ingredients to your liking. A scoop of tomato sauce on top of the peppers wouldn't hurt, either.

> **2 large green bell peppers and 2 red bell peppers**
> **3 cups fresh bread crumbs (use French or Italian bread)**
> **2 garlic cloves, finely chopped**
> **1 can flat anchovies, rinsed and chopped (reserve oil)**
> **6 tablespoons capers, rinsed in cold water and finely chopped**
> **8 Sicilian, black, dry-cured olives, pitted and finely chopped**
> **4 tablespoons finely chopped fresh Italian parsley**
> **¼ cup freshly grated Parmesan cheese**
> **salt and freshly ground black pepper**
> **olive oil**

1. Cut the peppers in half, lengthwise, and remove stems and seeds.

2. In a large bowl, combine the bread crumbs, garlic, anchovies, capers, olives, parsley, Parmesan, salt, and pepper. Combine ¼ cup olive and anchovy oil. Slowly drizzle over crumb mixture, tossing lightly until the crumbs are slightly moistened but not wet.

3. Spoon the stuffing into the pepper halves and arrange them in a single layer in an oiled baking dish.

4. Bake in the middle of a preheated 400-degree oven for about 30 minutes, or until the peppers are tender, but not limp, and the stuffing is golden brown and crusty.

5. Let peppers set until they reach room temperature before serving.

Serves 8

 # Zucchini Stew

⅓ cup olive oil
½ pound ground beef*
1 small onion, chopped
2 cloves garlic, chopped
1 small green pepper, chopped
2 stalks of celery, chopped fine
2 pounds small zucchini, washed and cut into ¼-inch rounds
2 medium-size potatoes, cut into thin slices
¾ cup canned tomatoes OR 1 tablespoon tomato paste
salt, pepper, and red pepper flakes to taste
Parmesan cheese (reserve)

1. Using a large skillet, heat the olive oil. Saute the ground beef, onion, and garlic in the oil until browned.

2. Transfer the beef into a large soup pot and add the remaining ingredients (except the cheese) with 1½ cups of water.

3. Cover the pot and cook over medium-low heat for 30 minutes or until the zucchini is tender. Be sure not to overcook the zucchini. Serve in soup bowls and toss with Parmesan cheese if desired.

Serves 4

* Vegetarians may omit the beef and still be pleased with the result. The ingredients may need to be slightly altered to taste.

TO ROAST LEFTOVER VEGETABLES

Sprinkle scraps of parsley, lettuce, escarole, onions, or other leftover vegetables with olive oil and salt to taste. Broil until crispy brown but not burned. Serve on top of any cooked meat as a garnish.

 # Zucchini Frittata

ZUCCHINI OMELETTE

8 eggs
½ teaspoon salt
black pepper
¼ cup Parmesan cheese
2 medium zucchini, sliced thin
2 tablespoons chopped fresh parsley
2 tablespoons chopped fresh basil
1 tablespoon olive or salad oil

1. Beat the eggs with the salt and pepper. Stir in cheese, zucchini, parsley, and basil.

2. Preheat the broiler.

3. In a 10½-inch skillet, heat the oil. Add the eggs and cook undisturbed over low heat about 10 minutes. Carefully lift the edge to check the bottom—it should be golden brown.

4. Place the skillet under the broiler for 30 seconds until top is golden. Cut into wedges. Serve hot or at room temperature.

Serves 4

Batter-Fried Zucchini Sticks

Many popular restaurants feature this dish on their menus.

> **3 6-inch-long zucchini**
> **½ cup semolina or all-purpose flour**
> **2 teaspoons cornstarch**
> **1 large egg**
> **½ cup ice water**
> **olive oil for deep frying**
> **salt**
> **dried oregano**

1. Wipe the zucchini with a paper towel. Do not peel. Cut off the ends and discard. Cut the zucchini lengthwise into ¼-inch-thick strips, similar to carrot sticks.

2. In a medium-size bowl, stir together the flour and cornstarch.

3. In a small bowl, beat the egg until foamy. Add the water and beat to blend. Add the egg mixture to the flour mixture and stir just until moistened. The batter will be lumpy, but do not stir it again.

4. Pour olive oil into a heavy skillet until it is about 2 inches deep. Heat the oil. Dip the zucchini sticks into the batter and place them, uncrowded, in the hot oil. When they have nicely browned on one side, turn them over to brown the second side.

5. When the sticks are golden brown on both sides, transfer them to paper toweling to drain. Sprinkle with salt and oregano. Serve hot as an appetizer or as a side dish.

Serves 4–6

 Baked Zucchini  Casserole

This is another delicious appetizer or party dish. It can be assembled ahead of time and baked just before serving.

> 6 small or 2 large firm zucchini
> 2 eggs, beaten
> ¼ cup fresh bread crumbs
> 1 small onion, grated
> salt and freshly ground black pepper to taste
> 4 tablespoons butter or margarine, melted
> ¼ cup freshly grated Parmesan or Romano cheese

1. Wash zucchini, cut off tips, and slice in ¼-inch rounds. Cook in a small amount of salted water until soft. Drain well and mash coarsely.

2. In a large bowl, combine the beaten eggs, bread crumbs, grated onion, salt, and pepper. Mix well. Toss with the melted butter until the crumbs are coated. Add the zucchini and mix gently.

3. Transfer the mixture to a baking dish. Sprinkle with the cheese. Bake in a preheated 350-degree oven for 30 minutes.

4. Serve at room temperature.

Serves 6

 # Fried Zucchini
Blossoms

If you want to impress your friends with something exotic, here is the recipe for you. And the best part is that the preparation is simple. Your biggest challenge will be finding zucchini blossoms. These are the flowers that grow on a zucchini plant, so find someone who grows zucchini and you'll be all set.

24 zucchini blossoms
1¾ cups flour
pinch of salt
3 teaspoons baking soda
2 eggs, slightly beaten
¾ cup milk
¼ cup water
6 cups vegetable oil

1. Do not wash the flowers. Clean by carefully removing the pistils.

2. Combine the flour, salt, baking soda, eggs, milk, and water. Stir until a smooth batter is obtained.

3. In a heavy frying pan, heat the oil to boiling. Dip each flower into the batter, then carefully spoon into the hot oil. Fry the flowers until they are golden brown on both sides. Remove with a slotted spoon and drain on paper toweling.

4. Sprinkle with salt and serve hot. These blossoms are best when served immediately.

Serves 4

 Zucchini Fritters

This is a very old recipe that is used often in our homes. Zucchini is always available and at an inexpensive price. If you are making these fritters for a large gathering, you will need to increase the recipe.

2 cups coarsely grated zucchini
2 eggs
½ cup flour
½ cup bread crumbs
2 tablespoons Parmesan cheese
salt and pepper to taste
1 cup olive oil

1. Grate zucchini, using large holes of grater.

2. In a large bowl, beat eggs thoroughly with a wire whisk.

3. Add remaining ingredients, except oil, and mix well.

4. Let mixture stand 20–30 minutes.

5. Meanwhile, heat oil in a medium-size heavy skillet.

6. Drop zucchini batter by the tablespoons into the hot oil, bearing down with fork until slightly flattened. Fry on each side until golden brown.

7. Remove to a platter lined with paper towels and serve warm.

Serves 4–6

 Eggplant Parmigiana  with Meat Sauce

This dish is a favorite in my home. A duplicate of my mother's, it is a sure hit. Make the best sandwiches in the world with it, use it for an appetizer or with pasta, or carry it along when picnicking. It also makes an exciting house-warming gift. Eggplant has many uses, and once you get a system, you will find it easy to prepare.

2 small, dark, firm eggplants
1½ cups oil, or more as needed
flour
4 eggs, beaten
1 recipe Quick Meat Sauce (page 51) or a plain marinara sauce
¾ cup mozzarella cheese, sliced or grated (optional)
1 cup freshly grated Parmesan or Romano cheese
chopped fresh parsley for garnish

1. Remove the stem from each eggplant. Cut the eggplants crosswise into slices about ¼ inch thick. Do not remove the skin as this helps to hold the eggplant together.

2. Heat the oil in an electric frying pan on the highest heat, or use a large heavy skillet.

3. Dust each eggplant slice with flour, dip into the beaten eggs, and fry on both sides until golden brown. (I like to use tongs to handle the eggplant.) Use more oil as needed. Drain on paper toweling. (If you prefer a thicker coating, you may dip the slices into coarse bread crumbs after dipping them into the egg wash.)

4. Line a 2½-quart shallow baking dish with a little of the tomato sauce. Arrange a layer of eggplant slices over it. Cover with a layer of mozzarella cheese, more sauce, and a sprinkling of grated Parmesan cheese. Repeat the layers until all ingredients are used. Pour leftover egg, if any, around the edges of the eggplant.

5. Bake in a preheated 350-degree oven for 30 minutes or until the eggplant is tender and golden on top.

6. Garnish with chopped parsley and serve.

7. For best results, let eggplant rest for at least 30 minutes before you cut it.

Serves 8–10

 # Caponata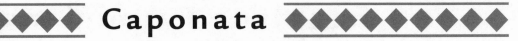

SPICY EGGPLANT

We usually serve this during Lent (Pasqua) or on Christmas Eve.

1 medium eggplant
⅓ cup olive or vegetable oil
1 medium onion, chopped
⅓ cup chopped green bell pepper
2 garlic cloves, crushed
1 4½-ounce jar whole mushrooms, drained, reserve liquid
1 6-ounce can tomato paste
½ cup pimiento-stuffed green olives
¼ cup water and/or mushroom liquid
2 tablespoons red wine vinegar
1½ teaspoons sugar
½ teaspoon dried oregano, crushed
1 teaspoon salt
⅛ teaspoon pepper
1 handful of unsalted capers
2 small, whole, red chili peppers (optional)
1 or 2 bay leaves

1. Pare and dice the eggplant. You will need about 2 cups.

2. Heat the oil in a large heavy skillet. Saute the onion, pepper, and garlic for 2 minutes. Add the eggplant and mushrooms. Toss to mix well, cover, and simmer over very low heat for 10 minutes, stirring once.

3. Stir in the remaining ingredients. Cover and simmer, stirring once, until the eggplant is tender, about 15 minutes.

4. Cool to room temperature. Refrigerate overnight. Serve cold or at room temperature.

Serves 4–8

 Broccoli and Cauliflower  Frittata

VEGETABLES FRIED IN AN EGG BATTER

This recipe makes a great appetizer or side dish.

> ½ *medium-size head of broccoli*
> ½ *medium-size head of cauliflower*
> *3 eggs*
> *salt and freshly ground black pepper*
> *1½ cups fine fresh bread crumbs*
> ½ *cup freshly grated Parmesan cheese*
> *oil*
> *1 large garlic clove*
> *lemon wedges for garnish*

1. Wash and trim the broccoli and cauliflower. Cut them into flowerets. Blanch them separately in salted boiling water about 4 minutes or until tender. Drain well and cool.

2. Beat the eggs in a shallow bowl with salt and pepper.

3. Combine the bread crumbs and grated cheese in a pie plate or shallow dish.

4. Dip the flowerets in the eggs, shaking off the excess. Coat with the bread crumb mixture and shake off the excess. Reserve.

5. Pour oil into a large heavy skillet, to about 1 inch deep. Heat over medium heat. Add the garlic and saute until golden, about 1 minute. Discard the garlic.

6. Fry the breaded flowerets in batches. Turn them over as they cook, until they are golden brown on all sides, about 3 minutes. Adjust the heat as necessary to keep the oil sizzling.

7. Transfer the flowerets to a baking pan lined with paper towels to drain. Keep them warm in the oven at the lowest setting until all of them have been fried. Serve with lemon wedges.

Serves 4–6

 Brocci di Rape  con Fagioli

BROCCOLI RABE WITH BEANS

Brocci di rape, or broccoli rabe, is a slightly bitter vegetable in the broccoli family. It is now a very popular item in our local restaurants, as well as in our homes. Just cook it with the water that remains on the leaves from washing. Although the rabe is wonderful when cooked alone, I like to add beans to the dish. I use canned cannellini or red beans. Even black beans are wonderful.

> **1 bunch broccoli rabe, rinsed in cold water**
> **olive oil**
> **7–10 garlic cloves, thickly slivered**
> **red pepper flakes to taste**
> **salt and pepper to taste**
> **1 19-ounce can of beans (cannellini, red beans, or black beans) (optional)**

1. Trim the broccoli rabe by cutting off the thick, dark leaves. Make several slits in the bottoms of the stems. Cut rabe in half, rinse in cold water, and drain.

2. Using a medium-size heavy saucepan, saute ½ of the garlic and a pinch of red pepper flakes in enough oil to cover bottom of the pan. When garlic is slightly browned but not burned, turn the heat on high and add the drained broccoli rabe a handful at a time, turning each batch over before adding the next.

3. Saute for a few minutes, turning often, adding salt and pepper to taste.

4. Shut off heat, cover, and steam for at least 10 minutes or until tender.

5. Remove broccoli rabe to a warm platter and return pan and juices to stove. Add remaining slivered garlic and a pinch of red pepper flakes and saute a couple of minutes.

6. Add whole can of beans with liquid to pan (optional) and let simmer until heated thoroughly. Adjust seasonings and pour immediately over broccoli rabe.

7. Serve immediately with crusty Italian bread.

Serves 3–4

Fusilli con Brocci di Rape

Once you acquire a taste for broccoli rabe (like my grandchildren have), it will always be included in many of your recipes for a wonderful, healthy meal. In this recipe the pasta can be cooked in advance and then tossed with the wonderful lemony garlic and raisin sauce. Naturally you will need plenty of freshly grated Parmesan and fresh black pepper. We like ours on the dry side, but you can add some of the reserved pasta water to your taste.

> ½ *pound fusilli pasta*
> 1 *bunch of broccoli rabe*
> ¾ *cup olive oil*
> 3 *cloves garlic, thickly slivered*
> *red pepper flakes*
> *salt and pepper to taste*
> ½ *lemon*
> ½ *cup golden raisins*

1. Cook fusilli in boiling salted water according to package directions. Strain, and reserve some of the cooking water.

2. Trim ends of the broccoli rabe and cut through thick part of stems to allow even cooking with the flowers. If the rabe is very large, cut leaves in half.

3. Soak broccoli rabe in cold water, then drain.

4. Meanwhile slowly heat the olive oil in a large heavy skillet. Add garlic slivers and red pepper flakes and simmer till golden. Raise heat and let oil get very hot.

5. Carefully add strained, wet rabe to the hot oil. It is best to do this over the kitchen sink to contain the splatter.

6. Return to high heat and stir constantly till slightly wilted.

7. Add salt and pepper to taste and juice of ½ lemon and toss well.

8. Shut off heat, cover, and let sit for 10 minutes, or until rabe is tender.

9. Return heat to high and add the golden raisins, tossing well.

10. Add strained cooked pasta and toss till mixture is hot and well coated with the garlicky sauce. Adjust seasonings. Add some of the cooking water if a soupy sauce is desired.

11. Place pasta in a large serving bowl and sprinkle with lots of freshly grated Parmesan cheese.

Serves 4

 # Lima Beans Italian Style

Serve these beans with any meat or fish dish. If you wish, you may refrigerate them for several days.

> **3 cups fresh, cooked lima beans or 1 16-ounce package frozen lima beans**
> **1 garlic clove, chopped**
> **4 tablespoons olive oil**
> **⅔ cup canned tomatoes**
> **pinch of dried oregano, red pepper flakes, and mint**
> **salt and freshly ground black pepper to taste**
> **1 cup hot water**
> **1 celery stalk, chopped**
> **freshly grated Parmesan cheese**

1. Drain beans well or, if using frozen beans, defrost.

2. In a medium saucepan, saute the garlic in the olive oil.

3. Add the tomatoes and seasonings. Simmer for 5 minutes, stirring often.

4. Add the water and let the sauce come to a boil.

5. Add the beans and celery, stir well, and let boil gently for a minute or two. Taste and add more seasonings, if desired.

6. Cover and gently boil for about 30 minutes or until the beans are tender. (Do not overcook.)

7. Sprinkle with grated cheese and serve.

Serves 3–4

 # Verdura

DANDELION GREENS

1 pound tender young dandelion greens
1 large baking potato
salt
1 garlic clove, minced
2–3 tablespoons extra-virgin olive oil
fresh black pepper
juice of ½ lemon or to taste
½ teaspoon sugar (optional)

1. Remove the stems from the dandelion greens. Wash the leaves. Cut the leaves into ¼-inch strips, cutting across the leaf.

2. Peel the potato and cut it into ½-inch cubes. Place the potato cubes in cold salted water, bring to a boil, reduce the heat, and gently simmer for 3 to 4 minutes, or until tender. Refresh the potatoes under cold water and drain.

3. Meanwhile, cook the dandelion greens in rapidly boiling salted water for 1 to 2 minutes, or until tender. Refresh under cold water and drain.

4. Mince the garlic. (The recipe can be prepared to this stage up to 12 hours before serving.)

5. Just before serving, heat the olive oil in a skillet over medium heat. Add the garlic and cook for 10 seconds. Add the dandelion greens and potatoes. Add salt and pepper to taste.

6. Saute the vegetables for 2 minutes, or until thoroughly heated. Add lemon juice to taste. If the greens are still bitter, add a little sugar.

Serves 4

 # Stuffed Escarole

1 whole escarole
1 cup fresh bread crumbs, coarsely grated
6 Sicilian dry-cured olives, pitted and chopped
4 garlic cloves
¼ cup grated Parmesan cheese
2 tablespoons fresh parsley, chopped
salt and pepper to taste
olive oil
red pepper flakes (optional)

1. Dip whole escarole continuously in cold water until all dirt particles are removed. Drain in colander.

2. Prepare stuffing in medium-size bowl. Mix together the bread crumbs, olives, 2 finely chopped cloves of garlic, cheese, parsley, and salt and pepper to taste.

3. Slowly drizzle crumb mixture with olive oil until slightly glistening.

4. Take drained escarole and stuff bread mixture into each leaf until stuffing is used up.

5. Tie escarole around the middle with string to keep the stuffing from falling out.

6. Using a large pot, add enough olive oil to generously cover the bottom of the pot. Heat oil on medium heat until warm.

7. Place escarole in pot, pour ½ cup water over escarole, and salt to taste. Add other 2 cloves of garlic, cut in chunks, and some red pepper flakes (optional).

8. Cover and cook until tender.

9. Remove from pan and let cool; remove string and cut in thick slices.

10. Serve warm as a side dish with any meat or fish.

Serves 4

 Escarole Saute

This is a simple, easy recipe that can be served hot or cold, as a side dish, or with beans for a delicious lunch. In some regions of Italy, cooks like to fry some bread crumbs separately in olive oil until crusty brown and add these to the top of the escarole before serving.

> **2 pounds escarole**
> **2 tablespoons olive oil**
> **2 tablespoons vegetable oil**
> **3–4 large garlic cloves, chopped**
> **¼ cup bread crumbs**
> **salt and pepper to taste**
> **red pepper flakes to taste**

1. Trim the escarole and wash thoroughly but quickly.

2. Bring a large pot of water to boiling and blanch the escarole for 5 minutes.

3. Drain escarole and chop coarsely.

4. Using a heavy skillet, heat the two kinds of oil on medium heat.

5. Saute the garlic until browned, and add ¼ cup bread crumbs, and cook till crusty brown.

6. Put heat on high and add drained, chopped escarole, turning it over a few times.

7. Add salt and pepper and red pepper flakes to taste.

8. Transfer to a serving platter and pour hot oil on top.

9. Serve hot or warm.

Serves 2–4

Marinated Mushrooms and Green Beans

This dish can be served as a side dish or over spinach or lettuce salad, tossed with croutons and grated cheese.

2 garlic cloves, chopped
¼ teaspoon grated lemon peel
¼ cup fresh lemon juice
¾ cup olive oil
1 tablespoon chopped fresh parsley
pinch of dried oregano
salt and pepper to taste
½ pound fresh green beans, tips snapped off
2 cups sliced fresh mushrooms
1 tablespoon sliced scallions

1. Combine the first seven ingredients and mix well. Set the dressing aside.

2. Steam the green beans until tender but not soft, then plunge them into cold water. Drain well.

3. Mix the beans with the mushrooms and scallions. Pour the dressing over the vegetables and let them marinate about 2 hours.

Serves 4–6

COOKING VEGETABLES

When cooking vegetables that grow under the ground, such as onions, potatoes, and turnips, cover the pan with a lid. Cook uncovered all vegetables that grow above the ground.

Baked Stuffed Mushrooms with Ricotta

These mushrooms are an excellent appetizer or side dish for a meat meal.

> **10 large fresh mushrooms**
> **¼ cup fresh bread crumbs**
> **2 garlic cloves, pressed**
> **1 tablespoon chopped fresh parsley**
> **2 medium eggs**
> **½ cup ricotta cheese**
> **2 tablespoons freshly grated Parmesan cheese**
> **salt and freshly ground black pepper to taste**
> **2 tablespoons olive oil**

1. Wipe the mushrooms with paper towels. Remove the stems and finely chop them. Mix the chopped mushrooms with the bread crumbs, garlic, parsley, eggs, ricotta, grated cheese, salt, and pepper.

2. Fill each mushroom cap with the stuffing. Place on a shallow ovenproof pan.

3. Lightly drizzle olive oil over each mushroom. Bake on the highest rack in a preheated 350-degree oven for 20 minutes. Let set for 10 minutes before serving.

Serves 5

 Marinated Mushrooms

Serve these mushrooms as an appetizer or put them over a fresh garden salad.

¾ pound small, white fresh mushrooms
4 tablespoons fresh lemon juice
½ teaspoon Dijon-style mustard
¼ teaspoon salt
¼ teaspoon freshly ground black pepper
½ teaspoon dried oregano
½ cup olive oil
2 garlic cloves, halved

1. Wipe the mushrooms with paper towels. Trim the stems.

2. In a large bottle with a tight-fitting lid (a mayonnaise jar will do), combine the lemon juice, mustard, salt, and pepper.

3. Stir until the mustard is blended with the juice and the salt has dissolved. Add the oregano, olive oil, and garlic. Cover the bottle tightly and shake well.

4. Add the mushrooms, cover, and shake again. Marinate in the refrigerator for at least 4 hours, shaking occasionally.

5. Drain the mushrooms before serving. If you are serving them as an appetizer, put them in a small bowl and serve with toothpicks.

Serves 2–4

 # Fanny's Jarred Vinegar Peppers

To purchase the type of vinegar peppers needed for home jarring, you will need to wait until the last week of August or the beginning of September. This is the only time of the year this type of pepper is available. They are shipped to produce centers and disappear fast. The type of pepper you will need is called Santa Nicola, or Saint Nicholas. They are the size of a large tomato and come in green or red. The red ones come either hot or sweet. I like to add a hot red one to my jar for an extra zing, though it is best to use the green ones when pickling, for the red peppers tend to get soft and mushy. The peppers can be packed in any size glass jar—quart, half-gallon, or gallon. The amount of liquid needed can be determined by following the measurement rule of thumb below. Adjust the seasonings according to the size of jar you will be using. This recipe is for a half-gallon jar.

If you first slice the peppers, they will be ready to eat in 2 weeks

30 to 36 peppers
⅓ part white vinegar, ⅓ part cider vinegar, ⅓ part water
1 heaping teaspoon kosher salt (with no iodine)
6 large cloves of thickly sliced garlic
1 heaping tablespoon oregano (preferably fresh dried)

1. Combine the vinegars, water, and salt in a large bowl and set aside.

2. Wash and dry the peppers. Cut large peppers in thick slices and smaller ones in half.

3. Place peppers, garlic, and oregano in jar in layers. Pack tightly in jar.

4. Add the mixture of vinegars, water, and dissolved salt to the jar, pushing the peppers down constantly, as they will try to rise to the top. Add enough liquid to cover the peppers completely. The peppers will absorb the vinegar, so keep adding the liquid mixture until the jar is completely full, keeping the proportions in mind.

5. Secure lid tightly and store in a cool place. The vinegar peppers will be ready to eat after 2 weeks.

As you remove peppers for eating, it will be necessary to keep the remaining peppers covered with extra vinegar mixture. Just repeat the vinegars and water combination.

 Seasoned Fava
Bollito

When I was a little girl visiting with my aunts, my grandfather would give each of us a small dish of fava beans sprinkled with extra salt and tons of pepper freshly ground from my grandmother's pepper mill. What a delicious treat it was to sit down together, pick off the skin, and eat the inside hulk.

1 pound dried fava beans, soaked overnight
3 tablespoons olive oil (use a very good-quality oil)
1 small onion, sliced
salt and freshly ground black pepper to taste
⅓ cup water
chopped fresh parsley for garnish
salt and pepper to taste

1. Shell the soaked fava beans and wash them in cold water. Drain well.

2. Heat the oil in a large heavy pot and saute the onion until golden.

3. Add the fava beans and stir until all of them are coated with oil. Add salt and pepper to taste.

4. Add the ⅓ cup of water and stir. Cover the pot and simmer over low heat until the beans are soft and the water has evaporated. Drain well.

5. Sprinkle with parsley and salt and pepper to taste. Serve immediately as an appetizer or a side dish.

Serves 4–6

 Risotto ai Funghi

RICE WITH FRESH MUSHROOMS

Risotto requires a little more effort than most of my recipes, but it makes a wonderful meal in itself or a side dish to accompany any meats or fish, This risotto recipe is richer than most.

3 tablespoons onion, finely chopped
1 clove garlic, peeled
3 tablespoons olive oil
1 tablespoon parsley, chopped
1 tablespoon celery, chopped
salt and pepper
10 ounces fresh mushrooms, thinly sliced
1 cup milk
1½ cup Italian Arborio rice
4 tablespoons cream
5 cups hot meat broth
1 tablespoon butter
1 cup freshly grated Parmesan cheese

1. In a casserole dish, over medium-high heat, saute the onion and garlic in oil.

2. Add the parsley, celery, and salt and pepper.

3. Discard the garlic when it becomes pale brown.

4. After about 5 minutes, add the mushrooms and cook over low heat. Stir frequently and add the milk to keep the mushrooms tender.

5. Add rice and cream.

6. Cook the rice by adding the meat broth, a ladleful at a time. Stir constantly and add more meat broth to rice mixture as liquid evaporates.

7. When the rice is cooked (approximately 25 minutes), add the butter and cheese. Serve immediately.

Serves 4–6

 # Stuffed Artichokes, Steamed

CARCIOFI ALLA ROMANA

A must for the holidays! After steaming the artichokes, let them rest for at least ½ hour to capture their full flavor.

6 medium-size artichokes
1 lemon, halved
1½ cups fresh bread crumbs (use day-old Italian bread)
¼ cup chopped fresh parsley
½ cup freshly grated Parmesan cheese
2 garlic cloves, chopped
salt and pepper to taste
olive oil
4 garlic cloves, halved

To Prepare Artichokes

1. Soak the artichokes in cold water for a half hour to release dirt.

2. Cut off the stems of artichokes with a sharp knife. Carefully cut straight across the top to remove the prickly tips. Stand the artichoke upside down and give it a firm whack to open the leaves slightly for stuffing. Repeat with the other artichokes.

3. Squeeze insides with fresh lemon juice.

To Prepare Stuffing

To eat the artichokes, scrape off pulpy ends between your teeth.

1. Mix together in a large bowl the bread crumbs, parsley, grated cheese, chopped garlic, salt, and pepper. Add enough oil to slightly moisten the mixture. Toss the crumbs with enough oil until they glisten slightly but are not soaked. Fill each cavity of the artichokes (inside the leaves) with stuffing until well packed. Squeeze lemon juice over the artichokes; reserve the used lemon. Lightly sprinkle a little salt over artichoke tops and sides.

2. Put 1 cup water and 1 tablespoon of salt in a deep saucepan.

3. Add the artichokes. Toss the 4 halved garlic cloves and used lemon into bottom of pan.

4. Drizzle the tops with olive oil. Cover and let the water come to a boil. Lower the heat, and let the artichokes simmer about 45 minutes or until tender.

5. Serve warm or at room temperature, not hot.

Serves 4

 # Joanne's Spicy White Rice

olive oil
1 large soft green tomato, chopped
1 large ripe red tomato, chopped
1 small onion, chopped
1 clove garlic, chopped
salt and pepper to taste
1 cup converted rice, washed and picked over

To serve 10–12: Use 5 cups water, 2 teaspoons salt; then add 2 cups rice.

1. Using a medium-size saucepan, add enough olive oil to just cover the bottom of the pan.

2. Using medium heat, saute the chopped vegetables until tender. Add salt and pepper to taste and 2½ cups water. Cover.

3. When the water comes to a boil, add the rice. Stir well and cover.

4. Let simmer for 15 minutes and then shut the heat off. Push the pan to the back of the stove and let it set until the rice is fluffy.

Serves 6–8

 # Leek Patties

These patties are a good accompaniment to fish or meat.

> **4 leeks, trimmed and thinly sliced**
> **4 slices white bread, cubed**
> **¼ cup milk**
> **1 egg**
> **salt and pepper to taste**
> **½ cup flour, preferably semolina**
> **1 onion, thickly sliced**
> **½ cup olive oil**

1. Cover the leeks in salted boiling water and cook until they are tender.

2. Meanwhile, soak the bread cubes in the milk.

3. Drain the leeks well. Mix them with the soaked bread (thoroughly squeezed), egg, salt, and pepper.

4. Roll into medium-size patties. Slightly flatten the patties with your hands and quickly coat both sides with flour. Place the patties on a large platter and reserve.

5. In a large heavy skillet, saute the sliced onion until transparent in the olive oil. (Do not burn.)

6. Discard the onion and gently fry the patties on both sides until golden brown. Transfer to paper towels to drain before serving.

Yield: 6–8 patties

 # La Giambotta

ITALIAN VEGETABLE STEW

When I was a child, my mother would collect all the leftover vegetables and cook them into this wonderful stew. We would eat this stew for lunch with lots of cheese and bastone bread.

1 garlic clove, chopped
1 large onion, chopped
½ cup olive oil
1 8-ounce can whole tomatoes
2 tablespoons tomato paste
salt and freshly ground black pepper to taste
pinch of dried oregano, red pepper flakes, basil, and mint
½ cup hot water
1 pound zucchini, cubed
2 medium potatoes, peeled and cubed
1 green bell pepper, thickly sliced
2 celery stalks, sliced
1 pound string beans, trimmed and cut in 1-inch pieces
grated Parmesan cheese (optional)

1. In a large heavy skillet, saute the garlic and onion in the olive oil for 3 minutes.

2. Add the tomatoes, mashing them slightly with a large fork. Stir well, and add the tomato paste, salt, pepper, and a sprinkle of the seasonings. Stir gently about 5 minutes until well blended.

3. Add the hot water and stir well. Let the sauce come to a gentle boil.

4. Add the zucchini, potatoes, green pepper, celery, beans, and additional seasonings to taste. Let the mixture come to a gentle boil, cover, and simmer until the vegetables are tender, but not mushy.

5. Shut off the heat and let the stew rest for about 15 minutes for a better flavor. Serve it in bowls, accompanied by crusty garlic bread and salad. Sprinkle with Parmesan cheese (optional).

Serves 3–4

 # My Nonna's String Beans and Potatoes

One evening my friend Barbara came for a visit. She mentioned her son Richard and how much he desired string beans and potatoes prepared the way his grandmother used to make it.. Naturally, I set forth to my mother's house. She gave me the list of ingredients needed, and we both stayed by the kitchen table while she prepared the vegetables. I sat and wrote down every step. Sometimes she slipped by and did things automatically—I couldn't take my eyes off her for a second. When the dish was finished, I had this wonderful recipe to pass on to you, straight from our peasant kitchens of years past..

1½ pounds string beans, trimmed
4 medium-size potatoes, peeled
olive oil
1 large onion, cut in large chunks
1 garlic clove, chopped
1 6-ounce can of tomato paste
1 (35-ounce) can peeled plum tomatoes
salt and pepper to taste
red pepper flakes
1 tablespoon fresh parsley, chopped
4½ cups water

1. Snap string beans in half and rinse in cold water. Reserve.

2. Wash potatoes, cut in medium-size cubes, and soak in enough water to cover. Reserve.

3. Using a wide 6-quart pan, add enough oil to cover bottom.

4. Using medium heat, saute onions and garlic until translucent.

5. Add tomato paste and, using a wooden spoon, stir mixture until well blended.

6. Strain tomatoes and put through blender until coarsely chopped. Add to sauce and stir well.

7. Add salt and pepper to taste, a pinch of red pepper flakes, and parsley. Stir well.

8. Let sauce come to a full boil and add 4½ cups water.

9. Return sauce to boil and add cut string beans. Stir a couple of times and cook about 15 minutes or until tender.

10. Remove beans and reserve to a warm place.

11. Bring sauce to a boil again, and add potatoes.

12. Stir a couple of times, then cook about 30–35 minutes or until tender, stirring only once or twice to prevent sticking.

13. Add string beans to potatoes in sauce, and bring to a soft boil. Adjust seasonings and simmer together for an additional 5–10 minutes just to blend.

14. Let mixture rest 10 minutes, then serve in bowls with garlic bread or crusty Italian bread.

Serves 6

 # Budino di Patate

MASHED POTATOES BAKED WITH EGGS AND CHEESE

This simple dish is simply delicious—and a great way to use up leftover mashed potatoes.

> **4 medium-size potatoes**
> **2 cups freshly grated Parmesan cheese**
> **2 eggs**
> **1 cup milk**
> **salt and pepper to taste**
> **6 tablespoons butter**

1. Preheat oven to 400 degrees.

2. Boil the potatoes whole until tender.

3. Drain and carefully peel potatoes while hot.

4. Place in a medium-sized bowl and mash.

5. Add the cheese, eggs, milk, and salt and pepper. Mix thoroughly until well blended.

6. Transfer to a baking dish smeared with butter, bake for about 30 minutes or until outsides look slightly browned.

7. Serve immediately.

Serves 4–6

 Spinach and Potatoes,  Ma's Way

Because we were poor when I was growing up, my mother would make our lunches for school by using any leftovers from the night before. We always had spinach in the refrigerator, and so we would bring our oil-sopped crusty Italian bread and garlicky spinach sandwiches to school. How wonderful this tasted, and how lucky I felt to bring something special from our kitchen at home.

> **1 cup water**
> **2 packages dry, cleaned spinach**
> **4 medium potatoes, peeled and cubed**
> **olive oil**
> **6–8 cloves garlic, thickly slivered**
> **1 tablespoon red pepper flakes**
> **salt and pepper to taste**

1. Using a large pan, bring 1 cup of water to a boil.

2. Add spinach, cover, and steam for 3 minutes, turning only once or twice.

3. Remove from heat, drain thoroughly, and set aside.

4. Boil potatoes, in enough salted water to cover, until tender. Drain, reserving some water.

5. Combine spinach and potatoes and place on a serving platter. Add salt and pepper to taste.

6. In a small skillet, slowly heat enough oil to cover bottom of pan. Saute chopped garlic and red pepper flakes until garlic is golden brown and almost burned.

7. Immediately pour hot garlic oil over spinach and potatoes. This will sizzle, so be careful.

8. Adjust seasonings. If more sauce is desired, you may add the heated reserved potato water.

9. Let mixture set and serve with strong, crusty Italian bread to sop the juices.

Serves 3–4

 Frittata con Spinaci

SPINACH OMELETTE

2 cups steamed spinach
2 tablespoons olive oil
salt and pepper to taste
pepper flakes
6 fresh eggs
¾ cup milk
¼ cup grated Parmesan cheese
3 ounces butter

1. Chop spinach, which has been steamed, and quickly saute in olive oil for one minute.

2. Season with salt and pepper to taste and red pepper flakes.

3. Using a fork or whisk, beat eggs with milk and salt and pepper to taste until fluffy.

4. Add grated cheese and beat until well blended.

5. Heat butter in a medium-size skillet on medium heat.

6. Slowly add beaten eggs, pushing with fork, until all the egg is used and slightly puffy. Cook until nicely browned.

7. Turn omelette over; cook for one minute.

8. Add cooked spinach to top of omelette and fold over.

9. Cut in serving size portions and serve immediately.

Eggs and spinach may be cooked in smaller portions for individual servings.

Serves 4–6

Pastries, Cookies, and Desserts

 Cannoli

Cannoli are made for holidays like Easter and Christmas. They store well in covered canisters and can be made at least a week in advance. The filling can be made a day or two ahead, but don't fill the shells in advance, as they will get soggy. You will need to purchase aluminum tubes from a specialty store. Buy a dozen. Aluminum will not sink to the bottom of the pan, so the cannoli shells cannot get oily. Make about 8 cannoli at a time. Remove cooked shells from the pan and start again.

Shells

$1\frac{3}{4}$ **cups all-purpose flour**
$\frac{1}{2}$ **teaspoon salt**
$\frac{1}{4}$ **teaspoon cinnamon**
1 tablespoon granulated sugar
1 egg, slightly beaten
2 tablespoons firm butter, crumbled
$\frac{1}{4}$ **cup port wine**
1 egg yolk, slightly beaten
1 can vegetable shortening

1. Sift flour with salt, cinnamon, and granulated sugar.

2. Make a well in center of flour mixture and add beaten egg and crumbled butter.

3. Work with fingertips to blend well until the flour is moist.

4. Add wine a little at a time, until dough just clings together.

5. Knead for at least 5 minutes, or until the dough is smooth.

6. Form dough into a loaf shape, flatten down, cover, and let rest for at least 20 minutes.

7. Cut dough into four portions.

8. Roll 1 portion at a time, on a lightly floured surface, until paper-thin.

9. Using a biscuit cutter, cut out circles of dough about 3½ inches in diameter. Patch all the scrap pieces and use for additional shells. Continue rolling and cutting until all the dough is used up.

10. Wrap each piece of cut dough loosely around the aluminum tubes, pressing ends of dough to flare slightly.

11. Seal middle edges together with beaten egg yolk. Press lightly with fingertips till middle edges are well sealed. This step is important, or shells will open during cooking and cannot be filled.

12. Heat shortening until very hot (350 degrees). Use a wide, semi-deep, heavy pan. Drop 3–4 cannoli, attached to aluminum tubes, in the hot oil (do not crowd) and fry 2–3 minutes, turning often with tongs, until golden brown but not burned.

13. Drain on paper towels, and let cool a minute.

14. With a clean dish towel, hold shell lightly and, with other hand, pull out tube. Be careful or shell will crumble if you bear down too hard.

15. Continue until all the dough pieces are cooked.

16. Finished cannoli may be filled with either ricotta or cooked cream fillings (recipes follow).

Yield: 25 shells

Ricotta Filling

> *2 pounds ricotta*
> *2 cups confectioners' sugar, plus extra for topping*
> *½ teaspoon cinnamon*
> *4 teaspoons vanilla (I use white)*
> *¼ cup semisweet chocolate chips, crushed*
> *2 tablespoons chopped citron*
> *½ cup lemon peel, grated*
> *chopped pistachio or walnuts (optional)*

1. Using a large bowl, mix ricotta with 2 cups of confectioners' sugar and add remaining ingredients except nuts until well blended.

2. Chill several hours or overnight.

3. When ready to serve, fill shells with ricotta mixture, using a long thin spoon or a pastry tube.

4. Sprinkle confectioners' sugar generously over cannoli.

5. Garnish ends with chopped nuts.

6. Serve immediately.

Panna Cotta, or Cooked Cream Filling

For a combination of fillings, use half the amount of boiled cream; then add the chocolate to the remaining half for a nice presentation. Be sure to sprinkle the cannoli with lots of confectioners' sugar before serving.

2 eggs, slightly beaten
⅔ cup sugar
¼ cup cornstarch
pinch of salt
2 cups whole milk
1 teaspoon lemon zest, grated (optional)
2 teaspoons vanilla flavoring (optional)

1. Whisk together the eggs and sugar in a small heavy saucepan.

2. In a small bowl whisk the cornstarch with ½ cup of the milk until slightly pasty. Add the pinch of salt and remaining milk. Mix well.

3. Slowly pour the milk mixture into the saucepan with eggs and whisk thoroughly.

4. Place over low heat and cook for 10 minutes or more, stirring constantly, until the mixture comes to a soft boil and is shiny and of pudding consistency. Do not allow to burn.

5. Remove pan from heat and stir in the lemon zest or vanilla.

6. Pour into a small bowl and cover with wax paper, placing the paper directly on the cooked cream to prevent a skin from forming on top.

7. Cool and refrigerate until needed. This keeps 3–4 days.

8. When ready to use, whisk until smooth if the filling has separated.

Yield: filling for 6–8 cannoli

For chocolate cream, whisk an additional ½ cup sugar with the eggs and add ¾ cup shaved unsweetened chocolate to the hot cooked cream, stirring well.

 Zeppole di San  Giuseppe

ST. JOSEPH'S DAY CREAM PUFFS

This recipe was donated by one of our senior citizens. Please enjoy.

1 cup hot water
1 stick butter
1 tablespoon sugar
½ teaspoon salt
1 cup sifted flour
4 fresh eggs
1 teaspoon grated orange peel
1 teaspoon grated lemon peel

1. Bring water, butter, sugar, and salt to boil in a saucepan.

2. Add flour all at once. Stir vigorously with a wooden spoon until mixture leaves sides of pan and forms a smooth ball (about 3 minutes).

3. Remove from heat and quickly beat in eggs, one at a time, beating until smooth after each addition. Continue beating until mixture is smooth and shiny.

4. Add grated peels.

5. Drop mixture by tablespoons onto a lightly greased baking sheet, about 2 inches apart.

6. Bake in a preheated 425-degree oven for 15 minutes.

7. Lower heat to 350 degrees and bake until golden brown, about 15–20 minutes more.

8. Remove to rack and cool completely.

9. Cut a slit in side of each puff, using a sharp knife.

10. Fill with cream filling or whipped cream.

Yield: about 16–18 puffs

Cream Filling

¾ *cup sugar*
⅓ *cup flour*
pinch of salt
2 cups scalded milk
1 teaspoon vanilla
2 eggs, slightly beaten

TO SCALD MILK

Before heating milk in a saucepan, rinse the pan with water. This way it will not scorch as easily.

1. Using a medium-size bowl, mix sugar, flour, and salt.

2. Add hot scalded milk gradually.

3. Pour into top of double boiler, directly over bottom pan of boiling hot water. Over medium heat, stir constantly until mixture thickens, about 2–3 minutes.

4. Remove pan from heat and cool for 10 minutes.

5. Add vanilla and quickly whisk in slightly beaten eggs.

6. Replace on top of boiler pan and cook for 2–3 minutes, using low heat.

7. Remove from heat, cover, and cool.

8. Chill in refrigerator and fill cream puffs as needed.

9. Sprinkle filled puffs with confectioners' sugar.

 Ricotta Cream Puffs

These are a lovely dessert and are easier to prepare than you may think. They also are very convenient to make for company. The cream puffs may be baked early in the day and filled a couple of hours before serving.

Cream Puffs

> *½ cup solid vegetable shortening*
> *⅛ teaspoon salt*
> *1 cup boiling water*
> *1 cup sifted flour*
> *3 eggs*

1. Add the shortening and salt to the cup of boiling water and stir over medium heat until the mixture resumes boiling.

2. Lower the heat. Add the flour all at once and stir vigorously until the mixture leaves the sides of the pan.

3. Remove the pan from the heat. Add the eggs, one at a time, beating thoroughly after each addition.

4. Shape on an ungreased cookie sheet, using a tablespoon of batter for each cream puff. You may use a pastry bag if you wish.

5. Bake in a preheated 450-degree oven for about 20 minutes. Then reduce the temperature to 350 degrees and bake for 20 minutes longer.

6. Remove the cream puffs from the oven and place on a rack to cool.

Ricotta Filling

> *¼ cup confectioners' sugar*
> *¼ teaspoon grated lemon or orange rind*
> *1 teaspoon vanilla extract*
> *1 pound ricotta, well chilled*

1. Add the confectioners' sugar, lemon or orange rind, and vanilla to the ricotta. Blend. Do not stir too long; just use quick strokes to mix all the ingredients or the ricotta will become too soft and milky and seep through the puffs.

To Finish Preparation:

1. Cut the tops off the cooled cream puffs. Save the tops.

2. Fill the puffs with the filling. Replace the tops and dust with sifted confectioners' sugar. Refrigerate up to 2 hours before serving.

Yield: approximately 2½ dozen

 # Easter Sweet Ricotta Pie

This pie is the star of stars at Easter time. In my neighborhood if you didn't include it on your Easter menu, then nothing else mattered. This recipe is foolproof. If you follow the directions and use only the freshest ingredients, you will make a beautiful pie.

Pasta Frolla

> *2 cups all-purpose flour*
> *1 cup confectioners' sugar*
> *½ teaspoon baking powder*
> *½ teaspoon salt*
> *4 egg yolks (reserve whites)*
> *4 tablespoons vegetable shortening, melted*
> *1 teaspoon vanilla or orange extract*
> *1 tablespoon ice-cold water*

1. Using a medium-size bowl, sift together flour, sugar, baking powder, and salt.

2. Make a well in the flour mixture and add, all at once, the egg yolks, melted shortening, and vanilla or orange extract.

3. Mix with a large fork until mixture resembles coarse crumbs.

4. Add just enough ice water to make dough just moist enough to stick together. If dough still seems dry, keep hands damp until dough clings together instead of adding more water.

5. Roll into a ball shape and wrap in plastic. Slightly flatten the package of dough and refrigerate while you make the filling.

6. When filling is completed, take dough out of refrigerator and break off ⅔ of the piece; keep other ⅓ wrapped.

7. Using a wooden board or counter, place dough between 2 pieces of waxed paper. Roll dough until it will generously overhang a 9-inch Pyrex glass dish or tin plate.

8. Roll out remaining dough between waxed paper into a 9½-inch round. Using a fluted cookie cutter, cut this round into lattice strips at least 1 inch wide.

Filling

> *2 pounds ricotta cream cheese, firm*
> *1 cup confectioners' sugar, sifted*
> *1 teaspoon cinnamon*
> *grated peel of 1 orange*
> *grated peel of 2 lemons*
> *1 teaspoon vanilla extract*
> *½ cup white chocolate chips, crushed (optional)*
> *4 egg whites, stiffly beaten*
> *milk*

1. Place ricotta cheese in a large bowl and stir with fork until mashed.

2. Add sugar, cinnamon, grated peels, and vanilla extract.

3. Using a large spatula, gently fold in stiffly whipped egg whites. Blend well.

4. Pour into prepared pie shell and form a criss-cross pattern with remaining lattice strips to make top crust.

5. Brush with milk and bake in preheated 350-degree oven for 50 minutes or until golden brown in color.

6. Cool on wire rack at least 2 hours.

7. Sprinkle with confectioners' sugar.

8. Serve warm or loosely cover with plastic wrap and refrigerate until needed.

9. Dust with additional powdered sugar before serving.

Serves 8–10

Because this is a rich pie, you will need a sharp knife that has been dipped in water to cut the pie into thin wedges.

 # Ricotta Cake

This is a light, pielike treat. It can be made a day or two before serving and kept refrigerated.

> **3 pounds ricotta cheese**
> **2 cups sugar**
> **8 eggs, separated**
> **½ cup sifted flour**
> **grated rind of 1 lemon**
> **1 teaspoon vanilla extract**
> **½ cup cream, whipped**
> **graham cracker crumbs (enough to coat pan)***

1. In a large bowl, using a wire whisk, beat the ricotta until smooth. Gradually add 1½ cups of the sugar and the egg yolks, beating after each addition. Beat in the flour, lemon rind, and vanilla.

2. In another bowl, beat the 8 egg whites with the remaining ½ cup sugar.

3. Gently fold the whipped cream and the beaten egg whites into the ricotta mixture.

4. Turn the batter into a 12-inch springform pan that has been well buttered and sprinkled with graham cracker crumbs.

5. Bake in a preheated 425-degree oven for 10 minutes. Lower the temperature to 350 degrees and continue baking for 1 hour.

6. Turn off the heat and allow the cake to cook in the oven with the door closed.

7. Refrigerate the cake until serving time. Top it with crushed sugared strawberries or cherries before serving.

Serves 12.

* For this recipe, you may substitute graham cracker crumbs with pasta frolla (a crust of butter and sugar combined with flour), or the crust for Pizza Rustica, or your favorite pie crust recipe.

TO MAKE CREAM WHIP

When cream will not whip, add the white of an egg to it. Refrigerate both cream and egg white thoroughly, try again, and it will whip easily.

 # Pizza Rustica

DEEP-DISH RICOTTA PIE

This is a truly excellent dessert. It is nice to serve at a party because it makes enough pieces to serve a large group.

Pastry

> *2 cups sifted flour*
> *¾ teaspoon salt*
> *⅔ cup solid vegetable shortening*
> *1 egg*
> *6–8 tablespoons cold water*

1. Sift the flour with the salt into a large mixing bowl. Cut in the shortening until the mixture resembles cornmeal.

2. Add the egg and water. Blend together with quick motions.

3. Roll out the dough in a large rectangle to fit a glass or metal baking dish about 12 inches long, 8 inches wide, and 2 inches deep. Press it into the baking dish. Set aside while you prepare the filling.

Ricotta Pie Filling

> *2 pounds ricotta cheese*
> *1½ cups sugar*
> *½ teaspoon salt*
> *4 eggs, separated*
> *2 teaspoons vanilla extract*
> *1 cup milk*
> *confectioners' sugar*

1. Put the ricotta, sugar, salt, egg yolks, vanilla, and milk in a large bowl. Using a wooden spoon, blend until smooth.

2. Beat egg whites just until foamy, but not stiff. Gently fold into the ricotta mixture. Carefully pour the filling into the pastry shell.

3. Bake the pie in a preheated 400-degree oven for 20 minutes. Reduce the heat to 375 degrees and bake 45 minutes longer. Remove from the oven and cool. Sprinkle with confectioners' sugar.

4. Cut into wedges and serve cold or at room temperature, or refrigerate if holding several hours.

Yield: approximately 20 pieces

 # Biscotti

I have been making this recipe for so long and yet I still get raves. My friend Nancy first helped me with the recipe, then I made a few changes to suit my style. Biscotti are dry, plain cookies enhanced by the flavor of anise. They are excellent with coffee, cappuccino, or espresso and make a nice snack to help curb your appetite before meals.

> **2 cups flour (King Arthur preferred)**
> **2 teaspoons baking powder**
> **½ teaspoon salt**
> **3 eggs, well beaten**
> **1 cup sugar**
> **1 stick butter or margarine, melted**
> **2 teaspoons vanilla extract**
> **1½ tablespoons anise extract**
> **1 cup chopped walnuts (optional)**
> **½ cup dried cranberries (optional)**
> **½ cup miniature chocolate chips (optional)**

1. Preheat oven to 350 degrees.

2. In a small bowl sift together with flour, baking powder, and salt.

3. In a large bowl beat together with an electric mixer on medium speed the beaten eggs, sugar, melted butter, and the 2 extracts.

4. Stir the flour into the bowl with egg mixture and stir on slow speed of mixer until smooth and firm.

5. Remove from mixer onto a floured board or counter.

6. Gently knead dough, using floured hands. If the dough is too soft to handle, add more flour as needed.

7. Knead in the walnuts, cranberries, and chips, if using.

8. Cut dough in 3 parts.

9. Put dough pieces on ungreased cookie sheet and form dough into 3 log shapes, each about 6 inches long. Flatten slightly. If smaller cookies are desired, make 6 smaller loaves instead.

10. Bake logs in hot oven for about 25 minutes for large logs or 20 minutes for small logs. It is best to keep cookie sheets on middle rack of oven and away from oven sides, or logs will burn on bottoms. You will have to check them periodically to prevent burning. Remove from oven when slightly browned. If bottoms burn, scrape with the smallest part of a cheese grater.

11. Cool logs on a rack for 5 minutes, then, while still warm, slice them diagonally into ½-inch slices using a long, small saw-like knife.

12. Place the slices cut-side down on the ungreased baking sheet and return to 350-degree oven to toast until they turn a light golden color (about 10–15 minutes).

13. Remove from oven, cool, and store in a covered container. They will keep fresh at least three weeks.

Yield: about 2 dozen large cookies or 45 small cookies

 # Chocolate Walnut
Biscotti

I love this recipe! Make the plain biscotti, and if you have the time, make this chocolate one also. These biscotti recipes are so easy to make, and the combination of the two of them looks inviting when served on a doily-lined decorative platter.

2 cups unbleached flour (King Arthur preferred)
½ cup cocoa powder (Hershey's preferred)
1 teaspoon baking soda
1 teaspoon salt
¾ stick unsalted butter
1 cup sugar
2 large eggs, slightly beaten
1 teaspoon orange extract
½ teaspoon cinnamon
1 teaspoon vanilla
1 cup walnuts, chopped
1 cup semisweet chocolate chips
confectioners' sugar

1. Preheat oven to 350 degrees.

2. Butter and flour a large cookie pan.

3. In a small bowl, using a wire whisk, mix flour, cocoa powder, baking soda, and salt.

4. In a large bowl, using an electric mixer, cream butter and sugar.

5. Add eggs, orange extract, and vanilla.

6. Stir flour mixture into bowl with egg mixture to form a stiff dough.

7. Remove dough from mixer, and using a floured board, gently knead walnuts into the dough. If dough is too soft to handle, add more flour.

8. Cut dough into 3 parts. Place all 3 pieces onto one baking sheet.

9. With floured hands, form 3 long log shapes, slightly flattening each one with hands. (By keeping the shapes long, cookies will cook well inside and will cut easily.)

10. Sprinkle tops with a generous amount of confectioners' sugar.

11. Bake for 25–30 minutes on middle rack of oven.

12. Remove baking sheet from oven and cool cookies for 5 minutes.

13. Remove to a cutting board and cut the loaves diagonally into ½-inch slices while still warm. You will need a long, small, saw-like knife. Work quickly or the cookies will break.

14. Return cookies, cut side down, to ungreased baking sheet and bake in 350-degree oven until crisp (about 10 minutes).

15. Remove from oven and cool biscotti completely.

16. Store airtight. Cookies will stay fresh at least 2 weeks; they also freeze well.

Yield: about 36 cookies

 # Tortoni

This is a good recipe, but one that requires careful attention. Take your time, and you will be pleased with the end result.

> **6 egg yolks**
> **pinch of salt**
> **3 tablespoons warm water**
> **¾ cup sugar**
> **¼ cup water**
> **1 tablespoon vanilla extract**
> **3 tablespoons sherry**
> **1 pint heavy cream**
> **½ cup chopped almonds**

1. Combine the egg yolks, salt, and warm water in the top of a double boiler. Over boiling water, beat until the yolks are light and lemon colored. Set aside.

2. Boil the sugar and ¼ cup water over medium heat, stirring constantly, until the syrup spins a thread from the end of a spoon.

3. Cool the syrup slightly, then beat it into the egg yolks, beating rapidly and constantly. Cook over hot, not boiling, water, stirring constantly, until thick, about 8 minutes. Remove from heat and cool to room temperature.

4. Add the vanilla and sherry and let the mixture cool some more.

5. Beat the cream until it is thick but not stiff. Stir the cream into the custard. Pour into 12 fluted paper cups.

6. Sprinkle the tops with the chopped almonds. Put the cups in the freezer.

7. Freeze until firm, about 3 hours, or for a few days. If desired, tortoni may be frozen in ice cube trays and served in sherbet glasses.

Serves 12

 # Biscuit Tortoni

Here is another tortoni recipe, but one that uses different ingredients. It makes a very elegant company dessert.

½ cup crushed Italian macaroons (without almonds)
½ cup crushed toasted almonds
¼ cup confectioners' sugar
2 cups heavy cream
3 tablespoons rum
6 maraschino cherries for garnish

1. Mix together the crushed macaroons, three-fourths of the almonds, confectioners' sugar, and 1 cup of the cream.

2. Whip the second cup of cream until it is stiff. Fold it into the macaroon mixture, alternating with the rum.

3. Spoon into small paper cups and freeze. After 2 hours, sprinkle with tops with the remaining crushed almonds. Place a maraschino cherry in the center of each cup. Return the desserts to the freezer until serving time.

Serves 6

 Zabaglione

Serve this in pretty dessert glasses as the perfect ending for an elegant meal or for a special dinner party.

4 egg yolks
4 tablespoons sugar
¾ cup port or Marsala wine
pinch of cinnamon

1. Beat the yolks until they are light and lemon colored. Gradually add the sugar, beating constantly. Add the wine and beat well.

2. Pour into the top of a double boiler and cook over hot, not boiling, water until thick, beating constantly with a rotary beater.

3. Pour into dessert dishes, sprinkle with cinnamon, and serve. Or chill and serve as a sauce over fruit.

Serves 6

 # Brandied
Cherries

These cherries must be stored for a month before using. This can be helpful if you are making them for a holiday when you will be busy with other things.

> **2 pounds Bing cherries**
> **2 cups brandy**
> **2 cups sugar**
> **1 cup water**

1. Wash the cherries and cut off half of each stem.

2. Place the cherries in two sterilized quart jars and cover them with the brandy. Cover the jars, but do not seal. Let stand overnight.

3. Boil the sugar and water together for 10 minutes. Skim the surface and cool.

4. Drain the brandy from the cherries and add it to the syrup. Stir well. Pour the liquid back into the jars over the cherries. Seal tightly. Store in a cool, dark cupboard.

Yield: 2 quarts

 # Marguerita Cake

This cake is a sweet, crisp, sponge-type cake with rum frosting. It is great for the holidays or other special occasions.

> **5 eggs (separated)**
> **½ cup confectioners' sugar**
> **1 tablespoon lemon juice**
> **¼ teaspoon almond extract**
> **½ cup potato flour, sifted**
> **½ teaspoon vanilla extract**

1. Preheat oven to 375 degrees.
2. Beat egg yolks until thick and lemon colored.
3. Add sugar gradually and beat for about 5 minutes.
4. Add lemon juice and almond extract.
5. Fold in sifted flour.
6. Beat egg whites until they hold a peak. Fold them into cake batter.
7. Grease a 10-inch square cake pan and sprinkle with additional confectioners' sugar.
8. Pour batter into pan and top with more confectioners' sugar.
9. Bake for approximately 30 minutes or until cake springs back when touched.
10. Cool on a wire rack and sprinkle cake with vanilla extract.

Chiacciata al Rum *(Rum Frosting)*

> **1 cup butter**
> **2 cups cocoa powder**
> **4 cups confectioners' sugar, sifted**
> **2 egg yolks**
> **2 tablespoons rum**

1. Cream butter, cocoa, and sugar until well blended.

2. Beat egg yolks until thick and lemon colored, add to cream mixture.

3. Add rum and beat thoroughly.

4. Frost cake and serve.

Serves 6–8

Savoiardi

LADY FINGERS

I like to serve these with a cup of coffee or use them in any recipe calling for lady fingers.

4 eggs, separated
⅛ teaspoon salt
10 tablespoons sugar
2 teaspoons vanilla extract
⅓ cup sifted flour

1. Cut a brown paper bag to line two cookie sheets.

2. Beat the egg whites and salt until foamy. Add 2 tablespoons of the sugar, and beat until soft peaks form. Set aside.

3. In another bowl, beat the egg yolks until thickened. Then gradually beat in the remaining sugar and the vanilla. Beat until very thick and lemon colored.

4. Sprinkle the flour over the egg yolk mixture. Then fold in the flour carefully. Now fold the egg yolk mixture into the egg whites.

5. Using a pastry tube or spoon, make 3-inch-long finger shapes of batter 2 inches apart on the brown paper.

6. Bake in a preheated 350-degree oven for 5 minutes, or until deep golden brown. Cool 2 to 3 minutes.

7. With a sharp knife, carefully remove the lady fingers from the paper. Store in an airtight container when dry and cool.

Yield: 3 dozen

 # Vincenzo's Zucchini Bread

Vincent was a former employer of the North End Union and very interested in health food. His zucchini bread was so rich and moist, it was like eating a complete meal. It became one of our favorite recipes.

> **3 eggs**
> **2¼ cups sugar**
> **2 cups shredded zucchini**
> **1½ teaspoons vanilla extract**
> **1 cup oil**
> **3 cups flour**
> **½ teaspoon baking powder**
> **4 teaspoons cinnamon**
> **1 teaspoon baking soda**
> **1 teaspoon salt**
> **1 cup chopped nuts**

1. Mix the first five ingredients in a large bowl.

2. Mix the next five ingredients in a second bowl.

3. Mix the dry ingredients into the zucchini mixture. Add the chopped nuts.

4. Grease and flour two 9x5-inch loaf pans. Pour in the batter.

5. Bake at 350 degrees for 1 hour. (They may take a little longer, so test with a toothpick.) Cool and serve at room temperature.

This bread may be frozen.

Serves 14

 # Sweet Wine Strips

STRICCIA

Wine strips are an excellent, fancy Italian cookie. They are so crisp and light, your guests will never stop eating them.

2 cups all-purpose flour
½ teaspoon baking powder
3 tablespoons sugar
¼ cup butter
½ cup Italian red wine
2 cups oil
½ cup confectioners' sugar
1 teaspoon cinnamon

1. Sift the flour, measure, and resift with the baking powder and sugar.

2. Cut the butter into the flour with your fingers until the mixture resembles cornmeal. Make a well in the flour and pour the wine into it. Mix the wine into the flour. Knead the dough until smooth, about 5 minutes.

3. Wrap the dough in waxed paper and set aside for 2 hours. Do not chill.

4. Roll the dough into a rectangle, ¼ inch thick. Cut it into strips 1 inch wide and 4 inches long.

5. In a deep heavy skillet or pan, heat the oil on medium-high heat.

6. Drop about 4 strips of dough at a time into the hot oil, and fry until they are golden brown. Turn them over as they rise to the surface (using a pair of tongs makes this easy).

7. Remove the strips from the oil with tongs or a slotted spoon and drain on absorbent paper. Repeat until all the strips are fried.

8. Combine the confectioners' sugar and cinnamon. Sprinkle it over the strips when they are cool. Arrange on a pretty platter and serve.

These will keep in a covered container for a while. Put a piece of paper toweling in the bottom of the container to absorb any moisture. Do not sprinkle with confectioners' sugar until just before serving.

Yield: 2½ dozen

 # Cenci

FRIED BOWKNOTS

These are light and delicate, oddly shaped cookies. They are very interesting for an afternoon tea or a special luncheon dessert. Some people like to drizzle them with honey and sprinkle on multicolored candies for a colorful effect.

> **4 egg yolks**
> **1 egg white**
> **½ teaspoon salt**
> **¼ cup confectioners' sugar, plus more for dusting**
> **1 teaspoon vanilla extract**
> **1 teaspoon rum**
> **1 cup flour**
> **1 3-pound can solid vegetable shortening**

These keep very well in a covered container, with a piece of paper towel on the bottom of the container. Do not sprinkle with the sugar until just before serving.

1. Combine the egg yolks and egg white. Add the salt and beat 8–10 minutes on high speed with an electric mixer, or use a wire whisk and beat rapidly.

2. Add the sugar and flavorings and beat until well blended, about 2 minutes. Add the flour a little at a time, lightly folding it in.

3. Transfer the dough to a well-floured surface and knead until the dough blisters, about 5 minutes. If no blisters form, and the dough seems quite smooth, cover it with a towel and let it rest for about 20 minutes.

4. Divide the dough into 4 parts. Roll out one part at a time on a lightly floured board to paper-thinness.

5. Cut into strips ½ inch wide and 6 inches long. Tie each strip into a loose bowknot or twist. Let dry for about 5 minutes or until the oil is ready.

6. Using a large, deep, and heavy pan, heat the shortening to 375 degrees. Fry the bowknots, uncrowded, until golden brown, turning once. Using a slotted spoon or tongs, carefully lift them out of the oil. Drain on paper towels. (The oil can be strained and stored for a future use.)

7. Transfer to a large serving platter and sprinkle with confectioners' sugar.

Yield: 3–4 dozen

Strufoli

We usually make this dessert for Easter and Christmas. Use your prettiest platter and shape the strufoli into a cone or Christmas tree or even an Easter bunny if you're artistic. So pretty, and delicious too!

2 cups peanut oil
2 cups sifted flour
¼ teaspoon salt
3 eggs
½ teaspoon vanilla extract
1 cup honey
1 tablespoon sugar
1 tablespoon multicolored candies

1. Heat the oil in a deep saucepan to 365 degrees. Meanwhile, mix the flour and salt in a large bowl. Make a well in the center of the flour.

2. Add the eggs, one at a time. Mix slightly after each addition using a fork or tossing the eggs with your fingers, squeezing slightly. Add the vanilla. Mix well to make a soft dough.

3. Turn the dough onto a lightly floured surface and knead for 5 minutes. Divide the dough into halves. Lightly roll each half into a ¼-inch-thick rectangle. Cut the dough with a sharp knife or pastry cutter into ¼-inch-wide strips. Use the palm of your hand to roll the strips to pencil thickness. Cut into pieces about ¼ inch long.

4. Add the pieces to the hot oil, being certain they can float uncrowded. Fry 3 to 5 minutes, or until lightly browned, turning often during the cooking time. Transfer with a slotted spoon to paper towels to drain. Finish frying all the pieces.

5. Meanwhile, cook the honey and sugar in a separate skillet over low heat for about 5 minutes.

6. Remove from the heat and add the deep-fried pieces. Stir constantly until all the pieces are coated with the honey-sugar mixture.

7. Remove the strufoli with a slotted spoon and set on a pan in the refrigerator to chill slightly. Transfer to a large serving platter and arrange in a cone-shaped mound. Sprinkle with multicolored candies. Chill in refrigerator to set the shape desired and cool the syrup.

8. Strufoli may be kept in a cake box for up to two weeks. Serve by breaking off individual pieces.

Serves 8–10

 # Christmas Frosted
Anisette Cookies

S-shaped cookies

1 cup granulated sugar
12 heaping tablespoons butter-flavored Crisco vegetable shortening
6 fresh eggs
½ cup milk (at room temperature)
5 cups King Arthur unbleached flour
6 heaping teaspoons baking powder
1¾ tablespoons anise or lemon extract

Have all ingredients at room temperature.

1. Preheat oven to 400 degrees.

2. In a large bowl, using an electric mixer, cream together sugar and shortening for about 5 minutes.

3. Add eggs, one at a time, mixing well after each addition.

4. Using the mixer at low speed, add ½ cup milk, 3 cups of the flour, the baking powder, and the extract.

5. Stir slowly for a few minutes as you add the remaining 2 cups of flour (or more if needed) until dough is soft and pliable and not stiff. Dough should be a little on the sticky side.

6. Using a large spatula, scrape dough from bowl onto a well-floured board.

7. Knead slightly with floured hands until dough is firm (about 2 minutes).

8. Break off small pieces to form 1-inch balls, keeping in mind that the dough will double in size while cooking.

9. Roll between hands to form a pencil-like shape.

10. Twist pencil-shape dough into a mound to form a pyramid shape. Seal the ends by pinching the dough. The dough can also be twisted into the letter S or the figure 8. All these shapes are traditional for these cookies.

11. As each cookie is made, place on an ungreased cookie sheet at least 2 inches apart.

12. Bake in hot oven for 8–10 minutes or until light on top and slightly browned on bottom. Check baking cookies periodically.

13. Remove from oven and, when cool, brush with anise frosting.

Frosting

1 pound confectioners' sugar
1 teaspoon anise extract
¼ cup milk (at room temperature), plus a little extra
multicolored sprinkles

1. Combine the sugar with extract and mix well.

2. Add milk to form a smooth paste. If mixture is too thick, add more milk. If too thin, add more powdered sugar.

3. Frost cookies; immediately sprinkle with candies.

4. Set on wax paper until frosting is firm.

5. When completely cooled (about 1 hour), place on a decorative platter and serve.

Yield: 3–4 dozen large cookies or 6–7 dozen small cookies

 # Brandied Chestnuts

Chestnuts must be blanched and shelled before they can be used. There are many ways to blanch them. This is an easy one: Cut slits in each nut before putting them in a pan covered with water. Boil gently until tender, about 30 minutes. Drain, then remove shells and skins. Chestnuts prepared this way are easily pureed or mashed. Brandied chestnuts must be stored for a month before using them.

1¼ cups sugar
1 cup water
1 pound chestnuts, blanched and shelled
1 cup brandy

1. Boil the sugar and water together in a small saucepan for 10 minutes. Skim the surface.

2. Put the peeled chestnuts in a bowl, and pour the hot syrup over them. Cover and let stand overnight.

3. The next day, drain the syrup from the chestnuts and combine with the brandy in a saucepan. Bring to a boil.

4. Put the chestnuts in a hot, sterilized quart jar or two pint jars, and pour boiling syrup over them. Seal tightly. Store in a cool, dark cupboard.

Yield: 1 quart

 # Pastiera Grano

EASTER WHEAT PIE

Pasta Frolla

> *2 cups flour (King Arthur preferred)*
> *¼ cup sugar*
> *pinch of salt*
> *1 cup butter-flavored Crisco vegetable shortening*
> *2 egg yolks, slightly beaten (reserve whites)*
> *1–2 tablespoons cold water, or more if needed*

1. Mix flour, sugar, and salt together in a large bowl.

2. Cut in shortening until dough is the size of large peas.

3. Add the 2 slightly beaten egg yolks and, using a fork, work until dough is well blended.

4. Add 2 tablespoons ice-cold water and gently knead until dough is manageable and holds together well, adding more water if necessary. Do not overwork dough or it will be tough.

5. Form into a flat ball, cover with plastic wrap, and refrigerate until needed.

Filling

Preheat oven to 350 degrees.

> *1 cup skinless grano wheat*, soaked overnight and drained*
> *1 cup water*
> *2 cups scalded milk*
> *1½ cups granulated sugar, plus ½ teaspoon*
> *1 teaspoon salt*
> *1 teaspoon freshly grated orange peel, rind only*
> *1 teaspoon freshly grated lemon peel, rind only*
> *2 teaspoons vanilla extract*
> *1½ pounds ricotta cheese, drained*
> *4 egg yolks, beaten*
> *reserved egg whites*

1. Buy only skinless grano wheat, wash well, and soak overnight in 2 cups water.

2. The next day, drain grano and simmer in a large saucepan with 1 cup water, 1 cup of the scalded milk, ½ teaspoon of the sugar, and 1 teaspoon salt.

3. Cook for at least half an hour or until soft and pasty. Add more water, if needed, to prevent wheat from sticking to pan. Grano will triple in amount.

4. Remove from heat and add orange and lemon peels and vanilla extract. Reserve.

5. In a large bowl, combine ricotta, 1½ cups sugar, and 4 beaten egg yolks. Use a large wooden spoon to mix until well blended.

6. Combine cooked grano and ricotta mixture thoroughly.

7. Refrigerate while you make pie crust.

To Finish Preparation:

1. Take out the pie dough and divide in half.

2. Using a well-floured board, roll one of the dough halves to form a round slightly larger than your pie plate (you will need a large, deep pie pan for this).

3. Line pie plate, leaving a slight overhang around the edge.

4. Roll out remaining dough and cut into latticed strips, about 1 inch wide, using a fluted pastry wheel. Reserve.

5. Beat 3 of the reserved egg whites till stiff and gently fold into grano and ricotta mixture, using a large spatula.

6. Pour mixture into lined pie plate; spread evenly.

7. Arrange lattice strips in a criss-cross pattern over filling.

8. Beat, slightly, the two remaining reserved egg whites and brush them over the lattice crust.

9. Bake in 350-degree oven for at least 1 hour or until filling is slightly firm but moist (it will set while cooling) and crust is golden brown.

10. Cool in oven with door open.

11. Sprinkle well with confectioners' sugar before serving.

*Can be purchased in specialty stores.

Serves 8–10

For a sweeter pie, sprinkle with confectioners' sugar before serving.

 La Pastiera Dolce

SWEET SPAGHETTI PIE

A much sought-after recipe, this is to be treasured! You will see this wonderful dish in most Italian homes, mainly at Eastertime. It's a great way to use up any leftover pasta. There are many recipes for la pastiera. This one is made with milk and sugar, which makes it like a dessert. Use freshly cooked or leftover pasta. Enjoy this wonderful meal at Eastertime or on any fast day when meat is not allowed. This also makes a great lunch or snack and can be eaten either hot or cold.

¾ pounds spaghetti
1 pound ricotta cheese
3 eggs, slightly beaten
½ cup sugar
¼ cup grated Parmesan cheese
1 cup whole milk
¼ stick butter
cinnamon

For a sweeter pie, sprinkle with confectioners' sugar before serving.

1. Preheat oven to 450 degrees.

2. Break uncooked pasta into irregular-sized pieces. Cook pasta in boiling, salted water until al dente. Drain well and reserve.

3. Place ricotta in a large bowl and stir until smooth. Add slightly beaten eggs, sugar, Parmesan cheese, and whole milk. Mix well. Add cooked spaghetti and toss until well coated with cheese mixture.

4. Pour into a well-buttered 10x8x2-inch baking pan. Dot with slices of the butter and sprinkle with cinnamon.

5. Bake in oven for 30–35 minutes or until puffy and golden brown.

6. Remove from oven and set in a warm place for at least an hour before serving. If you want to serve the pie at another time (or save its leftovers), it can be kept in the refrigerator covered with foil.

7. Cut in squares with a sharp, wet knife.

Serves 8–10

 # Aniseed Cookies

Enjoy this old-fashioned and easy dessert when you need a relaxing change. Be sure to have all ingredients at room temperature. These cookies need to be stored at least a week before you can eat them. They are great to give as gifts during the holidays or as hostess gifts.

½ cup unsalted butter, softened
1½ cups firmly packed brown sugar (you may also use granulated sugar)
3 eggs
few drops of anise oil
3 cups sifted all-purpose flour
freshly toasted aniseeds

1. Preheat oven to 350 degrees.

2. Using a food processor on low speed, cream the butter with the sugar.

3. Add eggs one at a time and beat well after each addition. Add anise oil at a point during this process.

4. Pour 2 cups of the flour into this batter and gently blend at low speed.

5. Remove bowl from appliance and stir in remaining flour. Mix well.

6. Drop teaspoonsful of finished dough onto greased cookie sheets and sprinkle with the toasted aniseeds. (Use toaster oven for toasting the seeds.)

7. Bake in hot oven about 12 minutes until bottoms are golden and tops are pale.

8. Cool and store in an airtight canister for a week to allow flavors to develop before eating.

Yield: 4 dozen

 # Italian Toto Cookies

These cookies are also called too toos or tatto cookies. The addition of cloves gives them a unique flavor that distinguishes them from your ordinary Italian cookie, especially when combined with cinnamon and orange flavoring. Though the recipe seems long, the ingredients are easily available and the directions very easy. It is always important when baking to have all ingredients at room temperature.

4 cups flour, sifted
4 teaspoons baking powder
5 teaspoons unsweetened cocoa powder
1 teaspoon ground cloves
½ teaspoon cinnamon
3 eggs, well beaten
1 cup milk
¾ cup vegetable oil
½ cup granulated sugar
½ cup brown sugar
1 teaspoon oil of orange or orange flavoring
1 teaspoon vanilla
1 cup walnuts, crushed coarsely
¼ cup miniature chocolate chips
½ cup maraschino cherries in jar, drained (optional)

1. Grease a large baking pan.

2. Using a large bowl, combine sifted flour, baking powder, unsweetened cocoa, cloves, and cinnamon. Mix well.

3. In a separate bowl, add beaten eggs, milk, oil, white and brown sugars, orange oil, and vanilla. Mix well.

4. Add egg mixture to flour mixture and mix thoroughly. Dough will be fairly thick and sticky.

5. Add crushed nuts and chocolate chips. If desired, add drained, chopped cherries.

6. Turn dough onto a floured board and knead until you can handle well, using more flour if needed.

7. Wet hands with oil or dust with flour. Break off pieces of dough and roll it into size of large walnuts.

8. Place on greased cookie sheet, 1 inch apart, and bake 15–20 minutes in a preheated 350-degree oven.

9. Cool, then frost.

Frosting

2 tablespoons melted butter
2 cups confectioners' sugar
1 heaping tablespoon unsweetened cocoa powder
½ teaspoon oil of orange or orange-flavored extract
1 teaspoon vanilla extract
2 tablespoons milk or black coffee

1. Mix well until smooth enough to spread. If mixture is too dry, add more milk or black coffee. If too soft, add more flour.

2. Spread on cooled cookies and place on waxed paper to dry.

Yield: 3–4 dozen cookies

Italian Sesame Seed Cookies

This is my wonderful tried-and-true recipe that has been handed down from generation to generation. It was given to us by one of the former owners of a pastry shop that once was noted for having the best Italian pastries in our neighborhood. The shop is closed now, but these cookies are one of its legacies.

> 1 cup melted butter or margarine
> 1 cup sugar
> 2 eggs, well beaten
> 2 tablespoons milk, plus additional for coating
> 1 teaspoon vanilla
> 3 teaspoons baking powder
> 3½ to 4 cups unbleached flour (King Arthur preferred)
> sesame seeds

1. Preheat oven to 375 degrees.

2. Melt butter and allow to cool.

3. In an electric mixer, on medium speed, cream melted butter and sugar.

4. Add 2 well-beaten eggs and mix.

5. Add milk, vanilla, and baking powder and mix well.

6. Add enough flour as needed; mix until dough is soft and pliable, but not sticky.

7. Remove from bowl and knead gently, adding more flour if needed.

8. Cover and allow to rest 15 minutes.

9. Pour milk in a deep bowl and put sesame seeds in a wide bowl.

10. Break off dough pieces the size of a walnut and roll in palm of hands.

11. Roll dough pieces in milk first, then in seeds, covering generously all over.

12. Place on greased cookie sheet, then flatten slightly. Cookies should have a short and wide rectangular shape for a better appearance after cooking.

13. Bake in oven for about 15 minutes or until lightly browned. Use middle rack, so bottoms of cookies will not burn.

Yield: 2½ dozen large or 3½ dozen small cookies

 Almond Ricciarelli  Cookies

CRESCENT-SHAPED ALMOND COOKIES

This recipe was donated by one of the lovely ladies who devoted many hours of volunteer work to the North End Union. Her name was never recorded, but her recipe will be remembered and enjoyed. These cookies are also known as Anise Tea Cookies.

2½ cups sifted all-purpose flour
½ teaspoon salt
¼ cup pecans, walnuts, or other nuts, chopped
1 tablespoon anise flavoring or 1 tablespoon anise seeds
⅔ cup vegetable oil
⅔ cup confectioners' sugar, plus more for dusting
3 tablespoons orange juice
2 teaspoons vanilla extract

1. Preheat oven to 350 degrees.

2. In a large bowl, combine sifted flour, salt, pecans, anise flavoring, and vegetable oil. Using an electric mixer, slowly beat these ingredients until well blended.

3. In a small bowl or blender, combine confectioners' sugar, orange juice, and vanilla. Mix briefly, then add to flour mixture in large bowl. Beat on low speed until well blended. Mixture should be rather crumbly and a little on the dry side. If necessary, add more orange juice until dough is handleable but not moist.

4. Shape into small balls, squeezing slightly with the palm of your hands.

5. Put on an ungreased cookie sheet and press dough slightly with your fingers to form a half-moon or crescent shape about 1½ inches long. Space cookies a couple of inches apart.

6. Bake until lightly browned about 20 minutes.

7. Remove from oven and, while still warm, roll cookies in confectioners' sugar.

8. Cool and store in a covered container.

Yield: 2½ dozen cookies

 # Pignoli Cookies

This traditional recipe is especially popular at Christmastime and Easter. To make it you will need almond paste and pignoli nuts, which you'll find in a gourmet or specialty store. Grease your cookie sheets and be sure to remove the cookies from the oven before the nuts burn.

> **1 pound pignoli nuts, left whole**
> **1 8-ounce can almond paste**
> **2 egg whites, slightly beaten**
> **1 teaspoon lemon extract**
> **½ cup granulated sugar**
> **½ cup confectioners' sugar**
> **¼ cup all-purpose flour**
> **pinch of salt**

1. Preheat oven to 300 degrees.

2. Lightly grease 2 cookie sheets.

3. Put pignoli nuts in a small bowl.

4. In a medium bowl, blend the almond paste, using an electric mixer, until smooth.

5. Add the egg whites and lemon extract. Beat until well blended and smooth.

6. Sift the 2 sugars and flour with salt.

7. Slowly add sugar and flour mixture to almond and egg mixture, mixing with electric mixer on slow speed. Dough should be slightly sticky.

8. Using wet hands, form dough into walnut-shaped balls.

9. Flattening slightly, press dough into pignoli nuts (on one side of the cookie only).

10. Place 1 inch apart on greased baking sheet.

11. Bake 20–25 minutes or until golden brown.

12. Cool completely and store in a cookie canister.

Yield: 2½ dozen cookies

Ricotta Cookies

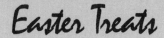

Easter Treats

Easter was always my favorite holiday when I was growing up in the North End. The subject on everyone's minds was food (and, of course, church). Everyone bragged about how they made the best ricotta pie or pizzagiena or zeppole. The windows of every bakery displayed incredibly beautiful decorated breads filled with colorful dyed eggs. During that time of the year, Woolworth's department store used to sell live baby chicks. I loved them so much that I always bought one or two. I kept them in a cardboard box and took good care of them, feeding and cleaning their boxes every day. Then, several weeks later when they had grown large, our family would enjoy a fresh organic chicken dinner!

These cookies are a nice surprise because they have the rich taste of butter, but the ricotta makes them light.

> *¼ pound butter, at room temperature*
> *¼ cup ricotta cheese*
> *1 teaspoon vanilla extract*
> *1 cup sugar*
> *1 egg*
> *2 cups sifted flour*
> *½ teaspoon baking soda*
> *½ teaspoon salt*

1. Blend the butter with the ricotta until creamy. Add the vanilla and mix well.

2. Gradually add the sugar, beating until well blended. Add the egg and mix well.

3. Slowly stir in the flour, baking soda, and salt, blending well.

4. Drop the batter from a teaspoon onto a greased baking sheet.

5. Bake in a preheated 350-degree oven for 10 minutes.

6. Cook, then transfer to a serving platter, using a spatula. They will keep for several weeks if stored in a covered container.

Yield: 36 cookies

 # Granita di Limone

LEMON ICE

Children will enjoy this lemon ice. It is also used as an after-dinner refreshment or as a cooling palate cleanser between the courses of a heavy meal.

> **1 envelope unflavored gelatin**
> **¼ cup cold water**
> **4 cups water**
> **1 cup sugar**
> **juice of 3 lemons**
> **4 lemon slices for garnish**

1. Soften the gelatin in the ¼ cup of cold water.

2. In a large saucepan, boil the 4 cups of water and sugar together for 5 minutes. Remove from the heat and add the lemon juice.

3. Add the softened gelatin to the syrup, stirring until dissolved.

4. Pour into a shallow pan and freeze until almost firm, about 2 or 3 hours. Transfer to the refrigerator 20 to 30 minutes before serving to allow the ice to soften a little. To serve, scoop into individual bowls and garnish with a slice of lemon.

Serves 4

 # Gelato

ITALIAN SHERBET

Another nice cooling dessert. This gelato is more like ice cream than the granita.

> **2 cups water**
> **2 cups sugar**
> **pinch of salt**
> **1 cup fresh lemon juice**
> **grated rind of 1 lemon**
> **2 egg whites**

1. Boil water, sugar, and salt together for 5 minutes over medium heat.

2. Strain the lemon juice into the sugar syrup. Add the grated lemon rind. Cool.

3. Beat the egg whites until stiff but not dry. Fold them gently into the cooled syrup.

4. Pour into a shallow pan, cover with waxed paper, and freeze until firm, about 3 hours.

Serves 4

 # Budino di Amaretti

MACAROON PUDDING

This recipe was given to me by the chef of a restaurant in Italy. The addition of macaroon cookie crumbs gives this pudding an especially light, delicate texture.

> ***½ cup macaroon cookie crumbs***
> ***3 ounces unsweetened chocolate***
> ***3 cups whole milk***
> ***4 eggs, slightly beaten***
> ***½ cup sugar***
> ***butter***
> ***whipped cream***
> ***maraschino cherries (for garnish)***

1. Put 4–5 macaroon cookies in a plastic bag and crush with a rolling pin until fine.
2. Heat chocolate and milk in a small saucepan, using low heat.
3. When chocolate is melted, beat with a small whisk until smooth. Remove from heat.
4. Beat eggs and sugar together until well blended. Slowly add egg mixture to hot chocolate mixture and stir constantly and vigorously with a whisk until completely smooth.
5. Return pan to stove and cook until thick, stirring constantly for 10 minutes.
6. Turn off heat, add macaroon crumbs to pan, and beat with whisk until smooth and shiny.
7. Cool slightly.
8. Pour pudding into a buttered one-quart baking dish.
9. Refrigerate for at least 3 hours before serving.
10. Top with whipped cream and cherry garnish.

Serves 4

 Original Arangini Balls

In years past, when a train stopped at a small station in Sicily, the attendant wheeling the tavolo caldo (a trolley containing hot food to be eaten on the train) would make his way to the platform, crying out, "arangeeeeeeeni," and travelers would be handed a piece of brown paper containing a warm mound of pale, orange-colored rice. The rice was eaten right off the paper, and then the paper was used to wipe the hands and mouth. This recipe for arangini balls comes close to the original one.

1 pound rice
4 tablespoons grated Parmesan cheese
1 egg, beaten
olive oil
salt and pepper to taste
¾ pounds lean ground beef
2 tablespoons chopped parsley
2 hard-boiled eggs, minced
½ cup cooked baby peas
bread crumbs, finely grated
paprika

1. Cook rice in boiling salted water.

2. Drain and mix with half the beaten egg.

3. Heat 1 tablespoon olive oil in a heavy pan and brown beef.

4. Place drained beef in a medium-size bowl and add cheese, parsley, minced eggs, and cooked peas.

5. Wet hands and take a handful of cooked rice. Place a generous amount of beef in center, closing the rice up to a round ball.

6. Repeat until all rice and filling is used.

7. Slightly dip the balls in balance of beaten egg.

8. Coat with fine bread crumbs mixed with paprika for color.

9. Deep fry in heavy pot in enough olive oil to cover balls. Cook until light golden brown.

10. Reserve to paper towels to drain.

Yield: 8 rice balls

Fave Dei Morte

BONES OF THE DEAD

There are several versions of this recipe, but this one is one of the most interesting. The fave dei morte consists of pastry shaped to resemble a large broad bean. In the old days in Italy the bean was a common funeral offering, and it was thought that the souls of the dead were enclosed in it.

> ¼ *pound sweet almonds, blanched and skinned*
> ½ *cup of sugar*
> *2 cups flour*
> 2⅓ *tablespoons of butter*
> *1 egg*
> *lemon flavoring or brandy*
> *1 egg yolk and additional flour*

1. Preheat oven to 350 degrees.

2. Pound the blanched and skinned almonds in a mortar with the sugar until the almonds resemble small grains of rice.

3. Place the flour in a large bowl and, with a fork, gradually add the butter and 1 egg.

4. Add the almond and sugar mixture to the flour mixture, and mix all thoroughly, adding sufficient lemon flavoring or brandy to make a stiff dough.

5. Roll out onto a floured board and, with a sharp knife, cut the dough into thick strips.

6. Use your hands to shape the strips into *fave*, or large broad beans.

7. Put these on a buttered pastry sheet and sprinkle with a little flour.

8. Brush them with the beaten yolk of one egg.

9. Bake until they are of even golden color, about 5–10 minutes.

10. Because they are small, these cookies are quickly done, so check them after 5 minutes and continue cooking only if needed.

Yield: 2–3 dozen cookies

 Fruit and Wine
D'Italia

This heavenly mixture of fruits, cherries, and wine is a great dessert when you need something light to pick you up. Serve it alone or with fresh whipped cream. (Whip one pint of cold heavy cream with 1 cup confectioners' sugar in a well-chilled bowl. Add a drop or two of vanilla or anise flavoring. Refrigerate immediately until needed.

**¼ cup golden seedless raisins
white wine
small bunch seedless red grapes
1 apple, peeled and chopped
1 orange, peeled and segmented
1 pear, chopped
½ cup maraschino cherries, pitted and halved
3–4 dates, cut in pieces
juice of half lemon
2 heaping tablespoons sugar
¼ cup maraschino liqueur
1 banana, peeled and sliced
whipped cream (optional)**

1. Soak the raisins in enough white wine to cover.

2. Drop the loose red grapes in a large bowl.

3. Chop the peeled apple in small chunks and add to bowl.

4. Add the orange segments, chopped pear, maraschino cherries, and dates.

5. Pour the raisins with wine into the large bowl.

6. Add juice of lemon, sugar, and maraschino liqueur.

7. Stir gently using a big spoon.

8. Chill for at least ½ hour.

You may add or substitute melon, strawberries, peaches, or any fruit in season.

9. Just before serving, add the sliced banana and stir gently.

10. Place in sherbet glasses with some of the syrup.

11. Top each serving with whipped cream, if using, and a single maraschino cherry.

Serves 6

Nonna's Sweet Easter Egg Bread Baskets

This is a recipe that I take particular pride in making, especially in my cooking classes. My students really enjoy sculpting baskets of different sizes. They can't wait to take them home and show off their creations to friends and family members. Don't forget to boil the eggs in advance.

Bread

> *½ cup lukewarm water*
> *1 cup sugar, plus 1 teaspoon*
> *2 packages dry granular yeast*
> *1 cup milk*
> *1 teaspoon salt*
> *¼ cup butter or margarine (½ stick)*
> *3 eggs, beaten*
> *6–7 cups unbleached flour (King Arthur preferred)*
> *1 4-ounce jar maraschino cherries, drained and chopped*
> *8 hard-boiled eggs, dyed in different colors*
> *multicolored candies*

1. Using a small bowl, mix ½ cup lukewarm water with 1 teaspoon sugar and, using your fingers, dissolve sugar.

2. Add 2 packages yeast to water and dissolve, using fingers.

3. Let rest until bubbly and foamy, about 10 minutes.

4. In a small saucepan, put 1 cup milk, 1 teaspoon salt, ¼ cup butter, and 1 cup sugar. Stir over low heat until milk is warm; reserve.

5. Using a large bowl, add beaten eggs and milk mixture. Beat these together with a wire whisk, then beat in 2 cups of flour, the yeast mixture, and chopped cherries. Mix well until smooth.

6. Add remaining cups flour, mix well with hands, and turn dough onto a floured wooden board.

7. Gently knead dough about 8–10 minutes until smooth, using floured hands (dough will be sticky because of the cherries).

8. Return dough to greased large bowl, cover with plastic, and allow to rest 1½ hours.

9. When double in size, punch down and divide into 9 equal parts. 8 parts will be for the baskets and 1 part will make the basket handles.

10. Twist 8 parts into a spiral shape, form spirals into circles, and knot ends to form a nest.

11. Put nests on a greased baking sheet and press a dyed egg into each one.

12. Break off 16 pieces of dough from the last of the 9 parts, allowing 2 small pieces for each dough basket (dough will rise considerably).

13. Slightly roll each piece of dough and make a thin cross shape with the two pieces of rolled dough. Place one of the 8 crosspieces over each dough basket, leaving some of the egg in each basket exposed.

14. Tuck cross ends under each basket and pinch together to secure.

15. Place baking sheet in a warm place and allow baskets to rise until double in size (about one hour).

16. Bake in a preheated 350-degree oven for 20 minutes.

17. Remove from oven and place each basket on a rack to cool.

18. While still warm, spoon glaze (recipe below) over each baked basket and sprinkle immediately with multicolored candies.

To Make Glaze:

Combine 3 tablespoons soft butter, 3 cups sifted confectioners' sugar, 5 tablespoons milk, and ¾ teaspoon vanilla. Stir with a large spoon until smooth. Use immediately.

Yield: 8 large baskets (or you can also divide dough further to make 16 small baskets)

Index

— F —

— G —

— M —

— T —

— U —

— V —

 # About the Author

Marguerite DiMino Buonopane has taught Italian cooking classes and for many years prepared and hosted the legendary luncheons at *The North End Union*, a non-profit community settlement house that has been a neighborhood landmark since 1892. She brings her talents and her history to this wonderful new edition.